BTEC
FIRST

BTEC

ALWAYS LEARNING

ENGINEERING

Published by Pearson Education Limited, Edinburgh Gate, Harlow, Essex, CM20 2JE.

www.pearsonschoolsandfecolleges.co.uk

Text © Pearson Education Limited 2012 (Units 1–2, 5–8), 2013 (Units 9–11)
Typeset by Phoenix Photosetting, Chatham, Kent, UK
Original illustrations © Pearson Education Limited
Illustrated by Phoenix Photosetting, Chatham, Kent, UK
Cover design by Pearson Education Limited and Andrew Magee Design
Cover photo © Getty Images/Blend Images/Jon Feingersh
Indexing by Indexing Specialists (UK) Ltd.

The rights of Simon Clarke and Alan Darbyshire to be identified as authors of this work have been
asserted by them in accordance with the Copyright, Designs and Patents Act 1988.

Units 1–2, 5–8 first published 2012
This full edition published 2013

17 16 15 14 13
10 9 8 7 6 5 4 3 2 1

British Library Cataloguing in Publication Data
A catalogue record for this book is available from the British Library

ISBN 978 1 446902 43 1

Printed in Slovakia by Neografia

Websites
There are links to relevant websites in this book. In order to ensure that the links are up to date,
that the links works, and that the sites aren't inadvertently links to sites that could be considered
offensive, we have made the links available on our website at www.pearsonhotlinks.co.uk. Search
for the title BTEC Engineering (Full Edition) Student Book or ISBN 978 1 446902 43 1.

Copies of official specifications for all Pearson qualifications may be found on the website:
www.edexcel.com

A note from the publisher
In order to ensure that this resource offers high-quality support for the associated BTEC qualification,
it has been through a review process by the awarding organisation to confirm that it fully covers the
teaching and learning content of the specification or part of a specification at which it is aimed, and
demonstrates an appropriate balance between the development of subject skills, knowledge and
understanding, in addition to preparation for assessment.

While the publishers have made every attempt to ensure that advice on the qualification and its
assessment is accurate, the official specification and associated assessment guidance materials are
the only authoritative source of information and should always be referred to for definitive guidance.

No material from an endorsed book will be used verbatim in any assessment set by BTEC.

Endorsement of a book does not mean that the book is required to achieve this BTEC qualification,
nor does it mean that it is the only suitable material available to support the qualification, and
any resource lists produced by the awarding organisation shall include this and other appropriate
resources.

Contents

The publisher would like to thank the following for their kind permission to reproduce their photographs:

(Key: b-bottom; c-centre; l-left; r-right; t-top)

Alamy Images: Andrew Fox 19, Bubbles Photolibrary 237, Culture Creative 89, Exotica.im 1 109, imagebroker 94, incamerastock 86, Juice Images 70, Science Photo Library 204, sciencephotos 158c, ZUMA Press, Inc 74; **Construction Photography:** David Potter 24; **Fotolia.com:** Arkadiusz Warmus 108, Kadmy 201, michaeljung 232, Paul Hill 90; **Getty Images:** PhotoDisc 63; **Honda Motor Europe Ltd:** 14; **Imagestate Media:** John Foxx Collection 58; **Pearson Education Ltd:** Clark Wiseman / Studio 8 30, Trevor Clifford 130, Coleman Yuen 50, Gareth Boden 54, 158l, Jon Barlow 136; **Photos. com:** Comstock 168, 198, 234, Jupiter Images 185; **Rex Features:** Sipa Press 4; **Shutterstock.com:** Alex Mit 93, U5, Andrey Erenim 64, auremar 110, 244, Catalonia Petloea 2, Charles Taylor 48, Chuck Rausin 33, U2, CREATISTA 41, Dale Berman 67, dekede 158r, Dmitry Kalinovsky 105, Eimantas Buzas 124, fasphotographic U8, 139, Fernando Cortes 82, Gwoeii 21, hansenn 26bl, Herbert Kratky 81, Ivan Montero Martinez 137, Jure Porenta 57, U6, Maksim Dubinsky 31, mangostock 161, manzrussall 69, michaeljung 5, Nadji Antonova U7, 111, 113, nikkytok 235, Nikonaft 199, Pedro Salaverria U1, Rehan Qureshi 135, Rido 26tl, roboot 34, teamdaddy 27, Vicky France 20; **SuperStock:** Cultura Limited 3, Design Plcs 169, Juice Images 91, Stocktrek Images 55; **The British Standards Institution:** 39, 52; **Veer/Corbis:** Creatista U11, hoack U10, lupobianco U9

All other images © Pearson Education

In some instances we have been unable to trace the owners of copyright material, and we would appreciate any information that would enable us to do so.

About this book

This book is designed to help you through your BTEC First in Engineering, and covers nine units of the qualification.

About your BTEC First in Engineering

Choosing to study for a BTEC First Engineering qualification is a great decision to make for lots of reasons. This qualification will give you the opportunity to gain specific knowledge and understanding in engineering, and will help you to sharpen your skills for employment or further study.

About the authors

Simon Clarke has spent over 20 years delivering BTEC qualifications across First, National and Higher National Certificates and Diplomas. His lecturing experience in FE has led to his appointment as an Advanced Practitioner and Head of Department. He has contributed extensively to various published resources.

Alan Darbyshire has worked as an advisor for BTEC on their mechanical engineering programmes. Prior to this, he held the post of lecturer and senior lecturer in mechanical and plant engineering at the Blackpool and Fylde College. He also spent 12 years working in the motor industry. He has written and co-written several engineering textbooks and tutor support materials.

Simon Goulden has been a teacher for 16 years in secondary and further education at a number of establishments in the north west and Wales. He has been Head of Subject for Engineering in a medium-sized school in Bolton.

Chris Hallgarth left school at 16 and started an apprenticeship as a toolmaker. On completing his apprenticeship, he focused on machining and moved into the field of injection moulding. Via various other roles, including work on CNC machines, he ended up as a designer for injection mould tools. Over the last 10 years, he has moved into teaching. He loves the challenge and opportunities that engineering can offer and finds it very rewarding to find solutions to many problems and create new and existing products.

Neale Watkins began his career as a toolmaker in South Wales where he served a four-year apprenticeship. He is now Head of Faculty at Lewis School Pengam. As well as almost 20 years of teaching experience, he has assessed and managed various engineering programmes. Throughout this time he has also been involved in the development of engineering specifications.

How to use this book

This book is designed to help you use your skills and knowledge in work-related situations, and assist you in getting the most from your course.

These introductions give you a snapshot of what to expect from each unit – and what you should be aiming for by the time you finish it.

How this unit is assessed

Learning aims describe what you will be doing in the unit.

A learner shares how working through the unit has helped them.

Features of this book

There are lots of features in this book to help you learn about the topics in each unit, and to have fun while learning!

Topic references show which parts of the BTEC you are covering.

Get started with a short activity or discussion about the topic.

Key terms appear in bold blue text and are defined in a key term box on the page. Also see the glossary for definitions of important words and phrases.

Activity 2.4 — Injection moulding

Identify a product that has been moulded with a hole through it and see if you can work out how this is done. A good example is a plastic pencil sharpener.

Activities will help you learn about the topic. These can be completed in pairs or groups, or sometimes on your own.

Assessment practice 1.1

1 Identify three hazards associated with using workshop machinery [3]:

Hazard 1: _____

Hazard 2: _____

Hazard 3: _____

2 A small engineering company produces bespoke printed circuit boards for a range of products. Outline the five main stages in PCB manufacture.

3 Match the following processes with the correct description [3]:

Forging → Pouring/injecting liquid metal into a mould, which then cools in the shape of the desired product.

Casting → Heating a metal, then applying a force to change its shape or size permanently.

Welding → Applying heat to join two pieces of metal together.

A chance to practise answering the types of questions that you may come across in your test or exam. (For Unit 1 and Unit 9 only.) Answers can be found on page 275.

Assessment activity 5.2 — Manufacturing children's toys   2B.P4 | 2B.P5 | 2B.M2 | 2B.M3 | 2B.D2

You are on a work placement with a firm that manufactures children's toys and have been asked by your supervisor to prepare a presentation on their use of sustainable materials. You must include information about:

- the environmental impact of the materials used in a children's toy
- appropriate forms of supply for the materials used, with reasons.

Tips

- Consider the environmental impact of each stage of the toy's life – including extraction and processing of its materials, manufacture and maintenance.
- Consider ways to make the product more sustainable.

Activities that relate to the unit's assessment critera. These activities will help you prepare for your assignments and contain tips to help you achieve your best results. (For all units **except** Unit 1 and Unit 9.)

Just checking

1 What are the letters used to define a 2D coordinate system?
2 What options are used to create and remove drawn lines?
3 What tools are used to define accurate geometry on-screen?

Use these to check your knowledge and understanding of the topic you have just covered.

Someone who works in the engineering industry explains how this unit of the BTEC First applies to the day-to-day work they do.

This section gives you the chance to think more about the role that this person does, and whether you would want to follow in their footsteps once you've completed your BTEC.

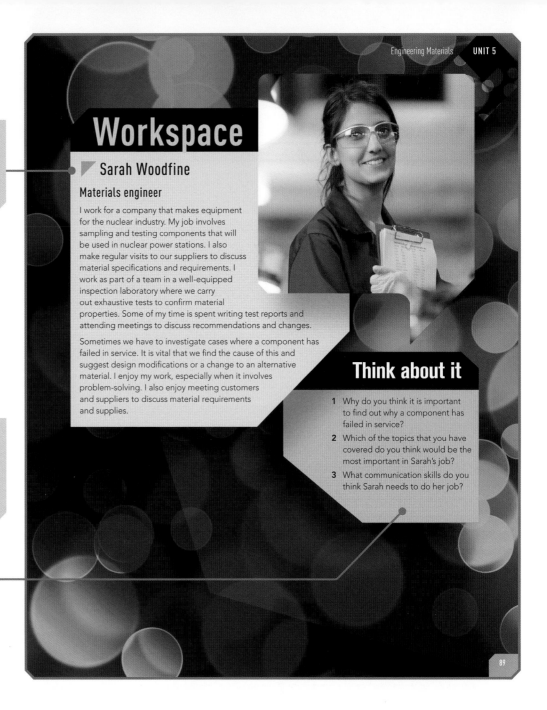

Workspace

Sarah Woodfine

Materials engineer

I work for a company that makes equipment for the nuclear industry. My job involves sampling and testing components that will be used in nuclear power stations. I also make regular visits to our suppliers to discuss material specifications and requirements. I work as part of a team in a well-equipped inspection laboratory where we carry out exhaustive tests to confirm material properties. Some of my time is spent writing test reports and attending meetings to discuss recommendations and changes.

Sometimes we have to investigate cases where a component has failed in service. It is vital that we find the cause of this and suggest design modifications or a change to an alternative material. I enjoy my work, especially when it involves problem-solving. I also enjoy meeting customers and suppliers to discuss material requirements and supplies.

Think about it

1 Why do you think it is important to find out why a component has failed in service?

2 Which of the topics that you have covered do you think would be the most important in Sarah's job?

3 What communication skills do you think Sarah needs to do her job?

BTEC Assessment Zone

You will be assessed in two different ways for your BTEC First Engineering qualification. For most units, your teacher/tutor will set assignments for you to complete. These may take the form of projects where you research, plan, prepare, andevaluate a piece of work or activity. The table in the BTEC Assessment Zone explains what you must do in order to achieve each of the assessment criteria. Each unit of this book contains a number of assessment activities to help you with these assessment criteria.

This table in the BTEC Assessment Zone explains what you must do in order to achieve each of the assessment criteria, and signposts assessment activities in this book to help you to prepare for your assignments.

For Unit 1 of your BTEC, you will be assessed using an onscreen test. For Unit 9 you will be assessed by a paper examination. The BTEC Assessment Zone for these units helps you to prepare by showing you some of the different types of questions you will need to answer.

The BTEC Assessment Zone in Units 1 and 9 helps you to prepare for your test by showing you some of the different types of questions you will need to answer.

◤ Planning and getting organised

The first step in managing your time is to plan ahead and be well organised. Some people are naturally good at this. They think ahead, write down commitments in a diary or planner and store their notes and handouts neatly and carefully so they can find them quickly.

How good are your working habits?

Improving your planning and organisational skills

1 Use a diary to schedule working times into your weekdays and weekends.

2 Also use the diary to write down exactly what work you have to do. You could use this as a 'to do' list and tick off each task as you go.

3 Divide up long or complex tasks into manageable chunks and put each 'chunk' in your diary with a deadline of its own.

4 Always allow more time than you think you need for a task.

◤ Sources of information

You will need to use research to complete your BTEC First assignments, so it's important to know what sources of information are available to you. These are likely to include the following:

Textbooks
These cover the units of your qualification and provide activities and ideas for further research.

Internet
A vast source of information, but not all sites are accurate – you should always double-check facts you find online.

Sources of information

Trade journals and magazines
These can be a useful source of information about recent developments in engineering.

People
People you may know who work in the engineering sector can be a great source of opinions and experience.

Take it further

If you become distracted by social networking sites or texts when you're working, set yourself a time limit of 10 minutes or so to indulge yourself. You could even use this as a reward for completing a certain amount of work.

Remember!

Store relevant information when you find it – keep a folder on your computer specifically for research – so you don't have to worry about finding it again at a later date.

Organising and selecting information

Organising your information

Once you have used a range of sources of information for research, you will need to organise the information so it's easy to use.

- Make sure your written notes are neat and have a clear heading – it's often useful to date them, too.
- Always keep a note of where the information came from (the title of a book, the title and date of a newspaper or magazine and the web address of a website) and, if relevant, which pages.

Selecting your information

Once you have completed your research, re-read the assignment brief or instructions you were given to remind yourself of the exact wording of the question(s) and divide your information into three groups:

1 Information that is totally relevant.

2 Information that is not as good, but which could come in useful.

3 Information that doesn't match the questions or assignment brief very much, but that you kept because you couldn't find anything better!

Check that there are no obvious gaps in your information against the questions or assignment brief. If there are, make a note of them so that you know exactly what you still have to find.

Presenting your work

Before handing in any assignments, make sure:

- you have addressed each part of the question and that your work is as complete as possible
- all spelling and grammar is correct
- you have referenced all sources of information you used for your research
- that all work is your own – otherwise you could be committing **plagiarism**
- you have saved a copy of your work.

Key terms

Plagiarism – If you are including other people's views, comments or opinions, or copying a diagram or table from another publication, you must state the source by including the name of the author or publication, or the web address. Failure to do this (so you are really pretending other people's work is your own) is known as plagiarism. Check your school's policy on plagiarism and copying.

Introduction

Have you ever wondered how electronic devices get smaller and smaller and yet become ever more complex? Or how Olympic athletes can be aided by new technologies to achieve greater heights in their individual sports? From jewellery to athletic equipment, to smartphones, laptops and televisions, examples of engineering can be found all around us in today's world. Engineers use their knowledge and understanding to make things happen and strive to solve many of the different problems that arise in the modern world. Engineering plays a vitally important role in many careers and industries: medicine, communications, automotive, electronics and aerospace are just some examples of sectors where engineers are the driving force behind new developments and advances.

Assessment: This unit will be assessed using an onscreen test lasting one hour.

Learning aims

After completing this unit you should:

A know about engineering processes used to produce modern engineered products

B know about developments in engineering materials and technologies

C understand how engineering contributes to a sustainable future.

> During my work experience placement I talked to different engineers about their jobs. This has helped me to decide which sector I would most like to work in. I also had the opportunity to view a range of machining processes.
>
> Laura, *16-year-old engineering student*

The Engineered World

1

Engineering sectors and products

Engineered products are used in all walks of life. Here a journalist wears a helmet and bulletproof vest to make his job safer.

Introduction

This topic will introduce you to some of the key engineering sectors, as well as a variety of products associated with them. You will need an understanding of these when you are choosing your career.

Types of products

You are probably already familiar with some of the main engineering sectors and products.

Table 1.1 Engineering sectors and products

Engineering sector	Description	Typical products
Aerospace	The design, development and manufacture of products through flight	Military aircraft, passenger jets, helicopters and rockets
Automotive	The design, development and manufacture of vehicles	Cars, motorbikes, commercial vans and lorries
Communications	The way information is used around the globe	Mobile phones, routers, satellites and computers
Electrical/electronic	The design, development and manufacture of electrical/electronic products	Televisions, Blu-ray players, calculators and microwaves
Mechanical	This is a branch of engineering that can be found in many different sectors and is associated with the design, manufacture and testing of machines and other mechanical devices	Engines, robots, lifts and machine tools
Biomedical	This is a sector that specialises in developing devices/procedures that solve medical problems using science and engineering knowledge	Artificial limbs, medical instruments, magnetic resonance imaging (MRI) systems and bulletproof vests
Chemical	The design and processing of equipment for the chemical industry as well as the manufacture of chemical products	Petroleum, medicines, cleaning fluids and a range of foods

WorkSpace

▶ Matthew Carlick

Aircraft Engineer

I work as part of a team of engineers that assembles aircraft engines in a busy aircraft maintenance facility. There are four engineers working on each engine at any one time. We work around the clock to assemble the various parts, taking it in turn to lead the team.

The engine itself comprises a number of sub-assemblies or modules: three gearboxes, a low pressure turbine, a compressor, a fan and booster and, finally, a series of bearings. My job is to help assemble these modules to produce a complete engine unit.

Other very important tasks I perform during assembly are 'stack measurement checks'. Each module should be a certain dimension, and it is my job to ensure that all the dimensions of the module 'stack up' when the engine is fully assembled. Once completed, the engine is transported to the test bed where I am on hand to fix any problems prior to, or during, the engine test. On numerous occasions I have had the opportunity to perform 'on wing' maintenance. This means I will fix engine problems at airports around the world.

I love my job because I enjoy working with my hands and I am fascinated by how an engine is assembled. I also really value working as part of a team, and have found that I am a natural team leader. It always gives me a sense of pride once the engine has been assembled and tested, and when I fly I am confident in the knowledge that trained engineers have serviced the engines that keep me in the air.

Think about it

1 Why are team-working skills so important in Matthew's job?

2 What are your strengths when it comes to teamwork? What areas would you like to improve?

3 If you were in charge of a team, how would you ensure that others carried out their tasks effectively?

Mechanical and electrical/ electronic engineering processes

Getting started

Consider an engineering product that you are familiar with, such as a hand vice or centre punch. Make a list of its important features. Think about its shape, size and how it helps you with an activity.

Introduction

In today's society, engineers need to have an understanding of the range of processes that will help them produce products or parts that perform a required function. This topic will introduce you to some of the main processes used to make or assemble products that meet the needs of customers and manufacturers, and will also outline important health and safety considerations.

Link

For more information see *Unit 7 Machining Techniques.*

Machining processes

The manufacture of engineered products or parts often requires the removal of material and some form of shape change. This is known as 'secondary machining' or 'forming'. Traditional secondary machining processes and the machines that perform them fall into three groups – turning, milling and drilling.

Turning

Turning involves the use of a lathe to produce a given shape, usually cylindrical. Lathes have one thing in common: the workpiece is held in a chuck and rotated while being machined to shape and size using a cutting tool.

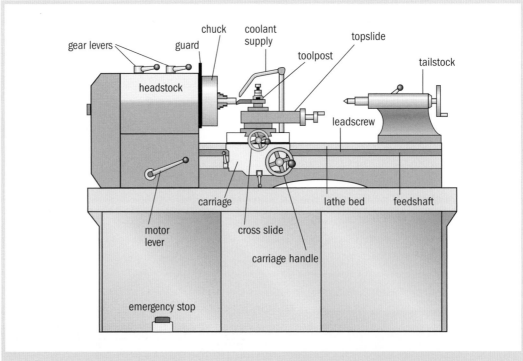

Figure 1.1 A centre lathe

Table 1.2 Machining operations

Operation	Description
Facing off	Removing material from the end of a workpiece to leave a flat or square surface
Drilling	Removing material from the inside of a workpiece using a drill bit
Parallel turning	Removing material from the outer diameter of the workpiece while maintaining the same size along its length
Taper turning	A process used to create a conical shape by feeding a tool at an angle to the length of the workpiece
Parting off	A process used to cut off the workpiece to the required length

Milling

This is a process used to shape products by removing excess material to produce a range of simple and complex shapes. A milling machine has a spindle that holds a rotating cutter in place. The workpiece will be clamped to a table or held in a vice and fed under the cutter to form the desired shape. There are two main types of milling machine – horizontal and vertical. In many cases, a universal milling machine combines both horizontal and vertical processes.

Drilling

Drilling is a process that creates circular holes in a workpiece. The cutting device is called a drill bit. It usually has a shank that allows it to be held in a drilling machine. To drill a satisfactory hole in any material, the correct type of drill bit must be used.

This is probably the most common machining operation you will perform and it is important that you do it correctly. Good-quality drill bits can be expensive but the key to good drilling is keeping the cutting edge sharp.

machine head
cutting tool
machine vice
cross traverse hand-wheel
knee
vertical traverse hand-wheel

Figure 1.2 The cutter can move up and down in a vertical milling machine.

Safety

Accidents during secondary machining processes are usually caused by:

- loose clothing snagging on a revolving part
- flying pieces of material entering the eye
- the hand or arm coming into contact with revolving surfaces/parts
- minor burns from hot material surfaces.

Make sure that you follow the correct procedures and wear the right personal protective equipment for each process (e.g. goggles and overalls/aprons), and ensure guards are in the correct position prior to any machining operation. Above all, listen to your teacher when they are demonstrating the correct use of a piece of equipment.

CONTINUED ▶▶

◤ Forming processes

Sometimes complex shapes such as engine blocks, tools and equipment cannot be achieved through traditional secondary machining processes. The two main forming processes that allow these parts to be made are casting and forging.

Casting

Casting is a process that usually involves pouring or injecting a liquid metal into a mould. The mould contains a cavity that takes the shape of the desired object where the metal is allowed to cool and solidify. The casting is removed from the mould and may require secondary machining to create the finished product, depending on the type of casting process used.

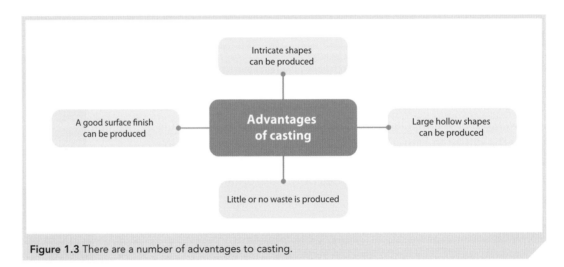

Figure 1.3 There are a number of advantages to casting.

Manufacturers use a range of different casting processes. The most common are:

- sand casting – used for large parts where dimensional accuracy is not as important as other features, e.g. manhole covers
- semi-permanent and permanent mould casting – used for products that require use with water pressure and in larger quantities than sand casting as tooling costs are relatively high, e.g. pressure valves
- investment casting – used for parts that require close dimensional tolerances and complex shapes such as compressor wheels for automotive turbochargers
- die casting – used for large quantities of parts that require close tolerances as tooling costs are quite high, e.g. toy cars.

Forging

Forging is a process that involves a metal being heated up and shaped by **plastic deformation**. It is usually achieved by applying some kind of squeezing force (compression) such as hammer blows using a large power press. Forging improves the physical properties of a metal by changing the direction of the grain flow to improve strength, toughness and ductility.

As with casting, forging can be achieved in a number of ways:

- drop forging – produces a range of small to medium-size shapes with good dimensional accuracy and high production rates through hammering in a closed die, e.g. engine camshafts
- press forging – uses a slow squeezing action to form the metal that penetrates the whole object making it suitable for forging large objects, e.g. aircraft landing gear
- upset forging – uses bar stock where usually one end needs to be forged. This is achieved by heating the end and gripping it in a fixed die so that the end that needs to be forged is projecting out. A moving die then delivers the hammer blow to create the simple shape, e.g. the head of a bolt.

Fabrication processes

Welding

More often than not, engineered products or parts need to be joined together in some way. Sometimes the solution is a simple nut, bolt and washer, but on other occasions a more permanent method is required. Welding is one of the most efficient methods of permanently joining two pieces of metal together. It can be done in many different ways but most methods use intense heat to fuse the metal together. A number of energy sources – a gas or electric arc, laser or ultrasound – can be used.

Did you know?

The word 'engineer' comes from the Latin word 'ingenium', meaning 'cleverness'.

Discussion

What processes do you use at your school/college? Consider the different machines that are available in your workshop and identify some of the processes that you have performed on them. Which did you enjoy doing the most and why?

Table 1.3 Welding processes

Welding process	Description	Advantages
MIG welding	This is probably the most common industrial welding process. It uses electricity to generate the heat required to weld materials. MIG stands for Metal Inert Gas.	- Suitable for large-scale production - Varying thicknesses of materials can be joined - Reduced cost because the production of neat and clean metal deposits on the workpiece means there is no need for extra cleaning
Oxy-acetylene	A gas welding process where a flame is produced using a mixture of oxygen and acetylene. No pressure on the product is required – the heat is there to control the welding of the parts.	- Ease of controlling the low and high temperatures needed for welding, brazing and soldering as the gas can be mixed manually - Relatively inexpensive in comparison with other welding processes and commonly found in school or college workshops
Spot welding	A type of electrical resistance welding generally used to join sheet material together. The basic principle uses a transformer with a primary winding and a secondary winding connected to copper electrodes. When the two electrodes trap the sheet material they generate enough heat to fuse the two together.	- The process is free from fumes or spatter - Requires little or no maintenance - Cost effective

CONTINUED ▸▸

Shearing

This is a process used to cut straight lines on a range of materials from sheet metal to angle and bar stock. An upper blade and a lower blade are forced past each other with a space between them determined by a required offset. Usually, one of the blades is stationary.

Materials that are commonly sheared include aluminium, brass, mild steel and stainless steel.

◤ Electrical/electronic processes

Circuit board manufacturing is a massive worldwide industry and circuit boards feature in all the high-tech gadgets we use every day.

Printed circuit board (PCB) manufacture

Printed circuit boards come in all shapes and sizes. Some are very simple, others extremely complex. To manufacture a circuit board you will need to work through some, or all, of the following basic steps:

1 Designing the layout

Usually, circuit boards are designed using computer software. Many packages allow you to construct circuits and position components. Alternatively, layouts can be drawn on paper or directly on to your board to ensure components will fit correctly.

2 Producing the artwork

If you are using computer software, your circuit diagram can be converted to a black and white image showing the component positions and the connecting tracks. This is known as 'artwork' and needs to be printed onto clear acetate material. Check that your printer supports the use of clear acetate first as it can damage some machines.

3 PCB etching

You then need to transfer the track and component layout to the copper-covered board. If you are making the PCB yourself you can draw the tracks straight on to the board using an etch-resistant pen. If you are using printed clear acetate you will need a photo etch board and an ultraviolet (UV) lightbox. Peel the protective covering from the board to expose the sensitive surface, place the artwork on it and put the board in the UV lightbox with the clear acetate between the board and the light. The artwork must be the correct way up or your circuit will be produced the wrong way around. Close the lid and switch the machine on to expose the board to the UV light for around 2½ minutes. From this point on, you will need to use plastic tongs as you are dealing with chemical solutions. Place the board in a developer solution and remove it after 10 seconds. Then place it in a solution of ferric chloride (an etching solution) until all the exposed copper is etched away. After **PCB etching** you are left with the copper tracks and component positions that make up your circuit.

4 Drilling the board

After etching, carefully drill the circuit board at the points indicated to mount your components. Accuracy is vital – an incorrectly drilled hole may cause your circuit to fail.

Printed circuit board (PCB) manufacture

1. Designing the layout

2. Producing the artwork

3. PCB etching

4. Drilling the board

5. Populating the board and soldering

Figure 1.4 The steps of PCB manufacture

Key terms

PCB etching – removing unwanted conductive material from the surface of a circuit board through a chemical process.

5 Populating the board and soldering

Finally, place the components in the correct positions and solder them in place. Again, take care when doing this, as you can easily mount a component in the wrong place or even on the wrong side of the board. Use your layout drawing as a guide.

| **Activity 1.1** | Producing a circuit board |

Using a given circuit, design the circuit layout using appropriate software. Use the finished circuit layout to produce a printed circuit board, fit the components and test the circuit to see if it works.

Surface Mount Technology

High-volume industrial PCB manufacture is achieved through a process called Surface Mount Technology or SMT. Virtually all of today's mass-produced electronic products are manufactured this way. SMT was developed in the 1960s but became more widely used in the 1980s. The process involves attaching electrical components to the surface of a conductive board rather than drilling holes for component legs.

The SMT process

1. Apply solder paste to copper pads.

2. Place components using pick and place robot.

3. Conveyor belts are used to transport the boards to the reflow soldering oven.

4. The board is heated to a temperature that melts the solder paste.

5. Components are soldered to the surface of the board.

6. The finished board is then inspected for imperfections.

Figure 1.6 The SMT process

Reduced cost of components, labour, protection, overheads

Components much smaller and lighter

Reduced human intervention – process highly automated

Advantages of SMT

Complex circuits produced on small boards

Increased production speeds

Figure 1.5 SMT has a number of advantages

Assessment practice 1.1

1 Give **three** hazards associated with using workshop machinery. [3]

Hazard 1: _____

Hazard 2: _____

Hazard 3: _____

2 A small engineering company produces bespoke printed circuit boards for a range of products. Name the five main stages in PCB manufacture. [5]

3 Match the **two** processes to the correct description. [2]

Process   **Description**

Forging — Pouring/injecting liquid metal into a mould, which then cools in the shape of the desired product.

Casting — Heating a metal, then applying a force to change its shape or size permanently.

Applying heat to join two pieces of metal together.

Scales of production

Getting started

Consider the following products: a paper clip, a magazine and a model of a new computer tablet. Discuss with a partner the costs of making these items. What processes would be used? What quantities would be required?

Link

For more information see *Unit 2 Investigating an Engineered Product*.

Key terms

Unit cost – the costs associated with manufacturing each individual product.

Dedicated machines – machines used specifically for a particular process and nothing else.

Introduction

When manufacturing products, the quantity required will determine which production method is used. This is referred to as 'scales of production'. Sometimes a large quantity may be needed so a production line might have machinery and equipment set up to make the same product over and over again. If a smaller quantity is required then it may mean that the production line is designed so that it can be changed to make different products.

One-off production

One-off production is used when a customer requires a product specifically for them or when a prototype needs to be made. There may be one person or a number of people working on the product from beginning to end but in each case the product is unique. This method of production usually results in high **unit costs** because a great deal of time is spent on producing one item, e.g. a prototype of a new smartphone.

Batch production

When a customer requires a certain quantity of identical products they are usually produced through batch production. There is flexibility in this production process: large quantities can be produced, but it is also relatively easy to change the production line to suit another type of product. Examples include specific sizes and quantities of flat bar aluminium or alloy wheels.

Mass production

This production method is used to produce products in very large quantities. It usually involves **dedicated machines** and assembly lines that will repeat the manufacture of the same product over and over again. There may be a number of stages along the production line with workers repeatedly performing their tasks to assemble the finished product. If a range of products is to be made by the same company then there may be separate production lines for each product type. Examples include the production of cars and televisions.

Activity 1.2   Mass production

You are working as an engineer in a small company, manufacturing air conditioning units. One particular unit is extremely popular and your manager has asked your opinion on having a dedicated production line to manufacture this unit only. What will you need to take into consideration for this to take place? Produce a short report on your findings.

Continuous production

As the name suggests, this method involves the continuous production of products over a period of time. This method usually means that the product is relatively inexpensive to purchase as thousands of identical products will be produced. Examples include machine screws, paper clips and plastic sheet material.

Table 1.4 Characteristics of different scales of production

	One-off	Batch	Mass	Continuous
Unit cost	High	Medium	Low	Low
Tools and equipment	General	Specialised	Specialised and dedicated	Specialised and dedicated
Initial investment	Low	Medium	High	High
Production efficiency	Low	Medium/high	High	Very high
Labour type	Skilled	Skilled/semi-skilled	Semi-skilled/unskilled	Unskilled
Labour costs	High	Medium	Low	Low

Assessment practice 1.2

1 Which type of production has the following characteristics: high unit cost, low initial investment, skilled labour? Select **one** of the options. [1]

A Batch production

B Mass production

C One-off production

2 Give **one** advantage of using mass production to produce Blu-ray DVD players. [1]

_____

_____

_____

Discussion

Use the internet to investigate car assembly lines. How does this type of automated production help organisations meet health and safety requirements?

Modern production methods

Getting started ▶▶

Consider how the mobile phone has changed from the 1980s to the present day. Write a brief report about the changes in the way that phones are used and also consider the methods used to manufacture them.
You may wish to use sketches to show how the technology has developed.

Introduction

New sophisticated production methods have helped to transform manufacturing in terms of speed, accuracy and efficiency. Not so long ago, many processes were carried out manually, which had a large impact on the price of goods because of the number of hours taken to produce a product or series of products. Today, many of the same products are manufactured using highly automated systems, often requiring a different type of labour force.

Robots

Although you may think of a robot as something resembling a human being, robots can come in all shapes and sizes, and are already very much a part of the manufacturing industry around the world. So what exactly are they? Robots are usually mechanical devices that can move in every direction using sophisticated electronics to control that movement. 'Robot' is a Czech word that simply means 'worker'. They were first used in the 1960s to carry out hazardous operations, including handling radioactive and toxic materials.

Many organisations rely on robots to produce their products cheaply, accurately and consistently over long periods of time. This is possible if there are processes in place to monitor the performance of each and every robot. Examples of the functions that robots perform in today's world include the following.

A Honda-produced ASIMO robot – the world's most advanced humanoid robot.

Exploration

Space exploration and the search for ships lost at the bottom of the ocean have been made possible through the use of remote operated vehicles (ROVs). Fitted with cameras and sensory devices, they allow personnel to control the vehicle well away from any danger at the site of the exploration.

Assembly

Manufacturing systems use robotic arms to perform dangerous tasks such as welding the frame of a car and spray painting parts without endangering the life of the workers.

Packaging and dispatch

Have you ever wondered how all airport baggage is sorted and arrives, more often than not, at the correct destination? Airports use highly complex programmable logic controllers (PLCs) to control the movement of the baggage through a series of sensors, cameras and conveyor systems.

Computer numerically controlled (CNC) machinery

A **CNC** machine uses programming information to automatically execute a series of machining operations. For example, a CNC milling machine has the same basic functions as a traditional milling machine but it also has a computer that controls the spindle and the movement of the table, allowing for a range of shapes and forms to be cut accurately. Most CNC machines also have a facility that will monitor and detect any wear in the cutting tool as a result of continuous use and adjust or change the tool automatically without stopping production.

Today CNC machining is often referred to as computer-aided manufacturing (**CAM**). This is essentially the same type of machine but CAM usually relies on the use of computer-aided design (**CAD**) programs to create drawings of products that can be directly converted to the CAM machines for manufacture. This impacts on the speed of production and the accuracy and consistency of the finished engineered products. These benefits come at a cost as the software and machines, together with the necessary maintenance and training, are very expensive. But organisations striving to improve their product and production quality should see this as a good investment for the future.

Activity 1.3 Machining an engineered product

Ask your teacher to give you a sample of a printout of a program for machining an engineered product. See if you can work out what each of the codes and numbers mean.

Assessment practice 1.3

1 Give **three** hazardous tasks that robots can perform. [3]

Task 1: _____

Task 2: _____

Task 3: _____

2 Give **one** advantage of using PLCs in a parcel sorting office. [1]

_____

_____

3 Match the **two** types of technology to the correct description. [2]

Technology   **Description**

CAM

> The use of programming information to execute a series of machinery operations.

> A type of software that is used to create drawings of products.

CAD

> The use of CAD information to execute a series of machinery operations.

Link

For more information see *Unit 6 Computer-aided Engineering.*

Key terms

CNC – computer numerically controlled.

CAM – computer-aided manufacturing.

CAD – computer-aided design.

Discussion

With a partner, think about some of the traditional machining techniques that you perform in your workshop and discuss what the impact of replacing them with CNC machines would be. What new skills would you need to learn?

Materials and their processing in engineering

Getting started

Think about the different products you use every day and the materials used to manufacture them. Where do the materials in your workshop come from? Use the Internet to look at material stockists' websites and suggest suitable types and shapes for the products you have looked at.

Link

For more information see *Unit 5 Engineering Materials*.

Key terms

Composite material – a material that is made from two or more constituents for added strength and toughness.

Smart material – a material that can have one or more of its properties changed in a controlled manner by an external stimulus.

Introduction

Why do we need such a range of modern materials? The answer lies in the function or purpose of the engineered products and the properties they need to be successful. You will need an understanding of these materials and processes before you decide how to manufacture an engineered product.

Materials

Table 1.5 Materials and their properties and uses

Material	Properties/characteristics	Applications/uses
Modern composite materials		
Glass reinforced plastic (GRP)	Good strength-to-weight ratio, easily moulded/shaped, resistant to corrosion, durable, electrical insulator, relatively inexpensive	Garage doors, boats and custom moulding to produce furniture
Carbon fibre	Amazing strength-to-weight ratio, easily moulded/shaped, resistant to corrosion, rigid/stiff, electrical insulator and quite expensive	Monocoque structures of supercars and specialist bicycle frames
Kevlar®	High tensile strength-to-low-weight ratio, high chemical resistance, extremely tough, very stable and non-flammable	Bulletproof vests, helmets, ropes and cables
High-performance materials		
Titanium	Low density, high strength, resistant to corrosion, low thermal conductivity	Drill bit coatings, golf clubs and medical implants
Ceramics	Very hard but brittle, good wear resistance, corrosion resistant, very stable, chemically inert	Glassware, catalytic converters and electronic components
Super alloys	Excellent strength at high temperatures, very expensive, resistant to corrosion, hard-wearing	Jet engine turbine blades, valves for piston engines and submarines
Smart materials		
Shape memory alloys (SMA)	Return to their original shape after heating and deformation, lightweight, quite expensive	Spectacle frames, pipe and tube jointing systems
Shape memory polymers	Return to their original shape after heating and deformation, lightweight, resistant to corrosion	Sportswear, surgical sutures and orthopaedic surgery
Piezoelectric actuators	Have an ability to generate electric charge when squeezed or pressed	Sensors, actuators, high voltages and power sources

Metallic foams

A metallic foam is broadly similar to any other type of foam, but it is made of metal – usually aluminium. A typical metallic foam will have between 75 and 95 per cent of its structure made of pores or spaces that can be connected together (open cell foam) or sealed (closed cell foam) which traps gases inside the metal.

Metallic foams are rigid materials and, in a number of cases, they look very much like solid metal until you cut them open or pick them up, as they are very light. Metallic foams have properties that make them very useful for most engineering sectors, particularly the automotive and aerospace sectors, including:

- a high strength-to-weight ratio, particularly when aluminium is used
- the ability to absorb large amounts of energy when crushed
- being non-flammable in most cases
- allowing the transfer of heat energy very easily.

These advantages outweigh the main disadvantages, which are:

- their high cost means that they are only used with advanced technology
- once crushed they do not spring back to shape like polymer foams, therefore they can only be used once.

Typical uses of metallic foams

- Sound dampening in cars or aircraft to reduce noise for the driver or passengers.
- Energy absorption to improve safety so passengers of a car are less likely to be injured during a collision.
- Taking heat from sensitive electronic components to reduce risk of product failure.

Material processing

By examining a range of products from different sectors, it is clear that a wide variety of processes are required to get materials to the correct shape before any secondary machining takes place.

These processes include drawing, blending, rolling, casting, moulding, pressing, sintering, mixing, calendaring and extrusion.

Powder metallurgy

This is a highly evolved method of producing consistently shaped components by blending elements or pre-alloyed powders together. The powders are then compacted in a die and heated in a controlled furnace atmosphere to bond the particles. The process of powder metallurgy includes blending, mixing, pressing and sintering.

There are many advantages to powder metallurgy:

- It can be applied to all classes of materials.
- It requires relatively low processing temperatures.
- It produces a uniform microstructure.
- Complex parts can be produced with precision and close tolerances.
- The process can be automated, allowing high-volume production.
- Final products require little or no finishing.
- There is no waste, so materials are used efficiently.

> **? Did you know?**
>
> Aircraft windshields are heated by a transparent, electricity-conducting ceramic embedded in the glass to keep them clear of fog and ice.

> **Activity 1.4**   Processes
>
> Look at the processes listed under the 'Material processing' section below. Produce a list of suitable products that could be made by each one.

New technologies in engineering

Getting started

Think about an engineering organisation in your local area. With a partner, discuss how its facilities and processes may have changed over the years.

Introduction

As technology moves on, so does the industrial world. This topic will get you thinking about how the invention of new processes and materials helps to develop new products.

Optical fibres

Optical fibres are used in a variety of industries, although their greatest success has undoubtedly been in the communications sector. Originally considered to be too expensive for practical applications, optical fibres have since revolutionised the infrastructure of telephone networks. They bring two advantages over the original copper wire:

- the ability to transmit data at higher speeds
- the ability to do this with lower rates of transmission errors.

Hydrogen fuel cells

Hydrogen is a versatile energy carrier that can be used to power most devices. The key to making this happen is the hydrogen fuel cell – an energy conversion device that captures and uses the power of hydrogen efficiently.

Fuel cells are used for the following reasons:

- they directly convert the chemical energy in the hydrogen to electricity with pure water and useful heat as the only waste materials
- they operate very quietly and are very efficient – typically two to three times more efficient than traditional technologies
- fewer moving parts mean very simple construction and therefore mass production costs are low.

Surface nanotechnologies

These are chemical systems that provide **coatings** to a range of surfaces. Examples include:

- ceramics – produces hygienic surfaces
- metals – resistant to corrosion
- glass – cleaning process is much less time-consuming
- plastics – easier surface cleaning
- textiles – surfaces become water- and dirt-repellent
- minerals – longer-lasting materials.

Key terms

Coating – a layer of material deposited on a surface to enhance its properties.

Bluetooth – open wireless technology for exchanging data over short distances.

Telematics

Telematics is a combination of telecommunications and information communications technology (ICT). This technology has improved the efficiency of many organisations but has had most impact when used in vehicles. It provides an opportunity to monitor the location or movement of vehicles across the world using Global Positioning Systems (GPS) technology.

A GPS navigation system

Blended wing bodies

As rising fuel costs and pressure to cut emissions drive most of the aerospace industry to seek even small improvements in aircraft efficiency, the development of blended wing bodies has seen fuel consumption reduced by up to a third.

This hybrid design uses the wings of a conventional aircraft smoothly blended into a wide tailless body. With the airframe as smooth as possible, this reduces turbulent airflow, thus reducing drag. Combined with the use of lightweight composite materials, this improves the fuel efficiency of the aircraft.

Bionics

This is the science of applying electronic principles and devices, such as computers and miniaturised circuits, to solve medical problems. An example is the development of artificial pacemakers to correct abnormal heart rhythms or the development of prosthetic limbs using a **Bluetooth** connection and specially enabled software to control the limb movement.

Activity 1.5	Pros and cons of bionics

Bionics is an exciting field within the biomedical industry. Discuss the pros and cons of using this technology in sporting activities. What sports could it be used for? What problems could it cause?

Discussion

What products would benefit from using hydrogen fuel cells as a power source? How practical would it be?

Assessment practice 1.4

1 Give **two** advantages of using optical fibres in the communications sector. [2]

Advantage 1: _____

Advantage 2: _____

2 Give **three** benefits of using hydrogen fuel cells. [3]

Benefit 1: _____

Benefit 2: _____

Benefit 3: _____

Sustainable engineered products

Getting started

Choose a product that you have previously investigated. Produce a diagram of its life cycle, from its design to disposal.

Introduction

Engineering and manufacturing have helped raise living standards in some parts of the world, but at what cost? There are concerns about the effects of the depletion of the earth's natural resources as modern lifestyles require huge amounts of energy, much of which is still produced from fossil fuels. Producing sustainable products will help to conserve the earth's resources.

Key terms

Sustainable product – a product that has a minimal impact on the environment throughout each stage of its life cycle.

Life cycle – the different stages a product goes through from design to disposal.

Extraction – the removal of natural resources such as gas, coal and oil from beneath the earth's surface.

Life cycle assessment

Life cycle assessment (LCA) is probably the most important method for assessing the overall environmental impact of products and processes from design to disposal. This system looks at the entire life cycle of a product or process, and maps its environmental footprint.

When carrying out this assessment you should consider the impact of the product and its production processes at the following stages:

- raw material **extraction**
- material production
- production of parts
- assembly of products
- the product use
- product disposal/recycling.

LCA is carried out by firstly creating a list of all the inputs and outputs to the product or process, and then evaluating the environmental impacts of each one. These results can then be used to set specific objectives for an organisation in terms of reducing its environmental footprint.

Did you know?

Waste that enters the ocean can turn up anywhere in the world. In 1992, a container ship in the Pacific Ocean lost 30,000 rubber ducks off the coast of China. The ducks first travelled on the currents towards Australia, but 15 years later some turned up on the shores of the UK!

Eighty per cent of the world's energy comes from burning fossil fuels.

Minimising waste production in engineering

Introduction

Minimising waste production in engineering through effective waste management is a key factor in sustainable development. Finding ways to reduce waste usually starts with a focus on the four Rs: reduce, reuse, recycle and recover. In this topic you will find out about each of these methods and how they affect the way we think about the design and manufacture of engineered products.

The 'four Rs'

Reduce

This is probably the most important of the 'four Rs': preventing waste in the first place means there is less to dispose of in the end. Organisations need to consider reducing the amount of materials and energy used to manufacture their products. Examples could include making products such as mobile phones smaller or exploring different formats such as e-books.

Reuse

This is probably the next most important consideration because if you can reuse waste material then it will no longer be considered as waste. This will reduce costs of disposal and materials/products can be put to further good use. Examples include giving unwanted clothes to charity shops or stripping an old bicycle down and reusing its parts for another bicycle.

Recycle

Sometimes products can't be reused. Recycling keeps raw material in the system and slows down the depletion of the earth's resources such as fossil fuels and trees. If we can keep recycling products then we will cut the amount of materials going to landfill, while also reducing the need to extract gas, coal and oil.

Recover

Sometimes waste has to be disposed of, but finding ways to use this material to produce energy is what recovery is all about. Modern technology allows us to treat waste using thermal and non-thermal processes to produce heat, gas, oil or electricity.

How can you safely dispose of electronic waste?

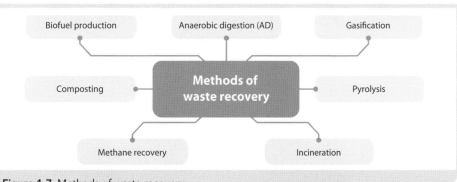

Figure 1.7 Methods of waste recovery

Lean manufacturing

Introduction

Japanese manufacturing techniques have been seen as the way forward in today's competitive business environment. They emerged in the post-World War II era and reached a peak in the 1980s. These techniques have made their way into worldwide manufacturing operations. Their main characteristics include the need to maximise manufacturing efficiencies and improve quality control. This topic will introduce you to some of the most common techniques.

Just-In-Time manufacturing

This involves a strategic approach to the development and operation of a manufacturing system. This means that the production process is organised in a way that ensures parts are available when they are needed.

Advantages of this system include:

- as products are made to customer orders, there is no overproduction, reducing the build-up of stock or inventory such as raw materials and finished goods
- a reduction in stock or inventory also reduces costs as there is less space required for storage of materials or finished goods
- it reduces production cycle times quite drastically through automation and the use of minimal manpower, further reducing costs
- it recognises waste in the movement of materials within an organisation and changes the layout of the manufacturing line to improve efficiency.

Kaizen

Also known as 'continuous improvement', this is a policy of constantly introducing small changes to improve quality and efficiency. This technique puts the workers at the heart of the decision-making as they are the best people to suggest improvements.

Advantages of this system include the following:

- Improvements are based on small changes rather than large changes as a result of research and development.
- As the ideas come from the workers they are less likely to be much different than existing processes and are therefore easier to implement.
- Small changes generally do not cost a great deal of money when compared with any major process/production changes.
- It encourages workers to take ownership of their work and reinforces team-working, leading to improved worker motivation.

Poka-Yoke

This is a technique for avoiding simplistic human error in the workplace also known as 'mistake proofing' and 'fail-safe work methods'. The idea is to take over all the repetitive processes/tasks performed by humans that rely on memory or vigilance and replace them with a simple system to improve productivity and quality.

Advantages of this system include:

- eliminating set-up errors, therefore improving quality
- decreasing set-up time and improving production output
- increased safety as workers do not get injured through lack of concentration
- reduced costs through improved production efficiencies and reducing the need for skilled labour
- improved motivation of workers, as tasks are not so mundane.

Did you know?

There are around 100,000 people directly employed by the British aerospace industry.

Discussion

Think about a product that you have manufactured. If you were to make a batch of these products, how could you make it easier to perform the same tasks over and over again?

Activity 1.6 Researching Japanese manufacturing techniques

- Produce a presentation to argue the case for using one of these Japanese manufacturing techniques to improve efficiency for a product of your choice.
- Use the internet or your resource centre to investigate the disadvantages of the three manufacturing techniques discussed here.

Assessment practice 1.5

1 Explain **two** characteristics of Kaizen that ensure continuous improvement within an engineering company. [4]

1: _____

_____

2: _____

_____

2 Give **three** advantages of Just-In-Time manufacturing. [3]

Advantage 1: _____

Advantage 2: _____

Advantage 3: _____

Renewable sources of energy in engineering

Getting started ▶▶

The number of cars on our roads is increasing dramatically every year. Consider current developments in making this form of transport much 'greener'.

Did you know? ?

Since 1900 the world's consumption of fossil fuels has nearly doubled every 20 years.

Introduction

There is an increasing demand for energy in our fast-developing world. Alternative forms of energy can slow down the depletion of the earth's natural resources and safeguard energy supplies for many generations to come.

Wind energy

Wind is a natural and clean source of renewable energy that produces no air or water pollution. Most wind energy is harnessed through the use of wind turbines. These are usually quite tall structures, sometimes as high as 100 m. The largest wind turbines can generate enough electricity to power small towns and villages. Wind farms sometimes contain hundreds of turbines and are usually positioned in windy areas, such as mountain ridges, for obvious reasons. Sometimes they are even positioned offshore where the wind can turn huge propellers connected to a generator to produce electricity.

Many governments also offer incentives for companies to use this form of energy. However, some people think they are ugly and spoil the surrounding landscape and the constant spinning of the propellers produces noise pollution. This is variable – but when there is no wind, no electricity will be produced.

Solar energy

Most solar energy is produced through a series of panels that contain photovoltaic cells. These cells convert the heat produced from the rays of the sun into electricity. Over recent years there has been an increase in the use of photovoltaic panels on people's roofs. The electricity produced can be used to power a home and even heat water directly.

Solar panels initially costs thousands of pounds to install, but if you have a south-facing roof they can significantly reduce electricity bills. In fact the government pays the householder for any extra energy produced that is fed back into the National Grid. However, some people think that these panels look unsightly. Today, an ever-increasing array of products, such as torches, mobile phones, small solar cell units and outdoor lighting, are powered by solar cells or panels. This is because panels not only produce electricity but are able to store it for use at night.

Domestic solar panels are becoming increasingly common.

Hydro energy

Water is another precious natural resource that can generate an unstoppable force.

Hydroelectricity is the use of running water – this could be a small stream, a large river or ocean waves – to generate electricity. Streams and rivers flow downhill and as water flows downhill it generates **potential energy**. Hydropower systems convert this potential energy into **kinetic energy** using a turbine. As water passes through the turbine, it spins the propeller blades, much like a wind turbine. The turbine is connected to a generator, which produces electricity. The faster the water flow, the more energy is produced.

This system usually comes in the form of a hydro dam where turbines are built at the base of the dam and water is released at a controlled rate to generate sufficient power. These systems can work 24 hours a day and produce electricity in abundance with no air or water pollution.

However, the initial cost of producing a facility to harness this natural resource's power is high and in periods of drought general water usage will need to be controlled around the country to ensure that there is enough water to keep producing electricity.

Geothermal energy

This system uses the heat from rocks in the earth's inner core that turns water into steam. Engineers drill down into the hot regions and the purified steam rises to drive turbines that produce electricity. Where there is no natural groundwater, cold water can be pumped down to create steam.

'Geothermal' comes from the Greek words 'ge' meaning 'earth' and 'therme' meaning 'heat'. This form of energy production does not produce any pollution so does not contribute to the greenhouse effect. There is no fuel required to run a geothermal power station and once built, the running costs are very low – just the energy needed to run a pump for the cold water, but even that can be taken from the energy being generated.

> ### Key terms
>
> **Potential energy** – energy that results from a body or a mass's position or configuration.
>
> **Kinetic energy** – energy created as a result of movement of a body/mass, whether it is vertical or horizontal.

> ### Discussion
>
> Why do you think it is important to use alternative forms of energy to generate power?

Activity 1.7   Renewable energy locations

Investigate the renewable energy production methods discussed in this unit and identify suitable locations for each one. Give some advantages and disadvantages of using these alternative energies in your chosen areas.

Assessment practice 1.6

1 A company is considering using tidal power to generate electricity. What would be the most appropriate location? Select **one** of the options. [1]

A On the coast near a quiet beach

B Near the mouth of an estuary

C In the middle of the ocean

Assessment Zone

This section has been written to help you to do your best when you take the onscreen test. Read through it carefully and ask your teacher/tutor if there is anything that you are still not sure about.

How you will be assessed

You will take an onscreen assessment, using a computer. This will be set over 15–20 screens and have a maximum of 50 marks. The number of marks for each question will be shown in brackets e.g. [1]. The test will last for one hour.

There will be different types of question in the test.

A Questions where the answers are available and you have to choose the answer(s) that fit. *Tip: Always read carefully to see how many answers are needed and how you can show the right answer.*

Examples:

Match the **four** products to the most appropriate engineering sector. [4]

Product	Sector
Aircraft landing gear	Chemical
Smartphone	Aerospace
Washing up liquid	Automotive
Flat bed lorry	Communications

Answers:

Aircraft landing gear	Aerospace
Smartphone	Communications
Washing up liquid	Chemical
Flat bed lorry	Automotive

Which **one** of the following types of energy source is considered renewable? [1]

A Coal

B Gas

C Oil

D Solar

Answer: D

B Questions where you are asked to give a short answer worth 1–2 marks. *Tip: Look carefully at how the question is set out to see how many points are needed.*

Examples:

What sustainable energy source is shown in the picture? [1]

Answer: Solar

Composite materials are used when manufacturing a range of parts for Formula 1 racing cars. Explain **one** advantage of this use of composite materials. [2]

Answer: Composite materials are lightweight. Therefore, they improve the overall speed of the car, helping it to go faster around the circuit. (Other appropriate answers will also be accepted.)

Disclaimer: These practice questions and sample answers are not actual exam questions and have been provided as a practice aid only. They should be used as practice material only and should not be assumed to reflect the format or coverage of the real external test.

C **Questions where you are asked to give a longer answer – these can be worth up to 8 marks.**

Tips: Ensure you answer **all** parts of the question in order to achieve full marks.

Check your answer – you may need to use the scroll bar to move back to the top.

Example:

> TNC Engineering is an engineering company that uses large amounts of water and energy during the production of exhaust systems. The company is looking to make the production process more environmentally friendly. Discuss how the company can use electricity and water in a more sustainable way. [8]
>
> **Answer:**
>
> The company should look to use more environmentally friendly sources of energy such as wind, solar or HEP. These would depend on the location of the factory. If it is located near a stream or river which flows all year, then HEP would be most useful. However, in most areas of the country solar energy can be a reliable source of electricity for most of the year, providing solar cells can face in a southerly direction. Either of these would reduce the reliance on fossil fuels and make the company operate in a more sustainable way. Wind energy is less reliable, particularly in built-up areas as the wind is blocked by other buildings. As a result, solar electricity would probably be the better choice.
>
> There are no carbon emissions from these energy sources, so there will be less impact on the environment. Greenhouse gases associated with the production of the exhausts will be reduced, and the company will be less reliant on fossil fuels such as coal for electricity production. The company's costs will also be reduced as renewable energy sources are much cheaper.
>
> To reduce the use of water, the company could begin to harvest rainwater by collecting water from the roof of the factory and storing it in tanks. They could also recycle the water used during manufacturing as greywater, which could be used as a coolant or to flush toilets.

Many questions will have images. Sometimes you will be asked to click to play a video or animation. You can do this as many times as you want within the time allowed for the test. Sometimes you may be asked to do a calculation – you can use the calculator provided in the onscreen test system if you need to.

How to improve your answer

Read the two student answers below, together with the feedback. Try to use what you learn here when you answer questions in your test.

Question

> The calculator pictured is powered using a renewable source of energy.
>
> Describe **two** other forms of renewable energy apart from solar panels. [4]

Student 1's answer

```
1 Wind energy

2 No attempt
```

Feedback:

The student has selected wind energy for answer 1, which would gain 1 mark. The student has not provided any justification for their selection so no further marks are given for answer 1.

Answer 2 has not been attempted, therefore no marks are given.

The student would achieve 1 mark overall.

Student 2's answer

```
1 Wind energy that turns a set of blades or propellers
  on a wind turbine. The blades are attached to a rotor
  that connects the main shaft. This spins a generator to
  create electricity.

2 Wave energy is power produced using the force of the
  ocean's tides. Tides move in and out twice a day and
  generate large amounts of force. This force is used
  to turn a turbine under the water which generates
  electricity.
```

Feedback:

The student has selected two different types of renewable energy – wind energy for answer 1 (1 mark) and wave energy for answer 2 (1 mark). The student has described how both wind and wave energy are produced through the use of turbines and generators, by using natural sources of energy (2 marks).

The student has provided an excellent answer that covers all the requirements of the question and will achieve 4 marks overall.

Assess yourself

Question 1

Describe the process of turning a product. [2]

Question 2

Using workshop materials such as a centre lathe can be dangerous. Give **three** safety procedures that you must follow when using a centre lathe. [3]

Question 3

TNC Engineering produces injection moulded components for the automotive industry. When parts are rejected after production, they recycle the plastic material. Describe **two** advantages for TNC Engineering of recycling these plastic materials. [4]

Question 4

Energy sources can be classed as either renewable or non-renewable. Complete the following table by identifying whether the energy sources oil, wave power and solar are renewable or non-renewable. [3]

Energy source	Renewable	Non-renewable
Tidal power	✓	
Geothermal	✓	
Coal		✓
Gas		✓
Oil		
Wave power		
Solar		

Question 5

State the main difference between MIG welding and Oxy-Acetylene welding? [1]

For further practice, see the assessment practice questions on pages 11, 13, 15, 19, 23 and 25. Answers can be found on page 275.

Hints and tips

- **Use the pre-test time** – make sure you have read the instructions, tested the function buttons, adjusted your seat and that you can see the screen clearly.
- **Watch the time** – the screen shows you how much time you have left. You should aim to take about 1 minute per mark. Some early questions will take less time than this and some later questions will take you longer.
- **Plan your longer answers** – read the question carefully and think about the key points you will make. You can use paper or the onscreen note function to jot down ideas.
- **Check answers at the end** – you should keep moving through the questions and not let yourself get stuck on one. If you are really unsure of an answer or cannot give an answer, then you can use the onscreen system to 'flag' that you need to come back to that question at the end.
- **Read back your longer answers** – make sure you view the whole answer if you are checking back. There is no spell check facility.
- **Do you find it harder to read onscreen?** – talk to your teacher in advance of your test about how the system can be adjusted to meet your needs. During the test, tools within the test player will allow you to apply colour filters, change the font size and colour, as well as allowing you to zoom in on the images and text.

Introduction

Have you ever looked closely at a product and thought how has that been made and why? By nature, engineers are very inquisitive and will pick up a product and examine it to see what its functions are, how it was manufactured, what materials were used and whether it is fit for purpose. This unit will help you to start looking at products through the eyes of an engineer.

You will investigate how products can be manufactured to the same standards time after time. Certain procedures must be put in place to guarantee quality and reliability. You will see, for example, how both quality assurance (QA) processes and quality control (QC) checks play an important role in the manufacturing process.

Assessment: This unit will be assessed by a series of assignments set by your teacher/tutor.

Learning aims

After completing this unit you should:

A understand the performance requirements of an engineered product

B understand the selection of specific materials for use in the components that make up an engineered product

C understand the selection and use of manufacturing processes in an engineered product

D understand the quality issues related to an engineered product.

After completing this unit, I always think about the different processes and quality checks that lie behind the production of an engineered product. I appreciate that – however simple some products may appear – a lot of thought and detail has gone into manufacturing them!

Ben, *16-year-old potential engineering apprentice*

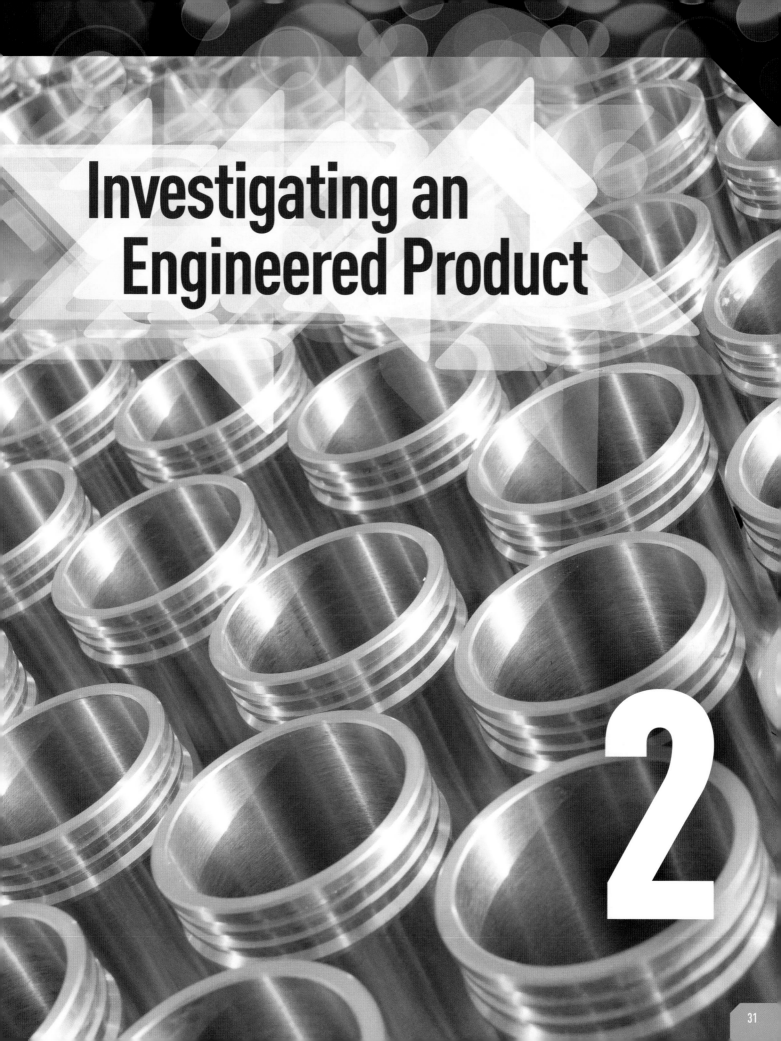

Investigating an Engineered Product

2

BTEC
Assessment Zone

This table shows you what you must do in order to achieve a **Pass**, **Merit** or **Distinction** grade, and where you can find activities in this book to help you.

Assessment criteria			
Level 1	Level 2 **Pass**	Level 2 **Merit**	Level 2 **Distinction**
Learning aim A: Understand the performance requirements of an engineered product			
1A.1 Identify relevant basic specification criteria for an engineered product.	**2A.P1** Outline relevant basic and advanced specification criteria for an engineered product. **See Assessment activity 2.1, page 37**	**2A.M1** Explain the importance of basic and advanced specification criteria for an engineered product. **See Assessment activity 2.1, page 37**	
Learning aim B: Understand the selection of specific materials for use in the components that make up an engineered product			
1B.2 Identify materials used in two components of an engineered product, stating engineering properties for each.	**2B.P2** Describe the engineering properties, qualities and environmental impact of materials in two components of an engineered product and suggest alternatives. **See Assessment activity 2.2, page 43**	**2B.M2** Compare and contrast the materials used in two components in an engineered product with reference to engineering properties, qualities, environmental impact and alternatives. **See Assessment activity 2.2, page 43**	**2B.D1** Evaluate the fitness for purpose of materials used in two components of an engineered product in relation to possible alternative materials making reference to properties, qualities, environmental impact and alternatives. **See Assessment activity 2.2, page 43**
Learning aim C: Understand the selection and use of manufacturing processes in an engineered product			
1C.3 Outline two production processes used in the manufacture of components in an engineered product.	**2C.P3** Describe two production processes used in the manufacture of components in an engineered product. **See Assessment activity 2.3, page 49**	**2C.M3** Explain reasons for the selection and use of two production processes used in the manufacture of components in an engineered product. **See Assessment activity 2.3, page 49**	**2C.D2** Compare and contrast the production processes used in the manufacture of components in an engineered product in terms of their environmental impact and the manufacturing need. **See Assessment activity 2.3, page 49**
Learning aim D: Understand the quality issues related to an engineered product			
1D.4 Identify quality control (QC) checks that could be used during the manufacture of an engineered product.	**2D.P4** Explain how quality control (QC) checks can help to improve the quality of an engineered product. **See Assessment activity 2.4, page 53**		
1D.5 Outline the quality assurance (QA) system that could be used during the manufacture of an engineered product.	**2D.P5** Explain why a specific quality assurance (QA) system should be used during the manufacture of an engineered product. **See Assessment activity 2.4, page 53**	**2D.M4** Analyse the fitness for purpose of a quality assurance (QA) system for an engineered product. **See Assessment activity 2.4, page 53**	**2D.D3** Evaluate the use of the quality control (QC) checks and quality assurance (QA) systems for an engineered product. **See Assessment activity 2.4, page 53**

How you will be assessed

This unit will be assessed by a series of tasks set by your teacher/tutor based around a given or selected engineered product consisting of two or more components. For example, you could investigate the materials, manufacturing processes and the required quality checks and quality assurance processes for a computer keyboard in relation to its function. You will also be required to disassemble and then reassemble the product in order to identify the different component parts.

Your assessment could take the form of:

- a written report or presentation detailing your product investigation
- photographic evidence of you disassembling/labelling the components as well as the reassembly.

Technical specification

Getting started

Think about a product you have used. Make a list of all the things you think the designer considered when they were drawing up a technical specification for the manufacturer.

Introduction

In this topic you will learn how technical specifications are used to communicate essential information about a product to the engineer who is to manufacture or maintain it. These specifications are produced to ensure that the final product performs in the way it should.

Basic specification criteria

When designing a product, an engineer must consider the following basic criteria:

- **Form** – why is the product shaped as it is? Why does it have a specific style, colour or texture?
- **Function** – what is the main purpose of the product?
- **User requirements** – what qualities will make the product attractive to potential users?

When considering these points, it is important to state *why* each one is important, so that the manufacturer receives as much information as possible.

User requirements: to use function keys such as 'print screen' as short cuts to carry out complex operations.

Function: connected directly to the computer, which in turn is connected to the monitor. The computer receives the signal from the keyboard and relays this information to the monitor making a letter or number appear on the screen.

Form: coloured to match the computer case and the monitor surround.

Function: allow the user to enter text characters and numbers. When these keys are pressed on the keyboard, characters appear on the monitor.

User requirements: feet to enable the user to adjust the angle of the keyboard, making it more comfortable to use.

User requirements: to enter text characters that will appear as words on the screen. This enables the user to write documents and emails.

User requirements: to be able to enter numerical values, carry out calculations or simply enter the date.

Form: rectangular shape, with four rounded corners, so it can be placed in front of any monitor.

Form: texture of the outer case is smooth which makes it easy to clean.

Figure 2.1 A learner's specification for a computer keyboard using basic criteria

- On a sheet of A3 paper draw a keyboard that is a mirror image of a traditional keyboard, i.e. so that the number keys are on the left side, and the keys run from right to left. Discuss how easy or difficult you think it would be to use this keyboard.

- Draw a fully annotated diagram to show what you think keyboards will look like in 25 years' time. How do you imagine we will communicate with computers and with one another?

Advanced specification criteria

There are also more advanced criteria that should be considered when producing a technical specification:

- **Performance** requirements – what are the technical feats that must be achieved within the product?

- Material and component requirements – how should the materials and components perform within the product?

- Ease of **manufacture** – how can the product be manufactured in the most efficient way?

- Ease of **maintenance** – how can the product be maintained in the most efficient way?

- Legal and safety requirements – are there any recognised standards or pieces of legislation that must be complied with during the manufacture and maintenance of the product?

Again, you must ensure that the information you give in any specification is correct and supported by clear justifications.

Key terms

Form – the shape/style of a product.

Function – the purpose of a product.

Performance – a product's ability to do the job it is intended to do.

Manufacture – the process followed to make a product.

Maintenance – the process followed to keep a product working properly.

CONTINUED ▶▶

Key terms

Ergonomic – designed to be safe, comfortable and easy to use.

Table 2.1 A learner's specification for a computer keyboard, using advanced criteria

Performance

- The current layout 'QWERTY' for the letter keys is supposed to be the most **ergonomic** way of typing, allowing the user to type comfortably with both hands.
- The numerical keys appear in order which is the most comfortable way of entering them.
- The number keys are generally on the right-hand side of the keyboard or just above the top row of letters. Having them in two places allows both left- and right-handed users to enter numbers comfortably.
- The marks that appear on the characters F and J allow users to align their hands so that they know where the relevant keys are and do not need to look at the keyboard when typing. This makes typing quicker and also benefits those with impaired vision.

Material and component requirements

- The outer casing is made of a plastic material that will withstand the knocks and bumps the keyboard may receive.
- The material can be produced in different colours making the keyboard appeal to a wider audience.
- The material is relatively cheap which will reduce the cost of the keyboard to the customer.
- The easiest way to produce the case would be through injection moulding, which would ensure the same case is reproduced over and over again.
- To prevent the case from being accidentally damaged it needs to be manufactured from a suitable material that can be easily cleaned by household products.
- The product needs to be made from a suitable material so that it is insulated. This way, the customer will not receive an electric shock when using it. The cable must also be well insulated and flexible so that the keyboard can easily be moved by the user.

Ease of manufacture

- Must be easy to manufacture – the more complex the process, the more expensive the keyboard will be. This is why injection moulding is used for the casing – it is quick and produces a good-quality product over and over again.
- The downside is the cost for the initial tooling, but this must be offset by the number of keyboards manufactured.
- All the other components that make up the keyboard must be produced in the most economic way possible, e.g. the electronic circuit board will be produced on a production line.
- Complex methods of manufacture would increase the cost of the keyboard and deter users from buying it.

Ease of maintenance

- Must be easy to maintain as it will be used by people with a wide range of skills.
- For all users the basic maintenance requirements are to wipe the keys to keep them clean, to blow dust off the keyboard occasionally and not to eat or drink while using it.
- Users should also check the connections looking for bent pins if the keyboard does not work correctly.
- These checks should be done on a weekly basis or when a problem occurs.

Legal and safety requirements

- Must ensure the keyboard will not cause injury to any person using it or damage the computer it is connected to.
- As the keyboard is linked to a computer powered by electricity it must be well insulated to prevent the user from receiving an electric shock when typing. This can be done through the use of suitable materials or by putting in place protective measures within the electronic circuitry.
- The keyboard design must be original and not a copy of someone else's as this could lead to legal problems.

Discussion

Can you think of ways to input information into a computer other than by using a traditional keyboard? Discuss the advantages and disadvantages of each method and arrive at a conclusion as to which is the best.

Assessment activity 2.1   Producing a technical specification   2A.P1 | 2A.M1

You have been given the task of disassembling and analysing an engineered product of your choice. The product must have at least two components.

You will need to find out what the designer had to consider when designing this product. Present your findings as a technical specification using the following key headings:

- form
- function
- performance requirements
- user requirements
- material and component requirements
- ease of manufacture
- ease of maintenance
- legal and safety requirements.

Tips

- Include photographs of you carrying out the activity.
- Lay out all of the components on flipchart paper and clearly label them. Document this by taking a photograph.
- Make sure you include written information about the importance of each heading in your specification.

Selection of materials and components

Introduction

We are surrounded by many different products – all of which have been engineered in one way or another from many different materials. Each material has a different set of properties so it follows that some may be better suited to certain products or components than others.

▶ Properties of materials

Aesthetic properties

Different materials have different appearances. A product manufactured from well-chosen materials and with an attractive surface finish will appeal to the user. It is often possible to change the **aesthetic** appearance of a material by painting or coating it, or by giving it a different surface finish or texture to meet the designer's requirements.

Mechanical properties

Some materials are chosen for their mechanical properties, some of which are explained in Table 2.2.

Table 2.2 Mechanical properties of materials

Mechanical property	Description
Tensile strength	The ability of a material to withstand forces stretching it from side to side. Imagine you are holding a piece of material in both hands. The tensile strength would be determined by the amount of force you would have to apply to the material before it breaks by moving your hands outwards to the left and right.
Ductility	The ability of a material to be stretched out in tension before it breaks. The test for ductility is very similar to the test for tensile strength. The difference is that two marks are placed on the material a set distance apart before it is stretched until the material breaks.
Malleability	The ability of a material to be spread or deformed in many different directions, until it breaks. These forces can be the result of many different processes such as rolling, pressing or hammering operations. Copper is both ductile and malleable, while lead is extremely malleable but not very ductile and will soon fracture when loaded in tension.
Hardness	The ability of a material to withstand wear and abrasion. Hardness is usually tested on materials by striking it with a steel ball or diamond point, under a controlled load, and then measuring the size of the indentation made in the material. The smaller the dent, the harder the material is said to be.
Toughness	The ability of a material to withstand sudden shock or impact loading. The easiest way to explain toughness would be to place a piece of material in a bench vice and then strike it at a constant force until it breaks. The material toughness can be determined by the number of blows required to break the material.

Electrical properties

The electrical property of a material is its ability to allow an electrical current to flow through it. Materials which allow the passage of an electrical current are called **conductors** and those that do not allow it are called **insulators**. Copper is a good conductor which is why it is used on electrical circuits, whereas polymers and plastic are good insulators so they are used to cover the copper wires on electric cables making the cables safe to handle.

Chemical properties

Materials can react with chemicals in various ways so it is important to consider their applications carefully. The wrong choice of material could affect the reliability and function of the product. For example, a ferrous material such as mild steel will rust if left outside untreated, but if it is painted, it is protected and will not rust.

◤ Qualities of materials

Cost

It is important to consider the cost of materials when designing a product as this will affect the cost of the product to the customer. Extracting raw materials can be very expensive – it may involve the use of heavy machinery and the raw material may need to be processed before it is suitable for use in manufacturing.

There will also be a cost for the manufacture of the product.

Availability

The availability of materials can influence the cost: materials in short supply will be very expensive whereas those that are readily available will be cheaper. It is easy to locate materials and check on their availability using the Internet.

Durability

The durability of a material is its ability to withstand wear and tear. If a product is to be used a lot then the material it is made from must be very durable.

Reusability

Many materials can be recycled after they have been used for their original purpose. Most households have recycling bins where plastic bottles, cans, paper and card can be collected. These items are taken to a recycling plant where they are sorted and then sold to be reused. For example, paper can be reused to make newspaper and plastic bottles can be used to make plastic pipes and garden furniture. Products made from recycled goods often cost the customer less.

Safety

Safety is one of the most important considerations when selecting a suitable material for the design and manufacture of a product. Unsafe materials may cause injury, leading to complaints and claims for compensation against the manufacturer.

There are many industrial standards that relate to safety. Products often display Kitemarks and CE symbols to show they have passed certain safety tests.

Link

For more information about the properties of materials see *Unit 5 Engineering Materials*.

Key terms

Conductors – materials which have low resistance to the flow of electrons.

Insulators – materials which have a high resistance to the flow of electrons.

Just checking

1   What does it mean when a material is said to be malleable?
2   What does it mean when a material is described as being durable?
3   Give two benefits of reusing materials.

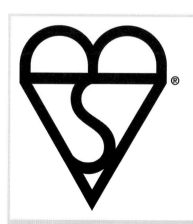
Figure 2.2 British Standards Institution Kitemark

Environmental impact

Introduction

Materials are not always readily available – most have to be sourced and extracted and then go through a series of processes before they can be used to manufacture products. In this section you will look at the impact this can have on the environment.

◤ Extraction and processing of raw materials

The extraction of **raw materials** involves the use of heavy machinery at the extraction site, as well as the different forms of transport needed to take the materials to a processing plant. During this transportation, exhaust fumes are released into the environment. When these materials are processed, further harmful waste products can be released. During processing, temperatures can reach as high as 1,800°C – this too requires a lot of energy.

The use of man-made materials can also be harmful. For example, plastics are formed through industrial processes where different chemicals are added together to produce materials that are suitable for particular applications.

It is always important to consider the environmental impact of the materials used in engineered products.

Case study

Polyvinyl chloride (PVC) is processed using salt and oil. It is commonly used for doors and windows in the building trade, and in children's toys and food packaging, because it can be manufactured in different colours. During the manufacturing process toxic chemical pollutants are produced which have a huge impact on the environment and can also lead to health issues for humans.

◤ Disposal of products after their useful lifespan

As a society we are keen to find ways to reduce the impact of waste materials on our environment and create a greener world. One way of doing this is to **recycle** these materials during the manufacture of new products. For example, the soft drinks can you are using today could be a wing panel on a car tomorrow.

But there remain some materials which cannot be recycled. These are sent to **landfill** sites which have a negative impact on the environment, giving off gases and attracting wildlife that feed on waste food.

It is important that you consider the **life cycle** of a product when selecting materials to be used in an engineered product.

Activity 2.2   Encouraging recycling

Produce a leaflet that can be distributed to parents showing how plastic bottles and containers are recycled. This should also be used to encourage recycling of plastic goods at home.

WorkSpace

Ben Lawton

Manager of a small engineering company

My company employs 20 staff. Within the team there are two design engineers, an engineer who creates all the CNC programs used to manufacture components, nine machine operatives who operate a range of 14 CNC machines and five bench fitters. These qualified engineers are supported by one person in the stores, one receptionist and one person dealing with orders and deliveries.

Recently, the company was asked to manufacture and supply a new product for one of our regular clients. The product needs to be durable and made from plastic. It will be mass-produced and production must be carried out using the most economical methods. The product will also need to comply with all relevant quality standards so that it can be sold in the UK and abroad.

As manager, I need to ensure that every stage in the production is carried out correctly, from drawing up the product specification to maintaining product quality during the production process.

Think about it

1 Who will produce the product specification?

2 Imagine you work for Ben's company.

   a How will you decide on a suitable plastic material?

   b How will you make sure the product matches the specification?

   c How will you check that quality is maintained throughout manufacture of the tooling and during the production run?

3 What standard tests must be passed to allow a product to be sold in the UK and abroad?

Alternative materials

Getting started

Create a list of as many different materials you can think of and group them under the headings 'Old' and 'New'. For each material give an example of a product that is made from it.

Key terms

Composite – made up from two or more constituents for added strength and toughness.

Link

For more information about plastics, see *Unit 5 Engineering Materials*.

Discussion

Identify two similar products that are made of different materials, e.g. a wooden rowing boat and a glass fibre boat, and describe the advantages and disadvantages of each type of material used.

Introduction

In recent years, materials have been developed that are much lighter than those we have used in the past. In this section, you will explore the use of some of these alternative materials and consider the benefits they bring to engineered products.

◥ Advantages and disadvantages

There are many advantages of using alternative materials:

- **Weight** – modern materials can be lightweight yet just as strong as traditional materials. For example, **composite** materials can be much lighter, yet stronger than some metals. Weight can be an important factor for engineers as the heavier the product, the more energy is required to move it. This is a big consideration for the automotive and aerospace sectors because lighter cars/planes will be more economical in terms of fuel consumption.

- **Shape** – modern materials can be easily shaped, for example, **glass reinforced plastic (GRP)** which is used on boat hulls and canoes. The ability to produce very smooth aerodynamic profiles is an important consideration when aircraft or road vehicles are being designed to operate economically or at high speed.

- **Mechanical properties** – the mechanical properties of composite materials are superior to – and sometimes uniquely different from – the properties of their constituents. By choosing an appropriate combination, manufacturers can produce mechanical properties that exactly fit the requirements for a part or structure.

- **Additional benefits** – altering the composition of modern materials can introduce additional benefits such as making a product flame retardant or very durable. Plastics can also be produced in many different colours which removes the need for painting. This, in turn, reduces the cost of the product.

- **Parts integration** – the ability to integrate parts can have several benefits including a reduced parts count, lower costs and faster assembly time. Integrating parts is the coming together of different parts to create a single product. The single parts can be produced and then used in many different products.

There are also some disadvantages to using alternative materials. For example, they may:

- be more expensive to buy
- be in short supply, which could cause problems with production
- need additional treatments, which could be expensive
- require specialist machining or manufacturing process, which will increase the cost of the finished product. This could also make it difficult to find a company able to carry out the manufacturing process in the time available.

Case study

Glass reinforced plastic (GRP) is used instead of sheet metal in the aerospace and automotive sectors because it has the following advantages:

- complex structures and shapes can be easily fabricated (important for both aesthetic and aerodynamic reasons)
- ability to integrate several parts into a single large component (impossible to do this with metal construction)
- freedom from corrosion
- combination of lightness and strength.

Despite these considerable advantages, it is important to mention that there can also be disadvantages to using alternative materials. These include:

- high costs depending on the raw materials used
- composites can often be brittle
- the repair of composite parts and structures requires specialised techniques and may take considerable time while hot or cold curing takes place.

Comparing materials

When selecting materials an engineer must consider how and where the product will be used, and also think about any other properties it may require. For example, if you were to use thermoplastic for the air filter cover on a car engine it would be fine while the engine is cold, but it would soften and lose shape as the engine heats up. In contrast a thermo set plastic would not be affected by a change in temperature.

Did you know?

The driver's seat in a Formula One car is made from carbon fibre and is moulded to suit the individual, making each seat different. Carbon fibre is used because of its high strength and weight.

Activity 2.3   What can modern materials achieve?

Bloodhound SSC is a project based in the UK that is trying to build a supersonic car that will travel at 1,000 mph to break the world land speed record. Visit Pearson hotlinks to see a website which explores how modern materials are helping to make this challenge possible.

Assessment activity 2.2   Consideration of a suitable material   2B.P2 | 2B.M2 | 2B.D1

Today's Formula One drivers are very well protected if they crash during testing or on race day because of the widespread use of modern-day materials in the construction of their cars.

Consider the different materials that are used in two components of your selected product from Assessment activity 2.1. Are these materials fit for purpose in terms of their properties, qualities and environmental impact? How would these compare to alternative materials?

Tips

- Areas of the car to look at are: the cockpit, seating, crush zone, nose cones and body along with the exhaust system.
- Consider the materials' properties, strength, lightness, durability, ease of manufacture and also the cost associated with your chosen product.
- Consider the environmental issues involved with obtaining raw materials, transportation costs, quality and also the ability to recycle the materials after the product has reached the end of its life cycle.

Selection of production processes

Getting started

Look around a room and identify three different products. See if you can identify the process through which each has been manufactured, giving a reason why you think this method was chosen.

Introduction

How a product is manufactured will depend on the number of components required, the materials used and the costs involved, as well as the application, function and quality of the product. This topic will look at some of the different processes used in the manufacture of engineered products.

Selecting the right process for the product

The decision about which production process to select can be informed by the number of products required by the manufacturer:

One-off production – where a single product is produced. These tend to be specialist parts and are very expensive to produce as you have all the set-up costs, material costs, design costs and manufacturing costs, including tooling and labour. These products are usually manufactured by highly skilled and well-paid engineers. They will generally be produced using manually operated machines such as mills, lathes and drills, with a large amount of manual skills, such as filing and polishing, being used.

Batch production – where a pre-determined number of products are produced. Set-up costs incurred to aid manufacture can be divided by the number of products being produced. This method is cheaper than one-off production. Examples of this type of production method include the use of computer numerically controlled machines (CNC) or moulding techniques.

Mass production – where there is a high demand for the product and thousands need to be produced. Here the set-up cost is offset by the production of much larger quantities. This method of production is the most economical. Methods used for mass production include CNC machines, injection moulding or die casting.

How each process meets the manufacturing need

One-off production processes will fully meet the manufacturing needs of the product. This is because a single part is produced to the customer's exact specification. These products are very expensive, with the customer paying a premium rate.

Both batch and mass production requires the production of a quantity of the same product. To achieve this a process that is capable of reproducing the same component over and over again must be selected, e.g. CNC machinery or injection moulding. Each component is expected to be of the same quality, so regular inspections must take place to ensure the products remain within the given tolerance or required accuracy.

Methods of manufacturing products

Here are some examples of different methods of manufacturing products:

- **Computer numerically controlled (CNC) machining** – the manufacture of products using machines controlled by computers. An engineer must first create a CNC program that will be fed from the computer into the control unit of the machine. The control unit will then use this data to move the machine to the required position. Products produced this way are very accurate and identical products can be quickly produced over and over again. CNC machining requires a highly skilled operative to set the machine up in the first instance, but once the program has been proved and the product passes the quality checks, a less skilled operative can take over.

- **Injection moulding** – a method used to manufacture many plastic components. This is a very clever process which allows different features, such as holes and strengthening ribs, to be moulded at the same time. An injection mould tool is produced and then placed into a press. The required plastic material is heated and then forced into the mould where it is allowed to cool slightly to retain its shape. The mould tool will then open and the component is ejected and falls to the bottom of the press. The press then closes and the process starts over again. The time taken to produce each component is called the **cycle time**. This is a very economical way of producing good-quality plastic components time after time.

Activity 2.4   Injection moulding

Identify a product that has been moulded with a hole through it and see if you can work out how this is done. A good example is a plastic pencil sharpener.

- **Blow moulding** – a process where a molten plastic or resin is injected into a mould tool. Once the resin has been injected into the mould, air is blown into it. This forces the molten plastic or resin to take the shape of the mould. The pressure forced into the mould causes the plastic or resin to form a uniform thickness in the shape of the mould. After a short period of time, the mould opens and the component falls to the bottom of the blow moulding machine, ready for the process to start again.

Activity 2.5   Blow moulding

Plastic drinks bottles and shampoo bottles are both produced by a process called blow moulding. Produce a presentation showing how this process works.

Just checking

1 What is the difference between one-off and batch production?
2 What is the difference between batch and mass production?
3 Which method of manufacture is the most economical and why?
4 What does CNC stand for?

Environmental impact

Getting started

Think about the mobile phone you have in your pocket, the computer you use every day or the television you watch at home. What impact has the manufacture of these products had on the environment?

Introduction

Energy is needed to operate tools and machinery. The energy used during production will impact on the environment – directly or indirectly. One of the biggest environmental considerations is the potential production of waste and pollution as a result of manufacturing.

The use of energy during production

An energy source of one form or another is used to manufacture every product we use today. Most common is the electricity used to power factories, providing lighting, heating and the energy required to run manufacturing machines. The bulk of the electricity used in the UK today comes from power stations that use either coal or gas.

In a coal-fired power station the environmental issues begin before any electricity is produced. The coal has to be mined then transported from the mine to the power station, where it is burnt to produce the energy required to heat the water used during the process of generating electricity. This production process produces many waste gases which are released into the atmosphere.

To combat this, power stations are investing huge amounts of money to reduce their environmental impact by cutting the amount of gases they release into the atmosphere.

But fossil fuels such as coal and oil will not last forever, so new energy sources must be found. Energy companies are investing in new technologies such as wind farms or the use of tidal waves to generate cleaner electricity with minimal impact on the environment.

Did you know?

When a car has burnt 1 litre of petrol it will have produced 2.28 kg of carbon dioxide – the equivalent of 1,268 litres.

Discussion

How are car manufacturers trying to reduce the amount of carbon dioxide pollution and what are the environmental benefits of doing so?

The use of resources during production

It is not only the use of energy during production that impacts the environment. The use of natural resources can also be damaging. An example is iron ore. As with fossil fuels, iron ore will eventually run out and, as it becomes scarcer, steel will become a lot more expensive. This is why engineers are working so hard to develop new materials.

Iron ore is one of the most commonly available engineering materials. It is used to make a range of the steels used in manufacturing. The ore is mined from the ground and processed in a blast furnace. Heavy machinery moves the raw material around the mine and it is loaded onto lorries or trains to be transported to the processing plant. The machines in the mine and the different modes of transport have an environmental impact because of the emission of fumes.

Once the raw material reaches the processing plant it is processed to separate out the iron. This involves burning the iron ore along with coke and limestone in a blast furnace at temperatures as high as 1,800°C. The molten iron is drained off and turned into different grades of steel through the addition of carbon and other materials.

Waste production and pollution

Poor or inefficient manufacturing methods can result in the production of waste materials, which then need to be disposed of. There are only two ways of disposing of waste materials: taking them to a landfill site or recycling them.

The pollution created is primarily from waste gases, such as those that are produced when plastic is melted during injection moulding processes. These fumes are **extracted** to the outside of factories where they are absorbed into the atmosphere. Manufacturers are required to reduce the amount of gas being emitted into the atmosphere by installing a filter system to absorb any pollutants so that only clean air is released into the atmosphere.

Link

For further information on landfill and recycling see *Unit 5 Engineering Materials*.

Key terms

Extracted – removed and taken away.

Acid rain – rainfall that contains trace elements of acid.

Activity 2.6   Exhaust fumes and pollution

Produce a poster that shows how car exhaust fumes contribute to pollution and the formation of **acid rain**.

Activity 2.7   Design a car of the future

Design a car of the future that can be built using recycled materials. Consider including a clean source of energy so that waste gases will not be produced and pollute the atmosphere.

Comparing production processes

Getting started ▶▶

Most people own a mobile phone. What process do you think is used to manufacture the outer casing and why?

Introduction

Every production process is chosen for a specific reason, for example, its suitability for the material used. This topic will look at the advantages and disadvantages of some of the most common processes.

Injection moulding

Injection moulding is a process used to manufacture many different products from plastic materials. The material is heated up and then forced into a mould tool. It is allowed to cool briefly, enabling the plastic to form in the shape of the mould. Examples of products produced using this process are mobile phone and games console casings.

Table 2.3 Advantages and disadvantages of injection moulding

Advantages	Disadvantages
• Once set up the process can often run with little supervision which reduces labour costs.	• The initial tooling costs are high as the mould has to be manufactured before any components can be produced.
• It is a relatively quick process with a short cycle time. There is very little work to be done to the product after it has been moulded.	• Tests are needed to ensure that the tool produces the required products. This will involve small batches being produced and checked before going into full production.
• It can produce the same product over and over again.	• When changing the material to a different colour, some waste products will be created containing a mixture of both colours.
• Different textured surface finishes and colours can be achieved.	
• It is possible to mould around different components so that complex shapes can be created.	• Transport costs will vary depending on the cost of fuel.

Why is die casting suitable for producing toy cars?

Die casting

This process is similar to injection moulding – the difference is the material used as products are made from cast metals such as aluminium or cast iron. During this process the metal is heated until molten and then cast into a die before cooling so the required component can be formed. When compared with manufacturing products from solid die casting it is a very cost-effective method.

Table 2.4 Advantages and disadvantages of die casting

Advantages	Disadvantages
• The same product can be produced over and over again. • The quality will remain high. • Complex shapes can be achieved. • Additional features can be machined after the product has been cast. • It produces complex parts at a fraction of the cost of machining them from solid.	• Again, initial set-up costs are high as tools have to be produced before any products can be made. • The tooling wears much quicker than an injection mould tool. • Additional operations have to be carried out after casting to remove the **feed gates** where the material enters the die. • The cycle time is greater than injection moulding. • Dies are often treated with **lubricants** between cycles which can be hazardous to health. • The casting process generally requires an operator to be present so increases labour costs.

Overall there are only a few differences in the way each method produces components:

- injection moulding requires less work after production compared with die casting and its tools will produce a lot more components before they need to be serviced
- die casting tools need to be a lot more robust because of the amount of pressure applied during each cycle
- die casting uses **toxic** chemicals throughout: injection moulding does not.

Discussion

Why do you think production runs are fewer when products are produced by die casting compared with injection moulding?

Assessment activity 2.3   Manufacturing processes   2C.P3 | 2C.M3 | 2C.D2

Select a child's toy with several different components. Suggest two methods of manufacture for the components of the toy, justifying your choices. Explore the similarities and difference of these two processes.

Tips

- What are the advantages and disadvantages of using your selected processes, with regard to cost, time, quality and the quantity required?
- What impact does the energy source used during the processes have on the environment?
- How are the waste products disposed of in an environmentally friendly way?

Quality control (QC)

Introduction

Products need to be manufactured to consistent standards. This can only be achieved by checks at various stages. Engineers will decide how often quality and function checks need to take place.

Materials supply

The materials used to produce products must be consistent to ensure the product will perform as it should. Manufacturers will often ask for a certificate of quality for their chosen material. This gives them assurance that the material contains the properties they require.

When materials are supplied without a quality check, the manufacturer should carry out their own checks prior to starting production. This could be as simple as checking the material's size or that the plastic is the correct grade and colour. Some products require a certificate to prove that the material supplied matches the exact specification. Materials need to be checked every time a new supply is received.

Production

Products are checked regularly throughout the production process to make sure they are being produced to the same quality each time. These checks will be carried out after a certain number of components have been produced or randomly throughout production. If a problem is identified then production will stop until the error has been corrected.

Products also need to be checked during production to make sure they fall within the given **tolerance**. If products are produced out of tolerance they may be **rejected** by the customer. Production checks can be carried out while the component is on the machine by fitting a probe to inspect features. Any necessary adjustments can then be made to bring the component back within tolerance.

Key terms

Tolerance – the size a component can be between two figures, for example, if a feature is 10 mm with a tolerance of ±0.5 mm then anything between 9.5 mm and 10.5 mm falls within the tolerance band.

Activity 2.8   Production quality

Locate two identical products and carry out a quality inspection check on them to see how accurately they have been manufactured. A good example to use would be three-pin plugs, as you can check the different features and identify the processes used to manufacture the different components.

Assembly

Products have to be tested once they have been assembled to make sure that all the different components fit together and that the product complies with the specification. These checks will cover:

- the function of the product
- its aesthetic appearance
- identification of any damaged parts
- identification of anything that could be a safety issue.

An assembly line is dependent on different components coming together that are consistently of the same standard and quality. When parts come together that are poor quality or damaged it can halt the production. This can affect sales, lead to poor customer relations and damage a company's reputation.

? Did you know?

Steel can be polished to give a mirrored finish, although it takes a long time to achieve. This type of finish is required when products like medical face masks are produced by injection moulding.

Discussion

You have just had your bedroom redecorated and added new furniture. The furniture comes flat-packed and you need to assemble it. As you begin building you notice that parts are damaged, holes for screws do not line up and parts are missing. How would this make you feel?

Following on from the discussion, write a letter that you could send to the supplier of the furniture explaining the problems you experienced.

Activity 2.9   Carry out a quality check

You are required to carry out a quality check. The product has four different diameters (17.60 mm, 27.20 mm, 76.30 mm and 100.20 mm). It has a hole in the end which needs to have a diameter between 12.64 mm and 12.80 mm. The outer profile has three shoulders that all need to be 18.50 mm long. Describe what tools you would use to check these features and justify your choice.

Just checking

1 Why is it important to carry out quality checks during a production run of products?
2 If a feature on a product is required to be 23.64 mm with a tolerance of ±0.05 mm, what is the range the feature can fall within?
3 Why is it important that parts required to make up an assembled part are checked?
4 Why might a material require a certificate to prove that it is what the customer is asking for?

Quality assurance (QA)

Introduction

Customers need to know that products meet quality standards and have been tested thoroughly. In this topic you will look at what checks and tests are carried out as part of this quality assurance (QA) system.

When and where quality control checks take place

There are two points at which quality control checks can take place:

- when the product is being manufactured – component parts could be randomly checked to make sure they are the correct size or even tested to destruction to make sure they are strong enough to carry any required load
- before products go into production for the first time – sample products are produced and rigorously tested to ensure they perform and function as required. If these are not carried out then faulty products could be manufactured and sold.

A simple example is a carrier bag put into the market without being tested. It is supplied to a supermarket that provides them to their customers. After a few hours the supermarket receives numerous complaints that the carrier bags are breaking and customers' shopping is falling out. If the bags had gone through a quality control check this problem would have been spotted and resolved.

There are different types of quality tests. For example, a product could be tested to the equivalent of its life expectancy based on slightly above average usage, or it could be tested to destruction.

What do QA checks consist of?

Tests are carried out to give customers some assurance of the expected life cycle of a product. A prime example of this can be seen in an IKEA showroom where there are lots of examples of products being tested. You will see drawers and doors being repeatedly mechanically opened and closed. This assures the customer that these products are built for reliability and will perform the required function over and over again.

How checks form part of the overall QA system

The overall quality assurance system is in place to ensure that products reach the required standards and give customers confidence that the product is safe to use.

The system usually involves products facing a range of quality tests. For example, in some workplaces you may see signs telling you the safe lifting load of a piece of equipment. This means that if you were to lift something above this safe weight the equipment could fail and the fault would lie with the user and not with the product. Once products have passed these quality assurance tests, they can be awarded an approved BSI standard, such as the British Kitemark or CE symbol. In order for a product to carry this sign the company must be awarded a BSI licence. The company

Figure 2.3 British Standards Institution Kitemark

will have to pay for this independent testing but its customers can be assured that they are purchasing a quality product. Even after a Kitemark has been awarded products should still be regularly checked to make sure standards are maintained.

Activity 2.10   Kitemark schemes

There are many different examples of Kitemark schemes for a range of products. Identify three different schemes and give examples of products that carry the mark.

Discussion

What other standard marks do you find on certain products? What do they tell you?

Fitness for purpose and meeting specification criteria

A product must be tested against its specification. For example, if the specification states the product will work at temperatures between $-20°C$ and $30°C$ it must be tested at each extreme to make sure it does function correctly. If products are not tested correctly against their specification and problems arise when they are used within the specified boundaries, customers may complain. If these complaints persist it could damage the reputation of the product and also the company. Many companies pay to have their products independently tested so that they can provide their customers with an assurance that the product they are buying will function as they expect it to.

Activity 2.11   A quality control process

Using a simple three-pin plug, for example, put together a quality control process that could be used during manufacture through to final assembly prior to dispatch for selling.

Assessment activity 2.4   A quality control process for the UK and rest of Europe   2D.P4 | 2D.P5 | 2D.M4 | 2D.D3

Select an engineered product and analyse what quality control checks and quality assurance systems you think have been used during manufacture, giving reasons why they would be needed. How have they contributed towards the quality of the end product?

Tips

- Once you have identified your product, look at it carefully to identify which features you think will need to be checked, why and how often. Then evaluate how these checks will contribute to the quality of the finished product.

- Think of the implications of not checking the quality of the products once the manufacturing process has begun.

Introduction

Engineers use a wide range of materials, and new materials are being developed all the time. This unit will give you an understanding of their properties and applications, as well as their availability and environmental impact. You will learn why engineers select certain materials for particular components. This might be because of their weight, cost or their ability to conduct heat – or a combination of these factors.

The materials that a product or component is made from are usually listed in its engineering drawing, production plans and service schedules (these are referred to when a component needs to be replaced). As an engineer, you will need to be able to identify raw materials and parts correctly, and ensure these are the required size. To do this you will need to know the symbols, abbreviations and colour codes that are used to identify them.

Assessment: This unit will be assessed by a series of assignments set by your teacher/tutor.

Learning aims

After completing this unit you should:

A know about the properties of common engineering materials and selection for engineering applications

B know about the supply and sustainable use of engineering materials and selection for an engineering product or activity.

> This unit has helped me to understand why different materials are chosen for engineering products. There are lots of things to consider, including the way materials perform and the impact they might have on the environment.
>
> Sarah, *18-year-old apprentice*

Engineering Materials

This table shows you what you must do in order to achieve a **Pass**, **Merit** or **Distinction** grade, and where you can find activities in this book to help you.

Assessment criteria			
Level 1	**Level 2 Pass**	**Level 2 Merit**	**Level 2 Distinction**
Learning aim A: Know about the properties of common engineering materials and selection for engineering applications			
1A.1 Identify an example of each type of material used in given engineering applications.	**2A.P1** Describe examples of each type of material and the properties of these materials in engineering applications. **See Assessment activity 5.1, page 77**	**2A.M1** Explain the choice of material for engineering applications. **See Assessment activity 5.1, page 77**	**2A.D1** Compare advantages and disadvantages of material choices for engineering applications. **See Assessment activity 5.1, page 77**
1A.2 Carry out a simple mechanical test on an engineering material.	**2A.P2** Carry out a range of simple mechanical tests on engineering materials and interpret the results. **See Assessment activity 5.1, page 77**		
1A.3 Describe a heat treatment process to alter a ferrous material's property.	**2A.P3** Describe two heat treatment processes that alter a ferrous material's properties. **See Assessment activity 5.1, page 77**		
Learning aim B: Know about the supply and sustainable use of engineering materials and selection for an engineering product or activity			
1B.4 Outline the environmental impact of a given engineering product or activity.	**2B.P4** Describe sustainable use of materials in a given engineering product or activity. **See Assessment activity 5.2, page 88**	**2B.M2** Assess whether materials have been used sustainably in an engineering product or activity. **See Assessment activity 5.2, page 88**	**2B.D2** Maths Analyse the sustainability of an engineering product or activity, including materials used and forms of supply. **See Assessment activity 5.2, page 88**
1B.5 Maths Identify the forms of supply for materials in an engineering product or activity.	**2B.P5** Maths Select appropriate forms of supply for materials in a given engineering product or activity. **See Assessment activity 5.2, page 88**	**2B.M3** Maths Justify the selected forms of supply for materials in an engineering product or activity. **See Assessment activity 5.2, page 88**	

Maths Opportunity to practise mathematical skills

How you will be assessed

In this unit, you will be assessed by your teacher/tutor through a series of investigative assignments. You will need to show an understanding of the properties, uses and forms of supply of a range of engineering materials.

Your assessment could be in the form of:

- a portfolio of investigations and observations which you have built up in the workplace
- written reports or verbal explanations based on workshop activities
- posters
- presentations.

Properties of materials

Getting started

Take a close look at a ballpoint pen. You should see at least two different kinds of plastic and two different metals. You may not know exactly what they are, but have a guess and make a note of the reasons why you think they have been chosen.

Key terms

Properties – the qualities or power of a substance.

Density – the number of kilograms contained in a cubic metre of a material.

Why must the lifting cables in cranes have high tensile strength?

Introduction

Materials can behave or react in different ways depending on their make-up. To describe this, we talk about a material's **properties**. A material can have mechanical, electromagnetic, chemical and thermal properties.

▶ Mechanical properties

Density

Density is the term used to describe the mass in kilograms of a cubic metre of a material (kgm³).The density of water is 1,000 kgm³. Materials with a lower density will float on water while those with a higher density will sink. The density of a material is sometimes compared with that of water and given as its relative density. For instance, the density of cast iron is 7,200 kgm³ so its relative density is 7.2. The densities of some common metals are given in Table 5.1.

Table 5.1 The tensile strength, density and melting point of common ferrous and non-ferrous metals

Metal	Tensile strength (MPa)	Density (kgm³)	Melting point (°C)
Aluminium	95	2,700	660
Cast iron	200	7,200	1,200
Copper	230	8,900	1,083
High carbon steel	900	7,800	1,400
Lead	Very low	11,300	327
Medium carbon steel	750	7,800	1,450
Mild steel	500	7,800	1,500
Tin	Very low	7,300	230
Titanium	218	4,500	1,725
Zinc	200	7,100	420

Tensile strength

The ultimate **tensile strength** (UTS) of a material is the maximum load that each unit of cross-sectional area can carry before it fails. We also call this the tensile stress at failure. Tensile strength is measured in Newtons carried per square metre. The SI name for this unit is the pascal (Pa). The pascal is a small unit and so we often have to use megapascals (MPa). 1 MPa = 1,000,000 Pa. The lifting cables used in cranes and hoists must have a high tensile strength.

Shear strength

Tin snips, guillotines and punches apply a shearing force to cut through a material. The **shear strength** of a material is the maximum shearing load that each unit of the sheared area can carry before it fails. It is measured in the same units as tensile strength but has a different value. The bolts and rivets used to join plates and sheet metal components together need to have a high shear strength.

Hardness

The **hardness** of a material is its resistance to wear, **abrasion** or **indentation**. Hard materials are difficult to cut (this is why very hard materials such as heat-treated steel often have be cut and polished by grinding). Cutting tools need to be hard and wear-resistant, whereas sheets of lead used on buildings have to be soft and workable.

Toughness and brittleness

The **toughness** of a material is its resistance to sudden impact and shock loading. Tough materials are able to absorb the impact energy when something strikes them. Hammers and punches made from toughened steel have this property. The opposite of toughness is **brittleness**. Glass and the pottery that we use for cups and plates are quite hard and wear-resistant, but they are very brittle and easily shattered.

Malleability and ductility

Malleability is when a material can easily be pressed or forged into shape. Some metals such as lead and copper are malleable when cold, but others such as steel often have to be heated to make them malleable. Rivets have to be malleable so that their heads can be formed to shape, and so does the aluminium sheet metal used to make car body panels and aircraft parts.

You should not confuse malleability with **ductility**. Ductility is the ability of a material to be pulled or drawn out in length to make thin rods and wire. Some materials are malleable but not very ductile. Some have both properties and behave rather like chewing gum.

Another way of looking at these two properties is to say that malleable materials can be formed to shape using mostly **compressive forces**, whereas ductile materials can be formed to shape using mostly **tensile forces**.

Elasticity and plasticity

An elastic material increases or decreases in size in proportion to the load that is applied. When unloaded an elastic material returns to its original shape. A plastic material is malleable and/or ductile. It stays in its deformed shape when the load is removed. Springs need to have **elasticity** while metal components formed to shape by pressing or forging need to have **plasticity**.

Key terms

Abrasion – wearing away by frictional contact with another material.

Indentation – piercing the surface of a material.

Compressive forces – press on a material tending to squash it.

Tensile forces – pull on a material tending to lengthen it.

Remember

Try not to confuse the term 'plastic material' with things that are made from plastic. Some plastics can be quite elastic and return to their original shape after being deformed.

CONTINUED ▸▸

▶▶ CONTINUED

Key terms

Corrosion – a chemical reaction, usually in the presence of moisture or oxygen in the atmosphere that causes a metal to become degraded.

Solvent – a chemical, usually in liquid form, that attacks plastics and rubbers.

Environmental degradation – the decay of timber and plastic materials because of the presence of moisture and/or sunlight.

Link

For more on electrical parameters, see *Unit 11 Electrical and Mechanical Science for Engineering*.

Electromagnetic properties

Electrical conductivity

Electrical conductivity is the ability of a material to conduct an electric current. Most metals are good conductors whereas plastics and ceramics are bad conductors – this is why they are used as insulation materials.

Electrical resistivity

All materials resist the passage of electric current to some extent. **Electrical resistivity** is a measure of this effect. If you can imagine a cubic metre of a material, its resistivity is the resistance to a current passing between opposite faces. Its SI unit is the ohm-metre (Ωm). For instance, the resistivity of copper is $1.72 \times 10^{-8}\Omega$m, measured at 20°C.

Paramagnetism, diamagnetism and ferromagnetism

Metals that contain large amounts of iron, nickel and cobalt can usually be made into magnets. They are called '**ferromagnetic**' materials (the Latin for iron is 'ferrum').

A **paramagnetic** material such as platinum cannot be made into a magnet but if a platinum rod is placed in a magnetic field, it will align itself along the lines of force.

If a bar of **diamagnetic** material, such as bismuth, is placed in a magnetic field, it will align itself at right angles to the lines of force.

Chemical properties

Resistance to corrosion

Some metals, particularly those containing iron, go rusty and eventually **corrode** away completely. This is because a chemical reaction occurs between the metal and the oxygen in air and in moisture. Other metals are not affected very much and we say that they have high **corrosion** resistance. Gold, for instance, can lie buried for hundreds of years and still be bright and shiny when it is dug up.

Resistance to solvents

Some rubbers and plastics are attacked by certain chemicals. We call these chemicals '**solvents**'. Other materials are very stable and are not affected. We say that they have a high solvent resistance. Petrol, diesel oil and lubricating oils can act as solvents and you must be careful to select rubbers and plastics with a high solvent resistance if they are going be in contact with these substances.

Environmental degradation

Unprotected wood will rot when exposed to moisture and certain plastic materials become very brittle when exposed to sunlight over a long period. We say that they undergo **environmental degradation**. Wood becomes more durable when painted or treated with chemicals. Plastics, such as those used for spouts and guttering on houses, tend to stay flexible for longer if coloured black – as many of them are.

Reactivity

Reactivity is the degree to which materials will readily combine in a chemical reaction. Some metals, such as iron, react readily with oxygen while others, such as gold, do not.

Activity 5.1	A five-step experiment in corrosion

1 Obtain three empty cans that have contained soup or baked beans, etc.
2 Take off the labels and thoroughly clean the outside surfaces.
3 Take a screwdriver or a scriber and scratch the outer surface from top to bottom in several places around each can.
4 Place one can in a dry place such as an airing cupboard, one outside in the open air and the other in a container filled with water.
5 Check them periodically every few days noting where corrosion takes place and how it progresses.

Thermal properties

Melting point

A metal reaches its **melting point** when it contains so much heat energy that its atoms can no longer stay in fixed positions. The melting points of some common metals are given in Table 5.1. Plastic materials do not behave in quite the same way. With thermoplastics, melting begins at a particular temperature and continues as the temperature rises with the material becoming more fluid. Thermosetting plastics and ceramics do not melt but may degrade or even disintegrate at high temperatures.

Thermal conductivity

Thermal conductivity is the ability of a material to conduct heat energy. As with electrical conductivity, metals are generally good conductors of heat, while plastics, ceramics and wood are bad conductors.

Thermal expansion

Most metals expand as their temperature rises and contract when it falls. **Thermal expansion** has to be taken into account in the design of aeroplanes, jet engines and steam plants which have to function over a range of working temperatures. Some plastics, such as those used for shrink wrapping, behave in the opposite way and will contract as the temperature rises.

Key terms

Reactivity – the degree to which a material will readily combine in a chemical reaction.

Melting point – the temperature at which a change of state from solid to liquid occurs.

Thermal conductivity – the ability of a material to conduct heat energy.

Thermal expansion – increase in the dimensions of a material owing to temperature rise.

Link

For more information about thermoplastics and thermosetting plastics, see Appendix 4.

Just checking

1 What is the difference between malleability and ductility in materials?
2 What effect does loading and unloading have on (a) elastic and (b) plastic materials?
3 How do chemical solvents and exposure to sunlight affect some plastic materials?
4 What materials generally make good conductors of heat and electricity?

Types of engineering materials – ferrous metals

Introduction

Iron is the main constituent of **ferrous metals**. In its pure form it is a soft grey metal and does not cast very well when molten or give a good surface finish when machined. However, the addition of a small amount of carbon greatly improves its properties, giving us a range of cast irons and plain carbon **steels**.

Did you know?

The chemical symbol for iron is 'Fe'. This comes from the Latin name for iron which is 'ferrum'. Iron occurs naturally in different kinds of rock that are called iron ore. The best of these is magnetite, which is so rich in iron that it can be picked up by a magnet. The iron is separated from the rock by heating it in a blast furnace.

Key terms

Ferrous metal – a material that is composed of or contains a large quantity of iron.

Steel – a mixture of iron and carbon.

Link

For more information about how case hardening and hardening and tempering are carried out see Topic A.4.

The different grades of steel and cast iron

Plain carbon steels

Mild steel is a mixture of iron and carbon. Mild, or 'low carbon' steel contains 0.1–0.3 per cent carbon. It is easy to machine, has good tensile strength and a fair degree of malleability and ductility when 'cold-worked'. When heated to a bright red colour it becomes much more malleable and ductile and can be more easily pressed, forged and rolled into shape.

Mild steel is the most commonly used engineering material. It is used for girders, pipes, ships' hulls, gates and railings and for general workshop purposes. Mild steel components are sometimes given a hard surface layer by a process called 'case hardening'. This makes them wear-resistant while retaining their strong and tough core.

Medium carbon steel contains 0.3–0.8 per cent carbon. It is stronger and tougher than mild steel and a little more difficult to machine. Its strength and toughness can be further increased by heat treatment processes called 'hardening and tempering'. Medium carbon steel is used for hammers, chisels, punches, couplings, gears and other engineering components that have to be wear- and impact-resistant.

High carbon steel contains 0.8–1.4 per cent carbon and can be made very hard and tough by 'hardening and tempering'. It is used for sharp-edged cutting tools such as wood chisels, files, screw-cutting taps and dies and craft knife blades. Mild, medium and high carbon steels are sometimes called 'plain carbon steels' because iron and carbon are their main constituents.

Stainless steel

In addition to iron and carbon, **stainless steel** contains chromium and nickel. It belongs to a class of ferrous metals called 'alloy steels'. These added ingredients make it corrosion-resistant and also very tough. It is widely used in food preparation areas, for surgical instruments, cutlery and very often for ornaments and decorative trim.

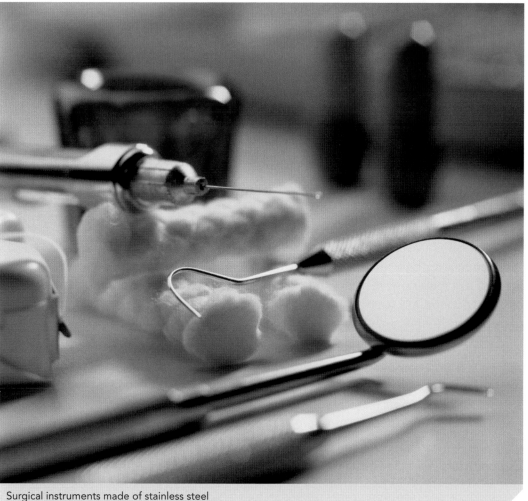

Surgical instruments made of stainless steel

Link

See Table 5.1 in Topic A.2 for the density, tensile strength and melting point of some ferrous metals.

Cast iron

Often called 'grey cast iron', **cast iron** has a carbon content of around 3–3.5 per cent which makes it very fluid when molten and enables it to be cast into complicated shapes. When looked at under a microscope you can see that it contains flakes of carbon in the form of graphite. This is the same material that pencil leads are made from. Not only does carbon make the iron easier to cast, it also makes it easier to machine and the graphite flakes act as a self-lubricant when cast iron rubs against another material.

Cast iron is widely used for engine parts, valve bodies, lathe beds, manhole covers and decorative garden furniture. Perhaps its main disadvantage is that it tends to be brittle unless it is specially treated, and should not be subjected to high tensile forces. It is strong in compression but weak in tension.

 Did you know?

An alloy is a mixture of metals. It can also be a mixture of a metal and a non-metal as long as the final product has metallic properties. Cast iron and plain carbon steels are really alloys but we don't refer to them as such.

Just checking

1 In which material can you find flakes of graphite?
2 What is the carbon content of mild steel?
3 What are the main constituents of stainless steel?
4 Which kind of steel would you expect a hammer head to be made from?

Types of engineering materials – non-ferrous metals

Introduction

A number of non-ferrous metals, such as copper and aluminium, are used widely in engineering in their almost pure form. Unlike most ferrous metals they are generally resistant to corrosion.

The different types of non-ferrous metal include the following.

Aluminium

Aluminium is probably the most widely used non-ferrous metal and is one of the lightest. It is malleable, resistant to corrosion and a good conductor of heat and electricity. It is widely used for cooking utensils and in overhead power transmission cables where a core of high tensile steel is surrounded by aluminium conductors.

In its pure form aluminium has low tensile strength compared with steel, but when alloyed with small amounts of copper, silicon, iron, magnesium and manganese its properties are greatly improved. Aluminium alloys are widely used in the aerospace and automotive sectors because of their low weight and resistance to corrosion.

Copper

Copper has a characteristic red colour. It is malleable, ductile, resistant to corrosion and an excellent conductor of heat and electricity. It is used in its almost pure form for water pipes, wires, cables and cooking utensils. Copper is not as strong as steel but it has fairly good tensile strength which can be improved by alloying it with tin to make bronze and with zinc to make brass.

Zinc

Zinc is soft but rather brittle. Like most non-ferrous metals it is highly resistant to corrosion. It is used in batteries and as a protective coating for mild steel (which is then said to be 'galvanised'). Galvanised steel is used for waste bins, metal buckets and building materials. Although galvanising adds to the cost of steel components, this is offset by the saving on maintenance costs because of the protection against corrosion.

Brass

Brass is an alloy of copper and zinc. The proportions vary between 70/30 and 60/40 copper to zinc, depending on its final use. A high copper content makes brass ductile and suitable for deep **drawing** into tubes and cartridge cases. A high zinc content makes the brass more fluid when molten and better suited for making castings. Valve bodies, bath taps and door handles are cast in brass.

Lead

Lead is a heavy grey metal that is very malleable and highly resistant to corrosion. It has low tensile strength and is used in its pure form as a roofing material and as

Galvanised steel is easy to recognise from the feathery pattern that the zinc forms on the steel surface.

a lining for tanks containing chemicals. When lead is mixed with tin it produces the range of alloys called 'soft solders'. Soft solder is used for joining copper components and for making electrical joints.

Titanium

In its pure form **titanium** is lightweight and highly resistant to corrosion. It is mainly used to produce a range of high strength alloys when mixed with aluminium, iron and other metals. These are widely used in aircraft production, and also in mobile phones and tennis racquets.

Tungsten carbide

Tungsten carbide is made from equal parts of tungsten and carbon. They are mixed together as a powder, then subjected to heat and pressure in a process known as 'sintering'. The materials fuse together to give an extremely hard and wear-resistant alloy widely used for cutting tools.

Superalloys

There are three types of **superalloy** or 'high performance' alloys.

- The iron-nickel range – developed from stainless steels.
- Nickel-based – containing smaller amounts of chromium, aluminium and titanium.
- Cobalt-based – containing smaller amounts of chromium and nickel.

Superalloys are used when high strength, resistance to corrosion and resistance to high temperature creep are required. For example, they are used in jet engines and steam turbines where the blades rotate at high temperatures and very high speeds.

Ceramics

Ceramics are non-metallic, inorganic materials produced mainly from naturally occurring earths and clays. Typical examples are bricks, tiles and pottery. In recent years two ceramics – boron carbide and boron nitride – have been increasingly used in engineering.

Boron is a chemical element which combines with carbon at very high temperatures to produce boron carbide. A very tough and light material, it is almost as hard as diamond and is used in cutting tools and dies as well as for tank armour and bulletproof vests. In pellet form it is used in nuclear reactor control rods and shields to absorb neutron bombardment and radiation.

Boron nitride contains boron and nitrogen. In its powder form, known as hexagonal boron nitrate, it has similar properties to graphite. Like the graphite in cast iron, it is added to other metals to give self-lubricating properties. In another form known as cubic boron nitride, it is used in cutting tools, grinding wheels and abrasive pastes.

Discussion

Why do you think that zinc is unsuitable as a coating for food containers?

Link

See Table 5.1 in Topic A.2 for the density, tensile strength and melting point of some ferrous metals.

You will also find more information about ferrous metals in Appendix 4.

Just checking

1 What are the main applications that copper is used for in your home?

2 What is the metal used to give galvanised steel its protective coating?

3 What are the main constituents of brass?

4 What is tungsten carbide widely used for in the workshop?

5 What are the three main classes of superalloys?

Types of engineering materials – thermoplastics

Getting started

The world would be a very different place without plastic materials, but where do the raw materials come from? Unlike metals they are not found in rocks. See if you can find out on the Internet or in your resource centre.

Key terms

Thermoplastic – a polymer material that can be softened by heating.

Introduction

Plastics have only been in use for the last 150 years. They have come to replace metals in many domestic and engineering applications. The word 'plastic' is used to describe something that is malleable and ductile, but some plastic materials can be quite hard and elastic. The description is more fitting at high temperatures where a group of materials called thermoplastics become soft and easy to mould.

Types of thermoplastic

In this section, we will look at different types of thermoplastic. Don't worry about the complicated chemical terms – you only need to remember the everyday names.

Acrylic

Acrylic is the common name for methyl-2 methylpropenoate or PMMA. You probably also know it by its popular trade name – Perspex. Acrylic is strong, rigid and transparent. It is used for lenses, visors, aquariums, aircraft windows and cockpit canopies, and also for protective shields and guards on workshop machinery. It may also be given a colour – this property makes it suitable for use in making dentures.

Polyvinyl chloride (PVC)

We know this best as **PVC**, which is the common name for polyvinyl chloride or polychloroethene. This material can be made hard and tough, or soft and flexible. When hard it is used for window frames, drainpipes and guttering. When soft it is used for the different-coloured insulation around electrical wiring and cables. It is also used in clothing, upholstery and inflatable products.

Polyethythene (PET)

Often shortened to **polythene** or **polyethythene (PET)** is a tough and flexible material. We use it as a thin film for wrapping and plastic bags. It is also used for squeezy containers, pipes, mouldings and insulation foam.

Polystyrene

Polystyrene is the common name for polyphenylethene. It can be used as a foam for packaging and disposable drinking cups. It can also be made into hard, tough and rigid mouldings such as those used in refrigerator interiors. Polystyrene is also used for CD and DVD cases and smoke detector housings.

Drinking cups are made out of polystyrene. Can you think of other products that are made out of this material?

Nylon

Nylon is also known as polyamide. This material can be drawn out into a strong thin fibre for use as bristles for toothbrushes, fishing lines, strings for musical instruments, nets or hosiery. Nylon is also very tough and flexible. It is used in engineering for moulded gears, cams and bearings.

Polycarbonate

This has similar properties to Perspex but it is stronger, scratch-resistant, highly transparent and can be used over a wider range of temperatures. It is, however, more expensive. **Polycarbonate** is used for spectacle and sunglass lenses and food and drink containers. In buildings it is used for dome lights and conservatory roofs.

 Take it further

Teflon is a plastic material that is also known as PTFE. Find out what these initials stand for and where you might find it: (a) in the home and (b) in an industrial application.

Types of materials – thermosetting polymers

Getting started

One of the first thermosetting polymers was called Bakelite and it is still in use today. Find out when Bakelite was introduced, who discovered it, what its properties are and what it has been used for.

Key terms

Thermosetting polymers – polymer materials which cannot be softened by heating.

Polymers – long intertwined chains of molecules, rather like spaghetti. They consist mostly of hydrogen and carbon atoms with the atoms of other elements such as chlorine attached to give them their different properties. Plastics and rubbers are classed as polymer materials or just polymers for short.

Introduction

In this section you will look at a range of thermosetting polymers. These are also sometimes called thermosets.

Thermosetting polymers are generally harder and more rigid than thermoplastics and cannot be softened by reheating. They undergo a chemical change under the effects of heat and pressure when they are being moulded to shape. The **polymers** become cross-linked together and, once formed, the cross-links cannot be broken, giving these materials their hard and rigid properties.

Thermosetting polymers begin the moulding process in either liquid or powder form. Often other substances, known as 'fillers', are added to improve their mechanical properties. These include very fine sawdust called 'wood flour', shredded paper and textiles, glass fibres and carbon fibres.

Types of thermosetting polymer

Formica

The chemical name for **formica** is urea-methanal resin. It is naturally transparent, tough and hard-wearing, and can be produced in a range of colours. Kitchen worktops and surfaces are often covered with a layer of hard-wearing formica laminate. It is also used for items of kitchenware, toilet seats and electrical fittings.

Melamine

The chemical name for **melamine** is methanal-melamine resin. It has similar properties to formica but is harder and more resistant to heat. It can also be moulded with a smoother surface finish. The white electrical plugs and sockets in your home are probably moulded from melamine. It is used for other items of electrical equipment, control knobs and heat-resistant handles, and can be used for kitchen utensils and plates.

Epoxy resins

Epoxy resins are generally formed by mixing together a liquid resin and a hardener. This triggers the cross-linking process and the resin can then be poured into moulds to solidify. Epoxy resin and its hardener are sold in tubes for mixing together as an adhesive. One of its trade names is 'Araldite'. It makes an excellent adhesive for joining together the thin layers of formica and melamine to make the plastic laminates used for kitchen worktops.

Polyester resins

Polyester resins have similar properties to epoxy resins with good heat resistance and a hard-wearing surface. They are formed in the same way by mixing together a resin and a hardener. The main application of epoxy and polyester resins is in **composites** with glass fibre and carbon fibre materials for use in automotive and aircraft components, luggage, furnishings, textiles and packaging.

Key terms

Composite – a material that is made from two or more constituents for added strength and toughness.

Link

For more information on composites for applications of epoxy and polyester resins see Topic A.1.

Did you know?

The earliest plastic was developed in the USA in the mid-19th century and used for billiard balls instead of ivory. Unfortunately, it was unstable and tended to explode on impact, causing people to reach for their guns.

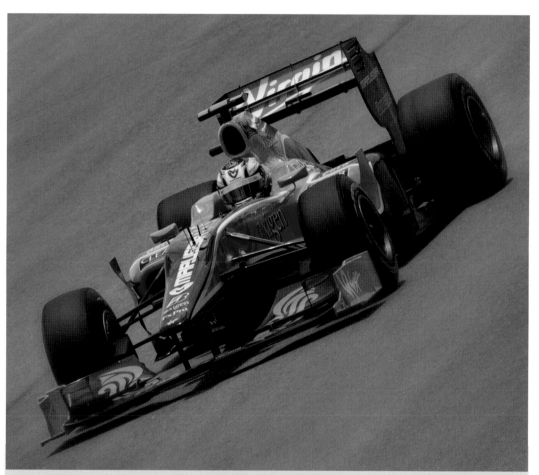

Why would polyester resins have been used in making parts of this car?

Just checking

1 What is the main difference between a thermoplastic and a thermosetting plastic?
2 What are the two properties of nylon that make it suitable for gearwheels and bearings in engineering products?
3 What is the thermoplastic polychloroethene better known as?
4 What is the thermosetting plastic most widely used to make white electrical plug tops and sockets?
5 What effect does cross-linking have during the formation of thermosetting plastics?

Types of materials – composite materials

Introduction

Composite materials are made from two or more separate materials that are bonded or fused together. In ancient times it was found that bows for hunting and fighting performed better if made from layers of wood and bone bonded together.

Types of composite material

Plywood

Plywood consists of thin layers of wood bonded together with their grain directions running alternately at right angles. This reduces the possibility of warping. Marine quality plywood is specially treated to make it suitable for outdoor use, particularly for boat-building, construction and outdoor cladding.

Plywood plays an important role in the construction of houses.

Fibreboard

Fibreboards are made from fine compressed wood fibres of differing size. They include hardboard and **MDF (Medium Density Fibreboard)**. MDF is manufactured by a dry process at a lower temperature than hardboard and with a different bonding agent. They are both used extensively for kitchen cabinets, furniture, tool racks and cupboards, panelling and door facings.

Glass reinforced plastic (GRP)

Glass reinforced plastic (GRP) consists of epoxy or polyester resins reinforced by glass fibres in the form of matting. The resin is mixed with its hardener and applied to the surface of a mould with the reinforcement matting. This is how canoe and boat hulls are made. Reinforced epoxy and polyester resins are strong, tough and have good electrical resistance. They are used for hot tubs, water tanks, pipes, roofing material and cladding.

Carbon fibre reinforced plastic

Here, as the name suggests, the resins are reinforced with carbon fibres. In tubular form **carbon fibre reinforced plastic** is strong, light and flexible, and used for fishing rods. When sheets of carbon fibre reinforced plastic are laminated with a core of plastic foam or aluminium mesh, the result is a light and rigid material widely used in aircraft.

Kevlar® composites

Kevlar® is an extremely strong polymer fibre that was developed by the American DuPont company. It is used for ropes, cables and as reinforcement for rubber in tyres. It is also used in textile composites for protective clothing, such as motorcycle clothing and flexible bulletproof vests. When Kevlar® is used as reinforcement for epoxy resin the resulting composite is light, strong and extremely tough. It is widely used by the military, police and fire services for protective helmets and body armour.

? **Did you know?**

Kevlar® has a tensile strength said to be five times stronger than steel of an equal weight.

Just checking ✔

1 What do the letters MDF stand for?
2 What are the materials commonly used to reinforce epoxy and polyester resins?
3 Why are the wood layers in plywood positioned with their grain directions at right angles?
4 What property improvements do reinforcing fibres bring to epoxy and polyester resins?

Types of materials – smart materials

Key terms

Alloy – a mixture of metals. (It may also be a mixture of a metal and a non-metal as long as the final product has metallic properties.)

Shape memory polymer – a polymer that returns to a pre-formed shape when heated.

Electrochromic materials – a material whose transparency can be changed by the application of electrical potential difference.

Did you know?

Today shape memory alloys are being used as dental braces. The temperature in the mouth causes them to contract and exert a force on the teeth.

Introduction

Many of the materials used in modern engineering have been developed to serve a particular purpose in relation to their properties. This is especially true of superalloys that are designed to work at high temperatures and smart materials whose properties can change very quickly in response to pressure, temperature, light or the presence of a magnetic or electrostatic field.

Types of smart material

Shape memory alloys (SMAs)

These are sometimes called 'memory metals'. After becoming deformed (e.g. as a result of heating, the application of external force and cooling) they return to their original or 'permanent' shape when reheated. They are **alloys** containing combinations of copper, zinc, nickel, aluminium and titanium. **Shape memory alloys** are now being used for vascular stents. These are small tubes made of alloy mesh that are placed in restricted blood vessels. When they are in position the body's temperature causes them to enlarge, improving the blood flow. Shape memory alloys are also used for dental braces, spectacle frames and to seal the connecting joints in oil pipelines.

SMAs that will return to their original shape when a magnetic field is applied are being developed, and it is thought that these may have a faster response than the heat-sensitive types. Possible applications are in electrical switchgear and control equipment.

Shape memory polymers

These have similar properties to shape memory metals. **Shape memory polymers** are used in helmets and small-scale surgical products. Shape memory foam is used to seal window frames where it expands at normal temperatures to fill in the gaps. Other types that return to their permanent shape by the application of light or an electric current are being developed. As with shape memory alloys, these will find applications in electrical and electronic equipment.

Electrochromic materials

The transmission of light can be controlled by applying a voltage across **electrochromic materials**. They are used for smart windows, mirrors and information displays. The applied voltage can change them from being transparent to frosted and then to completely opaque. This eliminates the need for window blinds and the property can be activated to give privacy.

Piezoelectric materials

With certain crystals, such as quartz, the application of a force or pressure causes a voltage to be set up across faces at right angles to the force. This is called the piezoelectric effect. It is put to use in pressure sensors, vibration recorders and microphones. **Piezoelectric materials** are also used to create the ignition spark in push-start gas fires and barbeques.

The piezoelectric effect can also occur in reverse where an applied voltage will produce stress in the material. This can cause it to twist or bend by a controlled amount. Smart materials with this kind of response are being investigated for possible use in aircraft control surfaces.

Quantum tunnelling composite

Quantum tunnelling composite (QTC) is a smart material that is an insulator in its normal state but when compressed it becomes an electrical conductor. In sheet form it is used to make touch switches on electrical and electronic equipment. It is also used in pressure sensors and its use is being investigated in textiles to make items of clothing that conduct electricity.

Key terms

Piezoelectric materials – materials that produce an electric charge when subjected to pressure or stress.

Quantum tunnelling composites – materials whose electrical conductivity increases with the application of pressure or stress.

Just checking

1 What are the special properties of a piezoelectric material?
2 What is quantum tunnelling composite (QTC) material commonly used for on electrical and electronic equipment?
3 How is the transparency of a smart window controlled?
4 What are shape memory alloys used for in vascular surgery?

Suitability of materials in engineering applications

Getting started

Designers have to decide what materials to use for engineered products. As well as looking at the material properties required, what other factors might a designer have to take into account?

Introduction

New materials are tested to find out their properties and to ensure they are suitable for use in engineered products. Raw materials supplied to engineering companies also need to be tested regularly to confirm that they are of the correct specification. Very often engineering components are tested during or after manufacture. This is especially important if they have been heat-treated to improve their strength, toughness or surface hardness.

Link

For more on mensuration, see *Unit 10 Analytical Methods*.

Simple mechanical tests

Industrial test equipment is expensive and can be complicated to operate. However, there are a number of simple tests that you can carry out in your training workshop or laboratory to confirm and compare the properties of different engineering materials.

Tensile/ductility test

Tensile tests determine the stress that causes a material to fracture. This is called the **tensile strength** and is calculated by dividing the load at fracture by the original cross-sectional area of the material. The test can also assess ductility by calculating the percentage increase in length that has occurred. If you haven't got access to a tensile testing machine the following test will be almost as accurate.

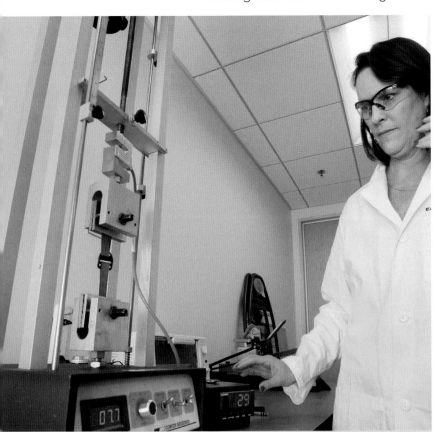

One stage of a tensile test

1 Take a length of copper or steel wire 2–3 m long and fix one end to a rigid support.

2 Record its length and measure its diameter using a micrometer or a vernier calliper.

3 Attach a weight hanger to the lower end and fix a ruler alongside it to measure the extension that occurs.

4 Slowly add weights up to the point of fracture and record the breaking load and increase in length.

5 Calculate the initial cross-sectional area of the wire in square metres (this will be a very small number) and the breaking load in Newtons.

6 Divide the breaking load by the initial cross-sectional area to find the tensile strength of the material measured in Newtons per square metre.

7 Divide the increase in length by the original length and multiply by 100 to give you the ductility of the material, measured as the percentage elongation.

Shear strength test

The shear strength of a material is not so easy to measure without the use of industrial test equipment. You can however compare the shear strength of different materials in a simple workshop test. For this you will need bench shears and thin strips of mild steel, copper, brass and aluminium sheet – all the same thickness and width. You need some way of measuring the load required to shear the specimens – the most convenient is to hook a suitable spring balance to the handle of the shears. You can now record the load that is required to shear each of the specimens and compare their shear strengths.

Hardness test

Industrial hardness tests are carried out by pressing a hardened steel ball (Brinall test for soft materials) or a pointed diamond (Vickers pyramid test for hard materials) into the surface of a material under a controlled load. The size of the resulting indentation is measured and used in a special formula to calculate a hardness number for the material. You can compare the hardness of different materials in the workshop by using a hammer and a centre punch and observing the relative sizes of the indentations.

Another way of comparing surface hardness is with a **scleroscope** (sometimes called a sclerometer). This instrument consists of a graduated glass tube containing a hardened steel ball which is allowed to fall on the surface of a material. The height to which the ball rebounds gives an indication of the surface hardness. You can carry out a similar test by dropping a hard steel ball bearing onto the surface of different materials from the same height and measuring the height of the rebound.

Impact test

Industrial impact tests measure the energy required to break a standard-sized material specimen using a large swinging hammer. You can carry out a similar workshop test to compare the toughness of different materials by striking them with a hammer while held in a vice. The specimens should be around 50 mm long cut from bars of the same diameter (5–6 mm is ideal) and with a saw-cut halfway through each one at around the mid-point. You should grip each specimen in the vice with the saw cut just above the vice jaws and of course you should try to use the same hammer force on each material. Some of the specimens may break and others may bend when they are struck. By comparing the effect, you can assess the toughness of each material.

Key terms

Tensile strength – the ability of a material to withstand tensile stress without fracturing.

Scleroscope – an instrument used for assessing surface hardness using the height of rebound of a hardened steel ball.

Take it further

A way of measuring hardness was put forward by the German geologist Friedrich Mohs in 1812. Find out about the Mohs scale of hardness and how a Mohs hardness test is carried out.

Just checking

1 How do you calculate tensile strength?
2 How is ductility measured from tensile test results?
3 What kind of indentors are used in industrial hardness testing?
4 How is the toughness of a material assessed in an industrial impact test?

Heat treatment processes

Introduction

Heat treatment processes are used to change or improve the properties of engineering materials. This involves heating the material to a specified temperature, followed by either rapid or slow cooling. Ferrous metals such as plain carbon steels can have their properties changed in this way. Industrial heat treatment is carried out in large temperature-controlled furnaces but you will be able to carry out some of the same processes in the brazing hearth or forge in your training workshop.

Annealing

Annealing is a heat treatment process used to restore a material to its soft condition after it has been formed to shape. Cold rolling, pressing and beating with hand tools increases the hardness of a metal. We call this 'work hardness'. In the annealing process steel components are heated to within the temperature range for their particular carbon content, shown on the graph in Figure 5.1. They are then allowed to cool very slowly – often in the annealing furnace as the heat dies away. This removes all traces of work hardness, enabling further cold working if required.

Normalising

This is very similar to annealing and is used to remove the internal stresses that may be locked inside a material. These can occur in hot forgings and castings that have cooled down unevenly. With iron and steel components the **normalising** process involves heating to within the temperature range shown in Figure 5.1 and then allowing it to cool in still air. Failure to remove internal stresses can cause a forging or casting to warp when it is machined.

Hardening

Medium carbon (0.3–0.8 per cent) and high carbon (0.8–1.4 per cent) steel components can be hardened by heating them to within the range shown in Figure 5.1 and quenching them in oil or water – a process known as **quench hardening**. Oil is preferable, as violent quenching in water can cause cracking. Not only does the process make the metal very hard, it also makes it brittle. To reduce the brittleness and toughen the material it must undergo a further heat treatment process called tempering.

Tempering

Tempering hardened steel components means reheating them in a temperature-controlled furnace to between 230°C and 300°C depending on their final use. There is a table showing the tempering temperatures for different components in the Appendix at the end of this unit. The metal can then be quenched or allowed to cool off naturally. An alternative method for single items such as chisels and screwdriver blades is to polish the surface and heat them slowly under a gas flame. Oxide colour films start to spread along the polished surface at the tempering temperature. As soon as the appropriate colour appears, the item is quenched.

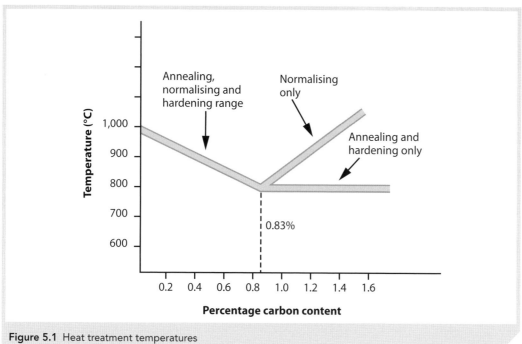

Figure 5.1 Heat treatment temperatures

Case hardening

Because of its low carbon content (0.1–0.3 per cent), mild steel cannot be quench hardened. It can, however, be made to absorb carbon into its outer surface, which can be hardened and tempered – **case hardened** – as required, leaving the mild steel with a tough core and a hard, wear-resistant surface. The surface carbon content is increased by heating the mild steel items in an iron box packed with a carbon-bearing material. Powdered charcoal and graphite, or a ready-prepared mixture such as Casenite, may be used. The sealed box is heated to 900–950°C and held at this temperature for 3–4 hours. The longer the 'soaking' time, the deeper the carbon penetration.

Assessment activity 5.1   An investigation of materials   2A.P1 | 2A.P2 | 2A.P3 | 2A.M1 | 2A.D1

Carry out an investigation of some of the materials used in your workshop and in engineered products found in the home. You will need to present your findings back to the group. Your survey should include:

- at least two examples of each type of material covered in this unit
- suggestions for how each material you have selected is used in the engineering world, and why

- evidence of tests you have carried out to determine the mechanical properties of some of these materials, and your interpretation of the results
- information about two heat treatment processes that can alter the properties of a ferrous metal.

Tips

- Describe the properties and applications of each material clearly. You could include images in your presentation.
- Explain why you think each material is suitable for its application.
- Consider the advantages of choosing one material over another for a particular application. Are there any disadvantages? You could present the advantages and disadvantages in a table.
- Practise. You will have more confidence if you know your presentation well and can look at your audience when you are talking.
- Ask your teacher/tutor how long your presentation should last. Time yourself to make sure you can finish on time.

Selection for applications

Introduction

When selecting materials for an activity or product, designers and engineers need to keep in mind several factors: suitability for the working environment, cost, method of manufacture, safety and sustainability. In other words a designer must select materials that are durable, are affordable to purchase and manufacture, meet health and safety requirements and, wherever possible, can be recycled or reused.

Selection of materials through activity

By selection of materials through activity we mean selection to meet the service conditions of a product, its manufacture, construction and the maintenance operations that will be needed during its service life.

Design

The task for the design engineer is to meet the **product design specifications** that have been agreed with the customer or which it is thought will meet a market need when offered for sale. The designer must select materials that are suitable for the working environment of the product, affordable, durable enough to withstand the forces acting on it, pleasing to look at and, wherever possible, they should be reusable or recyclable. Where possible, designers should avoid the use of **materials and substances hazardous to health**.

Manufacture and construction

The designer also has to consider the manufacturing facilities that are available and select materials that can be processed and handled by the existing plant and labour force. Investments in new machinery, training and safety equipment can add considerable costs to the manufacture and construction of a product.

Maintenance operations

An engineered product needs to be fit for its purpose and easy to maintain. In some cases a part may need to be replaced and a new one produced as a single item. This will be less costly if the material is readily available.

In cases where components need to be replaced as part of a **planned maintenance programme**, a number may need to be held in stock. This will be less expensive if they are made from a low-cost material.

Key terms

Product design specification – a detailed list of a product's requirements that takes into account function, performance, cost, aesthetics and production.

Materials and substances hazardous to health – materials requiring special storage, specific handling equipment and disposal procedures to protect the workforce and the environment.

Planned maintenance programme – operations and repairs that are carried out at regular intervals.

Selection of materials for use in a product

A skateboard is an everyday product made up from a number of parts; here you will consider the major components and the materials that are commonly selected for them (see Table 5.2). The alternatives would either be less durable or more expensive.

Table 5.2 Material selections for a skateboard

Component	Material	Properties required	Possible alternatives
Deck	Plywood – 7-ply maple	Strong and durable, able to be shaped	Glass or carbon reinforced epoxy resin
Shock pad	Rubber	Flexible, shock-absorbing	Polythene
Truck base plate	Aluminium alloy	Light, corrosion-resistant, able to be cast into shape	Titanium alloy
Truck hanger	Aluminium alloy	Light, corrosion-resistant, able to be cast into shape	Titanium alloy
Axle	Stainless steel	Strong, tough and corrosion-resistant	Medium carbon steel
Kingpin	Stainless steel	Strong, tough and corrosion-resistant	Medium carbon steel
Bushes	Rubber	Flexible, shock-absorbing	Polypropylene
Wheels	Polyurethane	Smooth running, hard-wearing	Rubber
Bearings	Hardened steel ball races	Low-friction, hard-wearing	Nylon

Link

For more information about product specifications, see *Unit 2 Investigating an Engineered Product*, Topic A.1.

Just checking

1 What is a product design specification?
2 How do manufacturing facilities affect material selection?
3 How can material selection be made sustainable?

Sustainable use of materials

Introduction

The demand for raw materials is increasing as a result of the growth of manufacturing in countries such as China and India and in the developing economies of Africa and South America. It is accepted that we must make better use of materials so as not to damage the environment and to safeguard future supplies of raw materials.

Raw materials

Extraction

Engineering metals begin their life in different kinds of rock known as mineral ores. They are extracted by mining and quarrying. Plastics are derived from the by-products of oil distillation and from vegetable sources. Timber, of course, is obtained from forestry.

These are all expensive operations and there are limits to the amounts that are available. To make their use sustainable we need to use less, recycle more and, in the case of forestry, replant for future generations.

Primary processing

Once material ores are extracted from their sources, they arrive at the steelworks or foundry for **primary processing**. Metals are **smelted** or otherwise extracted from their ores to produce blocks of different sizes known as **ingots**. The raw materials for plastics are converted into powders, granules and resins in chemical plants and timber is transported to **sawmills** for cutting and seasoning before use. Seasoning involves natural or forced drying to remove moisture from the wood.

Secondary processing of metals

Secondary processing may be carried out at the same location but, in many cases, the materials are transported on to other manufacturers. You could say that one person's product is another person's raw material.

Metal ingots are passed to rolling mills where they are reheated and passed backwards and forwards between powerful rollers. Girders, railway lines and thick steel plate are produced in this way. Further processing is carried out to make bars and sheet metal. Alternatively, the metal may be **forged** to shape or re-melted and used for **casting**. The final shaping of components is generally done by machining or presswork.

Secondary processing of plastics

In a similar way the powders and resins for thermoplastic materials undergo secondary processing into sheets, moulded components, tubes, pipes and the different kinds of complicated hollow sections that are used to make uPVC window frames and doors. This process is called **extrusion**. The raw materials are heated until soft and then forced through a specially shaped die. The process is rather like forcing toothpaste out of a tube. Some malleable metals, such as aluminium sections, are also formed by extrusion.

Lower volatile organic compounds

A lower **volatile organic compound (VOC)** is any chemical compound with a boiling point of 250°C or less that can endanger a person's health or cause damage to the environment. While some of these are essential to manufacturing processes, they must be used and disposed of with care. Examples include petrochemicals and industrial solvents used with paints and other protective coatings, cleaning supplies, glues and adhesives. VOCs may be given off in homes and offices by new carpets, wall coverings, furnishings and photocopying equipment. Adequate ventilation is needed as they can cause feelings of drowsiness and sickness.

Strict rules govern the use, storage and disposal of VOCs. Wherever possible, less toxic alternatives should be used – this is already happening in paint manufacture where there is a shift to water-based products. Some VOCs, such as chlorofluorocarbons (CFCs), have been banned completely in new products. They were used in aerosols and as a refrigerant in domestic and industrial refrigerators. Some of these are still in use and can only be disposed of by qualified authorities.

Reducing material use

Products made with fewer materials make less of an impact on our reserves of natural resources. They use less energy and can cost less to make.

Analysing a product to see if it can be made using less material is called '**lightweighting**'. Engineers create lightweight products by examining their shape, the forces acting on them, the types of material used and the manufacturing processes.

There are several ways that the use of materials can be reduced. For instance, the tubes of a bicycle frame are often made oval instead of round. This enables them to be made of thinner material but have the same strength. Sheet materials can be made thinner but corrugated and be just as strong and stiff. Expensive metals could be replaced by cheaper, lighter plastics. The use of recycled material and reusable parts can also reduce the use of raw materials.

Engineers must also think long-term. Good design can increase the lifespan of a product, meaning that better use is being made of materials. At the end of its life a product should be easy to dismantle so that the different materials can be recycled and the serviceable components reused.

How can you 'lightweight' a bicycle?

> **Key terms**
>
> **Volatile organic compound (VOC)** – any chemical compound with a boiling point of 250°C or less that can endanger a person's health or cause damage to the environment.
>
> **Lightweighting** – designing or redesigning products to use a minimal amount of material.

> **Did you know?**
>
> Bicycles made today are about 50 per cent lighter than those made 20 years ago. Cars, trains and domestic products are now also designed and updated with lightweighting in mind.

CONTINUED ▶▶

Reusing materials and products

A reusable product can be used over and over again for its intended purpose. Examples include returnable milk bottles, printer and toner cartridges, wooden storage pallets and shipping containers.

Before reuse, some reconditioning or refurbishing may be needed. Rubber tyres are re-treaded and automobile engines are factory reconditioned. Engineered products often contain components that are expensive to produce and show little wear after end-of-life dismantling. After careful inspection and testing to ensure that they meet the required specifications, these can be offered for reuse.

Case study

A waste product can be described as having 'new life' when it is used for a different function. Common examples include the use of discarded tyres for boat fenders and the use of power station ash to make building blocks. There are other examples of discarded items being used as building materials. In experimental 'eco-friendly' houses, earth-filled rubber tyres have been used for external walls and glass bottles built into internal walls to admit light.

The advantage of reuse is that it saves energy and raw materials. Disposal costs are reduced and sustainable use can provide employment in underdeveloped countries where reconditioning and refurbishment often take place.

Recycling or using recycled materials

Recycling reduces the demand for new raw materials. It also cuts the need for incineration, which can cause air pollution, and landfill, which can cause water pollution.

A number of systems are in place to collect recyclable materials.

- Industrial waste is collected in bulk by contractors. Manufacturing and engineering firms operate internal systems to ensure that different waste materials are kept separate and put in marked storage areas for collection.

- Local authorities organise doorstep collections and drop-off centres for domestic waste that has been sorted into the different categories.

- Metals can be recycled into quality supplies with a considerable saving in energy compared with their production from raw materials. This is especially true of aluminium which needs large amounts of electricity to extract it from its ore.

- Thermoplastics need to be sorted into their different polymer types. Automated systems have been designed to do this. They also need sorting into their different colours. After cleaning, they are shredded, melted and formed into pellets which are then used to make other plastic products.

- A high proportion of paper products are recycled, reducing the demand for wood pulp – the raw material needed for paper-making. Recyclable paper is generally divided into two categories:

A recycling plant for domestic waste

- pre-consumer waste, which includes cut-offs and paper damaged in production
- post-consumer waste, which includes newspapers, office paper, magazines and packaging. This category needs special processing to remove printing inks and colourings.

- Building waste can be recycled. Prior to demolition buildings are stripped of pipes, cable wiring and roofing material containing copper and lead. These can all be recycled, as can some of the timber used for floorboards and roof trusses. The bricks, roof tiles and concrete foundations are generally broken up and may be used as hardcore in the preparation of other building sites.

Waste management

Waste material that cannot be reused or recycled must be safely disposed of. The two main methods of disposal are **landfill** and **incineration**.

Landfill

Here, the waste is dumped at a designated site, compacted and buried. The decomposing materials can attract vermin and give off greenhouse gases. They can also generate flammable gases such as methane. Many landfill sites have buried pipes to take away the gas for burning. A properly managed landfill site can be hygienic and a cheap way of disposing of non-toxic waste. However, suitable sites are in short supply and authorities are encouraged to promote recycling and find alternative means of disposal.

Incineration

Incineration is one such alternative. The ash that remains from solid waste is around 20–30 per cent of its original volume. The hot gases from combustion can be used to raise steam, which can then be used to generate electricity.

Incineration is the best way of disposing of hazardous biological and medical waste. Strict rules apply for the treatment of hazardous materials. They must only be disposed of at approved sites and at prescribed temperatures.

The disadvantage of incineration is that it may produce pollutant gases. The decision over where to site incinerators is always controversial and it is desirable that they are positioned well away from towns and cities.

Did you know?

Large quantities of used oil from car services are collected from garages and service centres. While some of this is cleaned and recycled, it is not economical to recycle it all and the remainder is burned as a fuel.

Did you know?

Radioactive waste and waste containing heavy metals such as mercury must be separated and treated by encasing them in glass or concrete. They can then be stored at approved sites or, in some cases, buried.

Just checking

1. What is the difference between casting and forging?
2. In what forms are the raw materials used for making plastic products generally supplied?
3. What is a volatile organic compound (VOC)?
4. Name two types of container that can be reused.
5. What is the raw material from which paper is made?
6. What are the two major methods of waste disposal?

Forms of supply

Introduction

In this topic you will learn about the symbols, abbreviations and identification codes used to identify materials used on engineering drawings and maintenance schedules. You will also find out about the different forms and sizes in which engineering materials are supplied and stored.

▶ Symbols, abbreviations and identification coding

Engineering drawings usually give precise details of the material that is to be used for a product. Often, this is given in an abbreviated form together with other details such as the grade of material, size and surface finish required.

Figure 5.2 A typical title block on an engineering drawing containing information on the material to be used

Abbreviations for materials

The material specified in the title block (Figure 5.2) is bright drawn mild steel, abbreviated to BDMS, together with its British Standard (BS) specification: BS 970:040A10. Some other common abbreviations are shown in Table 5.3.

Table 5.3 Abbreviations for common metals

Abbreviation	Material
CI	Cast iron
SG Iron	Spheroidal graphite cast iron
MS	Mild steel
BDMS	Bright drawn mild steel
CRMS	Cold rolled mild steel
SS	Stainless steel
Alum	Aluminium
Dural	Duralumin
Phos Bronze	Phosphor-bronze

ISO and BSI materials coding system

As in the title block shown in Figure 5.2, the British Standards Institution (BSI) or International Organization for Standardization (ISO) specifications may be given for the material. The BSI issue codes that specify the constituents of the different kinds of metals and alloys in common use. In most cases they also specify the most appropriate uses and operating conditions, particularly for work at high temperatures and pressures. The codes have been updated in consultation with industry and, more recently, as a result of the creation of a common European numbering system.

There has been slow uptake of the new European system, BS EN 10277:2008 for steels, but it will undoubtedly become more widely used as time goes on. Some firms still use the BS 970:1991 codes (issued in 1991) and even the BS 970:1955 codes (issued in 1955) for steels. It would have been a mammoth task to change all the old material codes on drawings and service schedules when the changes were made, so you need to be aware of the different coding systems.

Table 5.4 gives examples of the codes for some common grades of steel. The systems are quite different and the full material specification can be obtained by referring to the latest standard. You will find that the same applies to the other metals and alloys where the same material may be coded in different ways depending on the age of the drawing or schedule you are working to.

Table 5.4 BS material codes for some common steels

Material	BS EN 10277:2008	BS 970:1991	BS 970:1955
Mild steel	1.7021	210M15	EN 32M
Medium carbon steel	1.0511	080M40	EN 8
Tool steel	1.3505	534A99	EN 31
Free cutting steel	1.0715	230M07	EN 1A
High tensile steel	1.0407/1.1148	605M36T	EN 16T

CONTINUED ▶▶

Suppliers' and organisations' colour codes

Suppliers and manufacturers often have their own coding systems and stores location codes. Metal bars are often painted with a colour code on their ends so that they can be easily identified on storage racks. There is no universal system so you should familiarise yourself with the local system. You will usually find it displayed on a chart in a prominent position in the stores area. A typical system used by one major supplier is shown in Table 5.5, but be aware that this may not be the same as in your place of work or training workshop.

Table 5.5 Typical colour codes for barstock

Material	Colour code	
Mild steel	Red	●
Medium carbon steel	Yellow	○
High carbon steel	Purple/white	◐
Free cutting steel	Green	●
High tensile steel	White	○

You may find that aluminium components are painted yellow. Again, this is not universal but the result of spraying them with an etching primer that better enables the finishing coat of paint to adhere to the surface.

In the absence of a storekeeper you may be required to update the stores records when you draw material or components. This may be a manual entry on a record card or a keyboard entry on the stores database. In either case it is important that you make the entry so that a low stock warning can be raised, manually or automatically, if the number falls below a certain level.

Colour-coded steel joists.

Material selection, forms, sizes and surface finish

Engineering materials are supplied in a variety of forms, as shown in Table 5.6. Steel barstock is supplied bright drawn or cold-rolled in circular, hexagonal, square and rectangular sections with a bright shiny surface. It is usually treated with oil to prevent rusting. It may also be supplied in hot-rolled condition in which case the surface will appear rough and black.

Table 5.6 Forms of supply

Metals	Polymers	Timber
Ingots	Powders	Planks
Castings	Granules	Boards
Forgings	Resins	Composite sheets
Pressings	Sheet	Rods
Bars	Mouldings	
Sheet	Pipe and tube	
Plate	Extrusions	
Pipe and tube	Film	
Wire		
Rolled sections		
Extrusions		

An engineering drawing or process plan may also state the required surface finish, surface protection, heat treatment and surface hardness (see Figure 5.3).

Figure 5.3 Examples of the information that might be included in an engineering drawing or process plan

In the case of bar, sheet, pipe, wire and fastenings some dimensional information may be given. This could be the diameters of bar and pipe, rectangular section dimensions or the distance across the flats of a hexagonal section bar. For sheet and wire a standard wire gauge number might be given.

Standard wire gauge (SWG) is a means of classifying wire diameters and the thickness of sheet metal. The higher the SWG number, the smaller the diameter or thickness. The most commonly used sizes lie in the range SWG16 (1.626 mm) to SWG42

CONTINUED ▶▶

(0.102 mm). The Greek letter Φ (phi) is used to indicate that a dimension is a diameter, for example, BDMS Φ50 would indicate bright drawn mild steel bar 50 mm in diameter. In the case of pipe or tube sizes, the outer and inner diameters might be given or the outer diameter and wall thickness. The 'extrusions' referred to in Table 5.6 are tubes and other shapes of metal and plastic cross-section that have been formed by pushing the material through a specially shaped die – rather like squeezing toothpaste out of a tube. Some of the abbreviations for this information are shown in Table 5.7.

Table 5.7 Material information abbreviations

Abbreviation/symbol	Interpretation
ISO	International Organization for Standardization
BS or BSI	British Standards Institution
BH	Brinell Hardness number
VPN	Vickers Pyramid Hardness number
SWG	Standard Wire Gauge
Φ50	50 mm diameter
MS, Hex Hd Bolt – M8 × 1.25 × 50	Mild steel hexagonal headed metric bolt, 8 mm diameter, 1.25 mm pitch, 50 mm long

Drawings may also contain BSI or ISO specifications relating to the use and safety requirements of the product.

The size of metric bolts and nuts are always shown as given in Table 5.7. Additional information on drawings and service schedules might state that fastenings such as nuts, bolts, washers or machine screws must be cadmium plated or otherwise treated to give corrosion protection.

Just checking

1 What do the letters CI indicate on an engineering drawing?
2 What do the letters BSI and VPN stand for?
3 What form of material supply are the letters SWG relevant to?

Assessment activity 5.2   Manufacturing children's toys   2B.P4 | 2B.P5 | 2B.M2 | 2B.M3 | 2B.D2

You are on a work placement with a firm that manufactures children's toys and have been asked by your supervisor to prepare a presentation on their use of sustainable materials. You must include information about:

• the environmental impact of the materials used in a children's toy
• appropriate forms of supply for the materials used, with reasons.

Tips

• Consider the environmental impact of each stage of the toy's life – including extraction and processing of its materials, manufacture and maintenance.
• Consider ways to make the product more sustainable.

Workspace

Sarah Woodfine

Materials engineer

I work for a company that makes equipment for the nuclear industry. My job involves sampling and testing components that will be used in nuclear power stations. I also make regular visits to our suppliers to discuss material specifications and requirements. I work as part of a team in a well-equipped inspection laboratory where we carry out exhaustive tests to confirm material properties. Some of my time is spent writing test reports and attending meetings to discuss recommendations and changes.

Sometimes we have to investigate cases where a component has failed in service. It is vital that we find the cause of this and suggest design modifications or a change to an alternative material. I enjoy my work, especially when it involves problem-solving. I also enjoy meeting customers and suppliers to discuss material requirements and supplies.

Think about it

1   Why do you think it is important to find out why a component has failed in service?

2   Which of the topics that you have covered do you think would be the most important in Sarah's job?

3   What communication skills do you think Sarah needs to do her job?

Introduction

Engineers are always trying to make the best use of computer technology in the manufacturing of products. Computer-aided design (CAD) involves the use of drawing software to design engineering products. These drawings carry all the information needed to manufacture the product, including measurements, materials and components. This unit gives you the opportunity to use CAD software using standard industry methods. You will also learn how given drawings can be easily adapted and modified.

You will then use computer-aided manufacture (CAM) techniques. This involves using the data from a CAD drawing to produce a computer numerically controlled (CNC) program, and then running the program on a suitable machine in order to produce an engineering component.

Assessment: This unit will be assessed through a series of assignments set by your teacher/tutor.

Learning aims

After completing this unit you should:

A use a CAD system to produce engineering drawings

B use a CAM system to manufacture an engineering component.

When I went on placement to a local engineering company I was given the opportunity to use CAD software to produce a new design. I then helped the technician run a program on the CNC machine to make the part.

Sarah, *16-year-old would-be engineering apprentice*

Computer-aided Engineering

This table shows you what you must do in order to achieve a **Pass**, **Merit** or **Distinction** grade, and where you can find activities in this book to help you.

Assessment criteria

Level 1	Level 2 **Pass**	Level 2 **Merit**	Level 2 **Distinction**
Learning aim A: Use a CAD system to produce engineering drawings			
1A.1 Produce a CAD drawing of an engineering component using a CAD system.	**2A.P1** Produce a fully dimensioned CAD drawing of an engineering component using basic and further CAD commands and BS conventions. **See Assessment activity 6.1, page 103**		
1A.2 Produce a circuit diagram using a CAD system.	**2A.P2** Produce a circuit diagram fully labelling all components using basic and further CAD commands and BS conventions. **See Assessment activity 6.1, page 103**		
1A.3 Identify drawing and modification commands used to produce engineering component and circuit diagrams.	**2A.P3** Describe drawing and modification commands used to produce engineering component and circuit diagrams. **See Assessment activity 6.1, page 103**	**2A.M1** Explain the importance of drawing and modification commands and the benefits when used to produce engineering components and circuit diagrams. **See Assessment activity 6.1, page 103**	**2A.D1** Justify the use of CAD in the production of engineering component drawings and circuit diagrams. **See Assessment activity 6.1, page 103**
Learning aim B: Use a CAM system to manufacture an engineering component			
1B.4 Load CAD data from a drawing into a CNC machine in order to produce an engineering component.	**2B.P4** Produce an engineering component by converting CAD data into an appropriate CNC program and loading the program into a CNC machine. **See Assessment activity 6.2, page 108**		
1B.5 Maths Check a component, produced using a CNC machine, for conformity with the design specification.	**2B.P5** Maths Describe how the component produced meets the design specification. **See Assessment activity 6.2, page 108**	**2B.M2** Simulate component production, identify improvements in programs and suggest solutions. **See Assessment activity 6.2, page 108**	**2B.D2** Evaluate CAM as a means of producing different engineered components. **See Assessment activity 6.2, page 108**

Maths   Opportunity to practise mathematical skills

How you will be assessed

The unit will be assessed by a series of tasks set by your teacher/tutor. You will be expected to show an understanding of CAD and demonstrate the ability to use CAD data to develop a CNC program in order to produce an engineering component. The tasks will be based on a scenario where you work in an engineering organisation. For example, your manager is considering production of a new component and asks you to design, using CAD, and manufacture, using CNC techniques, a new prototype.

Your assessment could be in the form of:

- an electronic portfolio
- CAD drawings and teacher/tutor observation records
- annotated photographs showing the safe use of a CNC machine to manufacture a component.

Use of a CAD system to produce an engineering drawing

Introduction

In this topic you will learn about the key features of a **CAD system**, and how to use this system to produce an engineering drawing with the correct information to ensure that a product is manufactured correctly.

Engineering drawings communicate to a technician the exact specification for a product. Engineers often use two kinds of drawings.

- Assembly drawings – showing how all the individual parts go together, as well as a parts list. Sometimes an exploded view drawing is used.
- Parts drawings – showing all the information that might be needed by the manufacturer of a part, including dimensions and materials.

CAD software can be used to produce these drawings quickly and effectively. A wide variety of CAD software packages are available although each varies slightly in the way it operates. You will receive guidance and instruction from your teacher/tutor on how the software you are using will allow you to complete the activities in this unit.

When you start the CAD software you will see an opening screen displaying a series of toolbars, drop-down menus and a drawing sheet (you can think of this as a piece of paper to draw on). Instead of a pencil you will have a cursor or pointer that moves as you move your mouse or pointing device. It is used to select menu options as well as for drawing and modifying objects.

Figure 6.1 A designer using CAD software

Drawing lines and circles

The first thing you might want to do when using a CAD system is draw some lines using a drawing tool. Once you have found this you can use the **snap** and **grid** function that allows the cursor to move from dot to dot and enables you to draw quite complex shapes.

Once you have drawn a few lines and produced some different shapes it is useful to know how to remove them from the screen. After selecting the erase tool, you should be able to select the lines you have drawn and remove them.

Drawing circles follows a similar process. Using the circle tool you should be able to select the centre of the circle then move the pointer to adjust the size (there is also an option that allows you to input the exact radius or diameter). If you are using the snap and grid function you can draw circles of similar sizes.

There are a variety of other drawing commands that you should experiment with:

- Arcs – parts of circles can also be easily constructed using the radius and centre point or end point positions, angles, etc.
- Rectangles – and triangles, hexagons and other polygonal objects can be quickly constructed using the tools available.
- Zoom/pan – zooming in and out allows you to view the whole of a drawing or particular details while panning allows you to move the view up/down or left/right.

Line types

You can use different types of line to represent different details on a drawing. Table 6.1 shows the types of line used and when you would use them.

Take it further

There are standards and conventions that should be used to present information on an engineering drawing, for example, a drawing should comply with BS8888. Carry out some research to find out about BS8888.

Link

To learn more about line types and the use of engineering information, see *Unit 9 Interpreting and Using Engineering Information*.

Table 6.1 The various types of line used in engineering drawings

Type of line	Appearance	Where used
————	Continuous thick line	Visible outlines and edges
————	Continuous thin line	Dimension, projection and leader lines, hatching, outlines of revolved sections, short centre lines, imaginary intersections
∼∼∼	Continuous thin wavy line	Limits of partial or interrupted views and sections, if the limit is not an axis
—⋁—⋁—	Continuous thin, straight line with zigzags	Break lines
- - - - - -	Dashed thin lines	Hidden outlines and edges
— — — —	Chain thin lines	Centre lines, lines of symmetry, trajectories and loci, pitch lines and pitch circles
⌐ —	Chain thin lines thick at the edges and changes of direction	Cutting planes
— — — —	Chain thin double dashed line	Outlines and edges of adjacent parts, outlines and edges of alternative and extreme positions of moveable parts, initial outlines prior to forming, bend lines on developed blanks or patterns

CONTINUED ▶▶

◤ Adding text

CAD software also allows you to add text. It is common practice for a designer to record the following on a CAD drawing:

- their name
- the date the drawing was produced
- the drawing number
- the scale
- the type of projection used
- the dimensions of the product
- the materials that should be used during the manufacture of the product.

This information is recorded in the 'title block' section of a CAD drawing.

◤ Coordinate systems

To construct and position lines precisely you need to have an understanding of three CAD **coordinate** systems.

TITLE:		DATE:	10/04/12
Bracket		SCALE:	1:1
DRAWN BY:			
AH		MATERIAL: MILD STEEL	
ALL DIMENSIONS IN mm		DWG NO:	0011

Figure 6.2 An engineering drawing for a bracket shown in orthographic view. See Activity 6.2.

Absolute coordinates

Absolute coordinates are like map references. They are based on a **starting point** or origin, which we call 0,0. This is normally in the bottom left-hand corner of the screen.

Points are entered using the x–y system so the point (100,50) is 100 units in the X direction and 50 units in the Y direction. Both are measured from the origin.

To draw using this system you need to know the start and end points of every line. This is a slow method and it is easy to make mistakes.

Relative coordinates

Relative coordinates allow you to measure from your current point. So instead of having to work out the position all the time you only need to know the length of the next line.

Polar coordinates

Polar coordinates are split into absolute and relative. However, instead of using the x–y system, the length of the line and the angle it makes with the horizontal are required.

Figure 6.3 shows a triangle, which has sides of 300, 400 and 500 units. Each view represents the same triangle but drawn using different methods of determining the coordinates.

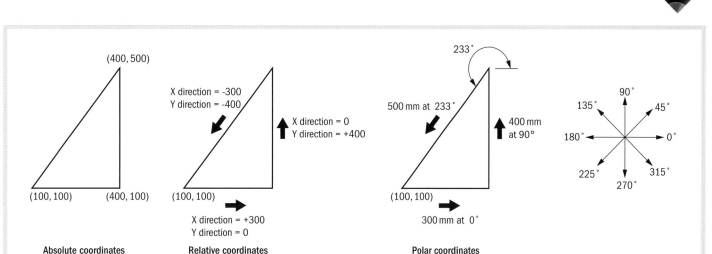

Figure 6.3 A triangle described in three different coordinate systems

Using drawing templates

Engineering drawings are produced using standard **CAD templates**. These are used to begin a new drawing with the necessary types of text, dimension settings, types of line and drawing layouts already prepared for the type of drawing being produced.

Activity 6.1   Creating a template

Using CAD software, work through the following steps to create a simple A4 template:

1 Activate the grid and snap and set both to 10 mm.

2 Use the draw/line option and when you are prompted for the starting point use the keyboard to input (10,10).

3 At the next point option input (287,10) then (287,200) then (10,200) and, finally, (10,10) again.

4 You should now have a rectangle, which is equivalent to an A4 sheet of paper but with a 10 mm border.

5 Using the zoom option make sure you are looking at the bottom right-hand corner of the screen.

6 Activate the draw/line option and use the snap and grid function to draw the title block, as shown in Figures 6.2 and 6.7.

7 Reset the snap/grid to 2 mm to add the text to the title block; use a height of 2 mm for the text.

8 Save the template drawing using the appropriate file format.

You can use this template as a starting point for all the other drawings you produce for this unit.

CONTINUED ▶▶

Key terms

Coordinates – a set of values that show an exact position in space.

Absolute coordinates – measured from the start point/origin, like plotting a graph in x–y.

Relative coordinates – measured from the current point, like using a ruler.

Polar coordinates – measured in terms of length and angle, like using a protractor.

CAD template – a standard layout that CAD operators use to produce drawings. It includes a border, title block and standard logo for the company or organisation. It also features standard settings such as units, types of line and colours.

Plotting/printing a CAD drawing:

1. Select the correct printer/plotter.

2. Select the correct paper size.

3. Select the layout (portrait or landscape).

4. Select the area to print (part of the drawing or all of it).

5. Select the printing scale (full size, half size, etc.).

6. Always review or preview if possible before printing.

Figure 6.4 Plotting/printing a CAD drawing

Key terms

Plotter – a mechanical drawing machine that reproduces what you have drawn on-screen onto paper or drawing film. Nowadays, any large inkjet or laser printer is often called a plotter.

Saving your work and outputting to a printer or plotter device

CAD drawings can be saved in a variety of formats, which are usually specific to the software being used. You can also often use the 'save as' feature to save as common formats such as .pdf or .jpg.

You may want to produce a hard copy of your drawing. This is often more complex in CAD than simply selecting the printer icon and collecting the printout from the printer.

You will need to select the 'plot/print' function. Next, you will be given a series of options, which you should carefully run through in sequence. Although each CAD software package does things slightly differently the procedure shown in Figure 6.4 is useful to follow.

You can use a normal A4 printer; however, it is often necessary to use a large-format printer or **plotter** to reproduce your CAD work.

Activity 6.2	Produce a CAD drawing

You have been given the following design brief:

Using the third angle projection system, produce a fully dimensioned CAD drawing using three views of a bracket similar to the one shown in Figure 6.2. The bracket measures 100 mm in width, height and length, and has a thickness of 10 mm. In addition, each face is to have a Φ40 hole centrally positioned.

- Have you checked that sufficient dimensions are in place to allow the component to be manufactured?
- Have you used the correct line types?
- Have you used the correct projection system?

Modifying and manipulating CAD drawings

There are many ways to save time and increase efficiency when using a CAD system. In this section you will look at different ways to modify and manipulate drawings so they can be viewed in different ways. Figure 6.5 gives examples of the techniques you can use.

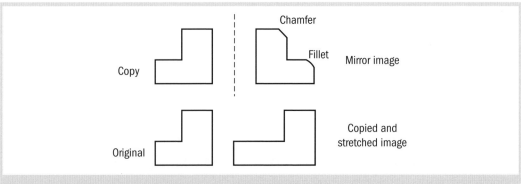

Figure 6.5 Ways that an existing drawing can be modified to produce a new one

Modify tools

Modify tools allow drawings to be adjusted quickly. You should experiment with these to see how you might be able to use them when you are constructing drawings or circuit diagrams (see Table 6.2).

Table 6.2 Modify tools

Type of tool	Use
Array/pattern	This can be used to produce multiple copies of an object or to create a rectangular or circular pattern without having to draw or copy the object over and over again.
Chamfer and fillet	These functions allow you to change the appearance of a sharp corner. They are often confused with each other. The fillet option rounds off the sharp corner to a given radius while chamfer cuts off the corner by a given angle or chamfer distance.
Change options	Use this to edit the properties of an object, for example, the radius of a circle, the colour of a line, the type of line or layer and the type of hatch pattern. You can also match the properties of an object to another similar object.
Copy/duplicate	Use this tool to duplicate/copy an object you have already drawn quickly and accurately.
Erase	You will inevitably make mistakes as you go along or need to change something you have already drawn. The erase command allows you to remove unwanted items. You can erase single objects or select groups of objects to remove. If you erase something accidentally the undo option will allow you to retrieve it.
Hatch	Used to fill a closed area with a pattern and useful for showing which parts of an object are solid material.
Move	If you have drawn something in the wrong place you can use the coordinate system to move it with accuracy and position it relative to other objects.
Rotate/revolve	If you draw an object that is shown in one position and then realise that it should be at a different angle this tool allows you to select the object and input the angle you need to rotate it by.
Scale	Use this to select an object and increase its size from a base point.
Stretch	This is a useful option if you have a feature or group of objects that are too long or short. It allows the objects to be stretched to connect with other objects or by a specific distance. You can often include the dimension lines too, and the dimension text will automatically adjust to the new measurement.
Trim	This is a useful option if you have been using guidelines or copy options and some lines overlap. This function allows you to remove overlapping elements with reference to other objects on screen.
Undo	Undo is a very useful option as it allows you to try something and experiment with the CAD tools and options. If it doesn't quite work out you can simply activate the undo option and try again. Sometimes you can use undo in the middle of a drawing operation to go back one step in the process.

Just checking

1 What are the letters used to define a 2D coordinate system?

2 What options are used to create and remove drawn lines?

3 What tools are used to define accurate geometry on-screen?

CONTINUED ▸▸

Projection techniques

CAD drawings are produced using standard drawing conventions:

- To represent objects in detail we use 2D views known as **orthographic projection**.
- To represent objects in 3D we use a technique called **isometric projection**.

Orthographic projection

When you need to show an object in detail it is common to use the 2D orthographic projection technique. There are usually six views of an object: front, back, left, right, top and bottom – think of a dice. Normally it is only necessary to draw three of these views, usually the ones that give the most detail:

- front elevation
- side elevation
- plan view (this is the top view).

There are two commonly used projection systems.

- First angle projection – this system requires you to draw what you see on the **opposite** side to where you are looking from. So looking at Figure 6.6 and starting with the front elevation, look at one side of this view and draw what you see on the **other** side. Then, again thinking of the front elevation, look from above this elevation and draw what you see **underneath** the front elevation
- Third angle projection – this system requires you to draw what you see on the **same** side as where you are looking from. So looking at Figure 6.6 and starting with the front elevation, look at one side of this view and draw what you see on the **same** side. Then, again thinking of the front elevation, look from above this elevation and draw what you see **above** the front elevation.

Figure 6.6 First angle projection (left), third angle projection (right). The centre view, shown in 3D, is a representation of the object.

Isometric projection

This technique is used to draw 3D objects. CAD software packages have settings and tools that allow you to produce an isometric (or 3D) view of an object very easily.

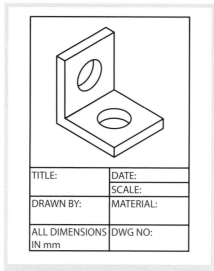

TITLE:	DATE:
	SCALE:
DRAWN BY:	MATERIAL:
ALL DIMENSIONS IN mm	DWG NO:

Figure 6.7 Example of an isometric model

Just checking

1 What techniques could you use to produce exact replicas or patterns of previously drawn objects?

2 What technique would you use to show the sizes of component parts on a drawing?

3 What techniques could you use to change the size of a previously drawn object?

4 What techniques can you use to remove part or all of an unwanted detail you may have constructed?

Use of a CAD system to produce a circuit diagram

Getting started

Take a look at a circuit diagram or refer to Figure 6.8. Draw one of the symbols using a pencil and paper. Consider how long it took to draw and how long it might take to draw an entire circuit diagram.

Introduction

Circuit diagrams are used to show how different components in a circuit are connected together. Examples include electrical circuits (e.g. for supplying electrical power to machinery), electronic circuits (typically used in control systems or computers), hydraulic systems (a typical example would be the hydraulic braking system in a car) and pneumatic circuits (such as those used to control dentists' drills).

Drawing circuit diagrams

CAD software can be used to produce circuit diagrams. This is a lot easier than using pencil and paper because CAD systems often have a library of pre-drawn parts.

Once you have drawn or selected a series of circuit symbols, you can turn these into a circuit using the 'drag and drop' technique. You will need to position the parts, add connecting lines and possibly rotate or manipulate individual elements.

Key terms

Circuit diagram – a drawing that shows how an arrangement of components can be combined to form a circuit.

Remember

You used the snap and grid function in Topic A.1. This very useful tool allows you to accurately position each component. This also makes it easier to produce the linking lines, which represent the pipework, or wiring that connects the parts.

Link

To learn more about using circuit symbols and circuit diagrams refer to *Unit 8 Electronic Circuit Design and Construction* and Appendix 3.

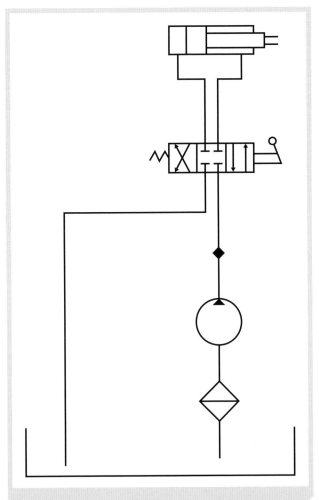

Figure 6.8 An example of a hydraulic circuit diagram

British/ISO standards are used to ensure that circuit symbols are drawn consistently and correctly to avoid any confusion when the real parts have to be assembled. Typical standards are BS EN 60617 for electrical symbols and BS 2917 for hydraulic/pneumatic symbols.

Modifying circuit diagrams

Many circuits are very similar and it can be convenient to open an existing drawing to change or add the necessary components and then resave the drawing with a different drawing number and description.

You should use a range of drawing and modifying commands, which will be specific to the software you are using. Look back at Topic A.1 to remind yourself how these techniques can be used.

Did you know?

Many software applications allow the simulation of circuit performance at the design stage. This can help designers decide whether components have been correctly selected and allows different designs to be tested without the need to spend time and money building a circuit and performing a physical test.

Assessment activity 6.1   Designing a spinning top   2A.P1 | 2A.P2 | 2A.P3 | 2A.M1 | 2A.D1

You have been given a design brief for a small model of a spinning top. Your model should incorporate space for a battery and an LED circuit, which is activated by the rotation of the spinning top. You have been asked to do the following:

a. Prepare a fully dimensioned CAD drawing of the spinning top using standard conventions. Then print out your drawing. **(2A.P1)**

b. Prepare a circuit diagram of the LED circuit, fully labelling all components and using standard conventions. Then, print out your diagram. **(2A.P2)**

c. Prepare a presentation to show how you used CAD drawing and modification techniques for tasks a and b, and the benefits of producing engineering drawings in this way. **(2A.P3, 2A.M1, 2A.D1)**

Tips

For the first task you should ensure that the drawing you produce contains all the information required for it to be manufactured. Using a template drawing will help, as this should prompt you to consider materials used, dimensional tolerances, etc. Ask yourself:

• Have I repeated any dimensions?

• Are there sufficient dimensions?

• Are the line types correct?

• Have I considered the surface finish?

For the second task you should consider using a template for the circuit diagram. Check that all components are labelled and that the drawing is drawn using BS conventions. Check that symbols are correctly used.

For the third task ensure that you have covered a considerable range of drawing and modification techniques. Look back through this unit – have you considered all the techniques listed? Have you explained the benefits of using these techniques and shown how CAD is such a powerful tool?

Use of a CAM system

Getting started

Think of a bicycle pedal crank. It is an individual engineering component, but it is also part of a more complex assembly of parts.

Working in pairs, decide which machines or processes might be needed to produce a one-off prototype of a bicycle crank. Can the part be manufactured using one machine or will it require the use of several machines?

Key terms

CNC (computer numerical control) machining – a system that allows the movements of a machine to be programmed rather than requiring a skilled operator.

CAM (computer-aided manufacture) – involves the use of software to control machine tools and other manufacturing systems such as robots.

Turning – a process that removes material by rotating or turning a workpiece using a lathe. The cutting tool is moved, usually parallel to the surface, removing material while it contacts the rotating workpiece.

Introduction

In this topic you will learn how CAM is used in the manufacture of engineering components.

CNC (computer numerical control) machining is a technique whereby machines are operated by a computer, rather than a skilled technician, during the manufacture of engineering components. The machines are programmed to carry out machining operations using information from CAD drawings.

This process is called **computer-aided manufacture (CAM)**.

CNC machining techniques

CAM technology can be used with machines big enough to fill a room or ones that fit on a tabletop. There are a variety of CNC machining techniques:

- Rapid prototyping (also known as 3D printing) – a technique used to create a 3D model using a CAD drawing. The CAD data is read by a machine, which uses a liquid or powder that is built up in very thin layers, to create a 3D model. The layers are melted or fused together with a laser to form the final product with minimal waste. This is an additive manufacturing process because material is being added instead of being removed. Rapid prototyping is an exciting way for designers to test their designs in CAD. It can be used before CNC manufacture or as part of the CNC process.
- **Turning** centres – are used in place of conventional lathes. Computers control the machining operations.
- Machining centres – are used in place of conventional **milling** machines. Computers control the machining operations.
- Electrical discharge machining (EDM) – uses a method known as spark erosion. An electrical current 'sparks' between two electrodes causing material to be removed from the workpiece.
- CNC **grinding** – a technique that allows a computer to control the grinding wheel, which removes material by an abrasive process to produce a smooth finish.
- CNC fabrication – allows metal and other materials to be cut, bent and assembled often with computer-controlled robots or cutting and punching tools.

The production of a complex component may require several different operations using a variety of tooling and machining processes. Modern machines can combine these techniques into a single machining centre or manufacturing cell.

Although there are a number of CNC machines, all follow the same basic principles. Because the workpiece is clamped to the table it can be moved forwards and backwards and from side to side (in the x and y directions) while the tool moves upwards and downwards (in the z direction).

A machining centre

Activity 6.3 Using a CNC milling machine

Think about how CNC milling machines work. In pairs, research:

- types of milling machine
- materials that can be cut using a CNC milling machine
- whether 2D or 3D CAD drawings can be loaded into a CNC milling machine
- how a CAD file can be loaded into a CNC milling machine in order to manufacture an engineering component.

Key terms

Milling – a process that removes material by moving a workpiece into contact with a rotating cutter.

Grinding – a process that removes material by abrasion. A grinding wheel, rotating at high speed, is brought into contact with the workpiece. Because the grinding wheel is very hard it causes the softer workpiece to wear or abrade.

CONTINUED ▸▸

Use of CAD drawings by a CAM system

Drawing files created using CAD software can be loaded into a CNC machine, replacing the conventional communication between designer and technician with an automatic communication. This can be done in several ways (see Figure 6.9).

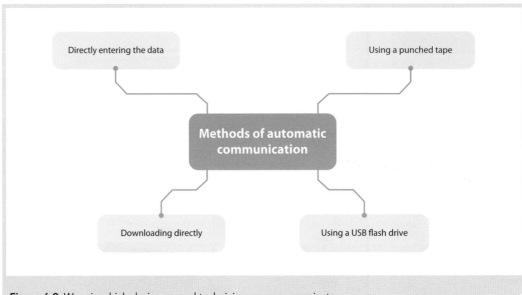

Figure 6.9 Ways in which designers and technicians can communicate

CAM systems and CNC machines will accept and interpret CAD files provided they have been saved in the correct format:

- STL (stereo lithography) – a file format used to portray surface texture. This format is widely used in rapid prototyping applications.
- DXF (drawing exchange format) – a file format that allows CAD files to be exchanged between different CAD/CAM applications.
- IGES (initial graphics exchange specification) – a file format that allows files to be digitally exchanged between applications.

Cutting tool data and machining information

Although CAD data can be directly transferred to machines, it usually requires some development. CAM software is used to generate the code for a CNC machine from the CAD file. It is this code that a CNC machine uses to produce the final components.

It is important to consider questions such as:

- What machine should be used?
- What tooling should be used?
- How and where should the workpiece be located in the machine?
- What coolant might be required?

Remember

If a part requires a series of 10 mm holes, a series of 20 mm holes and a series of 30 mm holes, you may need to consider the best way to sequence the drilling operation to ensure a minimum number of drill changes and the quickest way to move the drills around the workplace to save time and increase efficiency.

Key terms

Drilling – a process that removes material by moving a rotating cutter into contact with a workpiece.

The CAM software will decide which tools to use and how they will move around the workpiece in three dimensions. It will produce an image of the part on-screen and simulate the production of the part. This allows the designer to see the movement of the cutting tools and the sequence of operations. If there are concerns about the way the CAM program appears to be running, it is often easy to edit the way the software has planned the machining sequences.

Typical features of this simulation are shown in Table 6.3.

Table 6.3 Typical features of a CAM program

Feature	Use
Tool changes	As each different machining operation takes place, the CNC machine will need to change tools. For example, holes will need a drill while flat surfaces may need a milling cutter.
Cutter paths	As the tools move around the workpiece you can see the path each one takes. This information is converted into code for the CNC machines to use when real components are being produced.
Speeds and feeds	You will be able to see how quickly the tools move around and the amount of material they remove in each operation.

Link

For more information about setting machine tools see *Unit 7 Machining Techniques.*

Remember

Engineering workshops can be potentially dangerous environments to work in. You should always follow instructions and take appropriate precautions when operating CNC machines. Completing a risk assessment to ensure any potential hazards are identified is an important part of any practical engineering activity.

CONTINUED ▸▸

Unilateral tolerance – a tolerance that only deviates in one direction, e.g. 10 mm + 0.05 mm or 17 mm – 0.01 mm.

Bilateral tolerance – a tolerance that deviates in both directions, e.g. 15 mm ± 0.3 mm.

Calibration – the process of comparing the performance of an instrument against a known standard. For accurate measurements to be taken the tools must be regularly calibrated. This activity is undertaken by specialist organisations although instruments such as verniers and micrometers can be tested with the use of slip gauges.

Use of digital vernier callipers to check an engineering component

Checking and comparing components

It is important to check that each component has been produced to the correct size and standard by referring back to the specification and using measuring instruments.

If a feature has to be very accurate it is given a tolerance (either a **unilateral tolerance** or a **bilateral tolerance**). The tolerance is stated in the engineering drawing. For example, $\Phi10 \pm 0.05$ mm means the maximum size is 10.05 mm and the minimum size is 9.95 mm. This cannot be measured to this level of accuracy using a rule, so accurate and **calibrated** measuring instruments have to be used instead.

- Rulers – used to measure linear dimensions. Engineers use steel rules that have been carefully ground to give accurate measurements. They are usually either 150 mm or 300 mm in length and are accurate to ±0.5 mm.
- Vernier callipers – used most often to measure internal and external diameters. Engineers use verniers, as they are accurate to 0.02 mm.
- Micrometers – most often used to measure diameters, although different types and ranges of micrometers are required making them less versatile than vernier callipers. They are accurate to 0.01 mm.
- Height gauge – used to measure the height of components, these instruments use the same principle of operation as the vernier calliper.
- Dial gauge – used to test flatness and concentricity, they have the appearance of a clock with a plunger that moves across a surface and rotates a pointer.
- Slip gauges – used as an accurate measuring standard, slip gauges are precision ground blocks of metal used for reference measurement.

| Assessment activity 6.2 | Produce a working model | 2B.P4 | 2B.M2 | 2B.P5 | 2B.D2 |

You have been asked to produce a working model of the spinning top using CNC data from the CAD drawing previously created (Assessment activity 6.1).

a. Prepare a sequence of annotated photographs and screen grabs showing you developing the CAM program, simulating the component production, setting up the machine and loading and running the program to manufacture the spinning top. Make sure you include photographs or screen grabs indicating the improvements or changes you make to the program after simulating component production. **(2B.P4, 2B.M2)**

b. Use measuring tools and a checklist to make sure the spinning top has been produced correctly. **(2B.P5)**

c. Compare the use of CAM with traditional methods for the production of the spinning top. **(2B.D2)**

Tips

- Make sure you annotate each picture to carefully explain what is happening in each one.
- Ask a partner or your assessor to take photographs of you using a range of measuring instruments as you check the sizes of the spinning top.
- Make sure you consider the advantages and disadvantages of using CAM to produce different components.

WorkSpace

JAVED ALI

CAD technician

I work with a team of five other CAD technicians in the design office of an engineering company. My daily routine consists of working on new designs, making changes to engineering drawings and testing the designs I have produced.

When we first complete a design we often use the 3D printer to produce a rapid prototype. This is used to check that all parts will fit together, the sizes are correct and the product has the look and feel that we expect. Customers are often involved with this part of the process so we discuss any changes or modifications required with them.

Once this part of the process is complete I get the opportunity to transfer the drawing to our CNC machines in order to manufacture finished parts. Of course, we carefully check each one again to make sure all the sizes are correct and that the parts meet the specification required.

Think about it

1 Why is the customer involved in the design process?

2 Why is it important to check the parts produced by the rapid prototyping machine?

3 What sorts of measuring equipment might you use to check the finished part meets its specification?

Engineers design products to perform specific functions. To do this, the product's size and shape has to be carefully controlled. Machining techniques allow us to change the shape and form of workpieces by removing unwanted material. This is often done through a combination of three of the basic machining techniques: drilling, milling and turning.

This unit will provide you with the opportunity to use a range of machining techniques, work-holding devices and tools in order to carry out safe and effective machining operations.

You will be given the opportunity to create specific features using drilling techniques, as well as using milling and/or turning techniques to make workpieces. You will also learn how to check that these workpieces are made to specification.

Assessment: This unit will be assessed through a series of assignments set by your teacher/tutor.

Learning aims

After completing this unit you should:

A select and use tools and work-holding devices for drilling and for turning or milling

B make workpieces using drilling and turning or milling techniques safely.

" When I started as an apprentice I didn't know much about machining techniques. I first learned how a workpiece is positioned, then did it for myself. The part of my job I enjoy most is setting up my work on the machine, then making the piece and checking it is the right size and shape.

Claire, *16-year-old engineering apprentice*

Machining Techniques

7

BTEC
Assessment Zone

This table shows you what you must do in order to achieve a **Pass, Merit** or **Distinction** grade, and where you can find activities in this book to help you.

Assessment criteria			
Level 1	Level 2 **Pass**	Level 2 **Merit**	Level 2 **Distinction**
Learning aim A: Select and use tools and work-holding devices for drilling and for turning or milling			
1A.1 Outline the functions of simple tools used for drilling and turning or milling.	**2A.P1** Describe the functions of simple and complex tools used for drilling and turning or milling. **See Assessment activity 7.1, page 121**	**2A.M1** Explain why particular tools and work-holding devices are useful for different drilling and turning or milling tasks. **See Assessment activity 7.1, page 121**	**2A.D1** Evaluate the effectiveness of tools and work-holding devices for different drilling and turning or milling tasks. **See Assessment activity 7.1, page 121**
1A.2 Use simple tools for accurate drilling and turning or milling.	**2A.P2** Select and use simple and complex tools for accurate drilling and turning or milling. **See Assessment activity 7.1, page 121**		
1A.3 Use a simple work-holding device for accurate drilling and turning or milling.	**2A.P3** Select and use simple and complex work-holding devices for accurate drilling and turning or milling. **See Assessment activity 7.1, page 121**		
Learning aim B: Make workpieces using drilling and turning or milling techniques safely			
1B.4 Maths Set positional parameters before machining workpieces by drilling and turning or milling techniques.	**2B.P4** Maths Set positional parameters before machining and set and monitor dynamic parameters during machining by drilling and turning or milling techniques. **See Assessment activity 7.2, page 134**		
1B.5 Produce two given machined workpieces that demonstrate simple features of drilling and turning or milling techniques.	**2B.P5** Produce two machined workpieces that demonstrate simple and complex features of drilling and turning or milling techniques. **See Assessment activity 7.2, page 134**	**2B.M2** Maths Demonstrate high levels of precision and accuracy when using drilling and turning or milling techniques. **See Assessment activity 7.2, page 134**	**2B.D2** Maths Assess own levels of precision and accuracy, identifying strengths and weaknesses and safe working practices. **See Assessment activity 7.2, page 134**
1B.6 Describe and carry out visual checks made for compliance on a machined workpiece according to instructions.	**2B.P6** Describe and carry out visual and specific checks carried out for compliance and accuracy when producing the machined workpieces. **See Assessment activity 7.2, page 134**	**2B.M3** Explain why it is important to carry out checks on the accuracy of workpiece features both during and after manufacture. **See Assessment activity 7.2, page 134**	

Assessment criteria

Level 1	Level 2 Pass	Level 2 Merit	Level 2 Distinction
1B.7 Demonstrate safe practice when using drilling and turning or milling techniques.	**2B.P7** Demonstrate consistency in safety awareness and safe working practices when machining workpieces. **See Assessment activity 7.2, page 134**	**2B.M4** Explain the importance of safe working practices when using drilling and turning or milling techniques. **See Assessment activity 7.2, page 134**	

Maths   Opportunity to practise mathematical skills

How you will be assessed

The unit will be assessed by a series of tasks set by your teacher/tutor. You will be expected to show an understanding of how work-holding devices and tools are used, and demonstrate practical machining techniques. The tasks will be related to typical engineering activities. For example: your manager is considering the introduction of a new product and asks you to produce prototypes of two different ideas. In order to do this you will investigate the required tools and select and use these tools, as well as work-holding devices, to produce two prototypes, working safely and regularly checking your work.

Your assessment could be in the form of:

- a log book, including written observations, produced in an engineering workshop
- annotated photographic evidence of you carrying out practical activities
- a presentation of the activities carried out.

Tools – the parts of an engineering machine used to remove material from a workpiece. Different tools are fitted to a machine to carry out different operations.

Drill bit – the tool that is used to produce the drilled holes (sometimes called a twist drill).

Workpiece – the piece of material that is being machined in order to produce a finished component.

Threads – a spiral form used to locate a threaded part, e.g. a bolt.

Countersinking – producing an angled start to a hole used for a screw or bolt head.

Counterboring – producing a cylindrical, round-bottomed hole which enlarges an existing hole allowing a fastener to sit below the surface of the workpiece.

Spotfacing – producing a very shallow version of a counterbore – often used to ensure a small flat area for a seal or washer.

Introduction

A variety of tools are used for the machining operations you will perform in this unit. In this topic you will learn about the functions of simple and complex **tools** to help you decide which tool is most suitable for particular machining tasks.

Tools for drilling

Drilling is a machining operation used to produce holes in a workpiece. It is carried out using a drilling machine with a rotating tool called a **drill bit**, which is brought into contact with the **workpiece**. Although we often drill right through the workpiece we sometimes have to leave a '**blind hole**' (when the hole does not go all the way through).

Reamers are tools used for producing a very smooth surface finish after drilling to ensure a very accurately sized hole.

More complex tools are used to change the shape of a drilled hole. These are often required if a component or fastener such as a bolt or screw is being inserted into the hole. **Taps** are used to cut **threads** after a hole has been drilled. If the head of the fastener needs to be level or below the surface of the workpiece other techniques, including **countersinking**, **counterboring** and **spotfacing**, are used.

Tools for turning

Turning is a machining operation that removes material from a workpiece to produce different shapes. The machine used is called a **lathe**. This grips and rotates the workpiece, while a cutting tool is applied to the surface to remove material.

When performing a turning operation you can use simple **turning** and **facing tools** or more complex tools such as those used for **parting off** or producing threads.

Table 7.1 Different types of turning operation and the tools required

Type of turning operation	Function
Turning	Usually refers to the removal of material using a cutting or turning tool
Forming	Usually requires a specific profile or shape to be created using a **forming tool**. Specific forms such as knurled surfaces require a **knurling tool**
Forming threads	Requires the use of a **single point threading** tool although taps and dies can also be used with care
Boring	Hollowing out a workpiece using a drill, reamer, **boring bar** or **recessing tool**

Positioning the workpiece on a lathe often requires the use of 'centres' located in small holes on the workpiece. These holes are produced using a **centre drill**.

Table 7.2 Types of tools for turning

Type of tool	Function
Turning tool	Removes material from the workpiece
Facing tool	Removes material from the end of a workpiece to produce a flat surface. The tool is moved at right angles to the workpiece
Parting off	Produces deep grooves, which will cut off the workpiece at a specific length
Forming tool	Produces a very specific shape or profile such as a radius or stepped feature
Knurling tool	Produces a diamond pattern, known as a knurl, on the outside of the workpiece
Single point threading	Used when a thread form needs to be cut into the workpiece
Boring bar	Used on a lathe to carry out boring operations along the axis of a workpiece such as increasing the size of a drilled hole
Recessing tool	Often used after boring operations to produce internal features such as a recessed groove
Centre drill	A small drill used to make tiny location spots or 'centres' in a workpiece in preparation for turning operations on a lathe

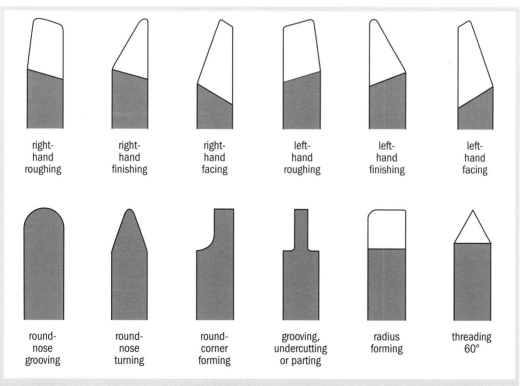

Figure 7.1 Each turning operation needs a different tool.

a) End mill

b) Slitting saw

c) Slot drill

d) Face milling cutter

e) Cylindrical cutter

f) Rough cut end mill

Figure 7.2 Examples of milling tools

◢ Tools for milling

Milling is a machining operation that removes material from a workpiece to produce complex shapes. A milling machine consists of a rotating cutter with teeth to remove material. The table or machine head can be moved up/down, sideways and forwards/backwards to bring the workpiece into contact with the cutter. The speed of the rotating cutter is varied depending upon the type of shaping operation and the material being used. This means that material can be removed from the top and sides of the workpiece, as well as working at an angle.

A wide range of milling cutters is available, for both horizontal milling and vertical milling. These range from simple **face mills** and **end mills** to more complex tools, for example, **slot drills**, **slotting cutters**, **slitting saws**, **profile cutters**, **twist drills**, reamers and **boring tools**. Table 7.3 shows examples of typical milling tools.

A mill can be used to create specific features such as:

● flat surfaces – produced using face and end mills

● grooves and slots – produced using slot drills, slotting cutters and slitting saws

● holes – produced with twist drills, boring tools and reamers

● other specific features – produced using profile cutters which create an individual profile, such as rounding off an edge.

Table 7.3 Types of milling tools

Type of tool	Function
Face mills	Cutter with multiple cutting tips – often called inserts – designed to move across the face of the workpiece
End mills	The most common tool used in milling, this has cutting teeth at one end and along the sides
Slot drills	A type of end mill designed to plunge into the workpiece like a drill then be moved across to create a groove
Slotting cutters	Cutters with multiple tips designed to move through a workpiece to create a channel or slot
Slitting saws	Discs with saw teeth around the perimeter designed for cutting deep thin slits into the workpiece
Profile cutters	Designed to produce a specific shape or profile such as gears or corner radii
Twist drills	Used to produce holes in the workpiece
Boring tools	Used to create a large hole by increasing the size of a drilled hole

Tooling materials

The choice of tooling materials depends upon the material of the workpiece and the conditions the tool is being used in.

Table 7.4 Examples of tooling materials

Material	Application
Solid high-speed steel	Used for a wide range of applications, it can withstand high temperatures without losing hardness. It is called high-speed because it can cut material much faster than high carbon steels and is resistant to wear.
Cobalt steel	Similar to high-speed steel but with additional cobalt. The advantage of drill bits using this material is that they remain very hard, even at high temperatures, so they are used to drill hard materials such as stainless steel.
Brazed tungsten carbide	Tungsten carbide is a very hard material that can cut faster than high-speed steel and produces a better surface finish. However, it is very expensive so only the cutting edge of the tool is made from tungsten carbide and this is attached by brazing to a steel body.
Indexible tips	An alternative to brazed tips, indexible tips are removable and contain multiple tool tips. They are typically triangular and screwed into place. When one tip wears and needs replacing you can simply rotate, or index, to the next tip.
Diamond tools	A cutting tool which has diamond particles bonded to the cutting surface. Because diamond is much harder than steel or tungsten carbide, diamond tools last longer and can be used on very hard materials to a very high degree of accuracy.

 Did you know?

Pilot holes are used when drilling very large holes. You drill a small hole and gradually build up the desired size using progressively bigger drill bits. This saves on tool wear and prevents heat building up which can damage the tool or the workpiece.

Just checking

1 Which tools are used for producing threads on a workpiece?

2 When using a lathe, what tool would be used to cut off a workpiece at a specific length?

3 What kind of milling cutter would be used to form a radius on a workpiece?

Work-holding devices

Getting started

Can you think of three ways that a workpiece can be secured? How can these methods be used for each of the machining techniques: turning, milling and drilling? Discuss your ideas in pairs and think about the similarities and differences between the techniques.

Introduction

In this topic you will learn about the different ways workpieces are positioned and secured to prevent movement, depending upon the type of machining operation taking place and the type of machine being used.

Work-holding devices are used to position and secure the workpiece. It is vital to select the correct work-holding device and ensure that you use it correctly. If the workpiece moves during a machining operation it will affect the quality of the finish. Similarly, an insecure workpiece can be very dangerous as, when the tool comes into contact with it, it can be forced off the machine and easily cause an accident.

Work-holding devices for drilling

Drilling operations are normally carried out with the workpiece clamped in a vice. However, alternative methods include:

- clamping directly to the machine table – using special T-shaped nuts that slide into grooves on the base of the machine
- angle plate – allows the workpiece to be positioned at any given angle, with slots or holes allowing the workpiece to be bolted onto the angle plate
- vee block and clamps – a vee-shaped block of metal that round workpieces can be positioned on. A clamp fits over the top to secure the workpiece to the vee block.

Angle plate resting on a surface plate

Vee block and clamp

Figure 7.3 Workholding devices: angle plates and vee blocks

Work-holding devices for turning

There are a variety of ways to position and secure the workpiece on a lathe for turning. The method you choose will depend upon the size and shape of the workpiece and the type of turning operation.

Chucks

The workpiece can be secured in a lathe by placing it in the jaws of a **chuck** and tightening it with a large key until the jaws hold it securely. Chucks normally have three jaws but there are also four- or six-jawed models. They grip the workpiece quickly and accurately. Hard jaws are often serrated to increase the grip but they can damage the surface of soft materials when tightened.

Centres

A **lathe centre** is an accurately machined cone-shaped tool that is clamped in a lathe's chuck to position a workpiece precisely and securely. The workpiece has a hole drilled centrally and the end of the centre tool is located in the hole. This ensures the workpiece remains central when machining takes place.

A **dead centre** must be lubricated regularly to prevent friction which would cause heat to build up, start to melt the material and cause the centre to bond or friction-weld to the workpiece.

A **live centre** has a bearing incorporated, allowing it to rotate, so it does not require the lubrication.

Faceplates

A **faceplate** is a circular metal plate with slots machined into it. It is used instead of a chuck when an awkward workpiece has to be secured. The workpiece is secured to the plate by nuts and bolts. T-nuts are often used as they can be locked into the slots. The faceplate fits onto the lathe spindle where it is securely fixed either by being screwed into place, held by a lock nut onto a taper or by cam locks.

Fixed and travelling steadies

Steadies are used to support long workpieces, held in a chuck or between centres, which could easily deflect. A **fixed steady** is clamped to the bed of the lathe. They normally consist of three jaws with plastic or bronze rollers that can be adjusted to support the workpiece. A **travelling steady** is attached to a **saddle**, which allows it to be moved along as machining takes place.

? Did you know?

Four jaw chucks are used for round, hexagonal and unusually shaped workpieces. However, they are preferred for machining square sections as they can grip each side more easily than three-jaw chucks. Four-jaw chucks can be adjusted independently. Six-jaw chucks are very useful if you have thin sections to grip.

CONTINUED ▶▶

Work-holding devices for milling

When you are using a milling machine you will be required to demonstrate a variety of ways of gripping the workpiece. Many of the methods are very similar to those previously mentioned:

- Using a machine vice, which is very similar to a bench vice with jaws that are brought together to hold the workpiece, the vice is clamped or fixed to the machine table.
- Clamping it directly to the machine table.
- Using an angle plate, which is then secured to the bed of the milling machine. Angle plates can be adjusted to allow the workpiece to be tilted if needed.
- Clamping the component in a vee block which is either magnetic or clamped in a vice. This method is used primarily for milling circular workpieces.
- Securing in an **indexing head**, this looks like the driveplate and centre of a lathe, and is often used with a tailstock. The devices are clamped to the table of the milling machine and the workpiece is positioned between them. The purpose of an indexing head is to allow movement through 90°.
- Clamping in a **rotary table**. The rotary table is clamped to the table of the milling machine and the workpiece is clamped to the table. This allows the operator to machine at regular intervals around the work.

Key terms

Indexing head – a device bolted to the machine table that allows the workpiece to be indexed or rotated to selected angles.

Rotary table – a device bolted on top of the machine table that allows horizontal rotary movement of the table to provide accurate angular movement.

Remember

Think about how different components need to be secured. For example, vee blocks are used to support round components that could slip from a normal vice.

Activity 7.1   Securing different workpieces

Consider a range of workpieces. How would you secure each of the following?

- Milling a flat feature along the edge of a 10 mm diameter round steel bar.
- Drilling holes along a 50 mm square section of nylon that is only 5 mm thick.
- Boring a feature on a cast aluminium gear box casing.

Activity 7.2   Preparing for a machining operation

Describe how you would use a chuck, a machine vice and an angle plate to hold a workpiece in preparation for a machining operation. You should sketch each work-holding device with an example of the type of workpiece you expect to be secured.

Assessment activity 7.1 — Setting up for machining operations 2A.P1 | 2A.M1 | 2A.D1 | 2A.P2 | 2A.P3

You have been asked to give a presentation and a practical demonstration to show learners on work experience how to set up two machines for machining operations. One of these must be a drilling machine; the other can be a milling or turning machine.

Consider the following tools:

- drilling tools – centre drill, counterboring tool

  and

- milling tools – face mill, slot drill

  or

- turning tools – facing tool, parting off tool.

and the following work-holding devices:

- work-holding for drilling – machine vice, vee block and clamps

  and

- work-holding for milling – machine vice, clamping direct to the machine table

  or

- work-holding for turning – three-jaw chuck with hard jaws, four-jaw chuck with hard jaws.

For each of the tools and work-holding devices listed, produce an annotated presentation slide showing why you would choose these tools, why they are used for different tasks and how effective they are. **(2A.P1, 2A.M1, 2A.D1)**

Demonstrate their use to drill and mill/turn given workpieces accurately and safely. Ask your tutor or assessor to provide an observation record to evidence this element. **(2A.P2, 2A.P3)**

Tips

- Make sure that when using tools and work-holding devices you follow health and safety guidance from your teacher/tutor.
- Set up the machine and locate and secure the tools and workpieces in preparation for carrying out machining operations. Take photos for use on your presentation slides.
- When you annotate the slides make sure you indicate why the set-up will produce accurate workpieces.
- Ask your teacher/tutor or assessor to complete an observation record to evidence your demonstration. You could also ask them, or a classmate, to take photos or video of this.

Features of the workpiece

Introduction

A variety of machining techniques are used to produce features in a **workpiece**. In this topic you will look in more detail at the drilling, turning and milling techniques that allow specific features to be produced.

To determine which features are required in a workpiece, an engineer will normally refer to the specification of the part, component or product they are working on. This often takes the form of an engineering drawing, which specifies sizes, tolerances and features, allowing you to select the correct tools, work holding and techniques.

Complex workpieces have different features. Sometimes a workpiece has a feature produced on a lathe; it then has holes produced using a drill and, finally, has extra features added using a milling machine. You should select tools and work-holding devices carefully to produce each of these features.

Features of drilling

Drilling is normally used for producing holes:

- through holes – pass all the way through a workpiece
- blind holes – do not pass all the way through a workpiece
- counterbored/countersunk holes – additional elements to a drilled hole to allow a part or bolt to sit below the surface of the workpiece
- flat-bottomed holes – a blind hole that has a flat base.

Reaming and **tapping** can then be applied to the drilled holes.

Key terms

Reaming – a technique used to produce an exceptionally smooth surface finish in previously drilled holes.

Tapping – a technique used after drilling a hole, in order to produce an internal thread.

Features of turning

Turning is normally used to produce features and profiles on round components:

- flat faces – a square end of a round workpiece
- parallel diameters – circular profiles produced using turning tools
- stepped diameters – circular profiles of different diameters on one workpiece
- tapered diameters – a sloping circular profile in a conical shape
- threads – formed either on the outside or inside of a circular component to allow a nut or other threaded component to be secured
- chamfers – an angled form, forming a bevel or small taper where sections or sizes change
- knurls – a diamond pattern allowing the workpiece to be gripped easily
- grooves/undercuts – ridges formed on the outside or inside of a workpiece
- profile form – a feature that is produced by following a given pattern to produce given diameters, chamfers, grooves, etc.

Features of milling

Milling is used to produce a variety of features normally on non-circular workpieces:

- flat/square/parallel faces – allows surfaces to be accurate and used as a datum for other operations
- angular/rotated/indexed features – produced by using special workholding devices
- steps/shoulders – produced by milling part of a surface away to leave a profile
- slots/recesses – cutaway parts of a solid workpiece
- serrations – a regular pattern on the surface of a workpiece.

Table 7.5 Examples of simple and complex features

	Drilling	Turning	Milling
Simple features	Through holes	Flat faces	Flat faces
	Blind holes	Parallel diameters	Square faces
More complex features	Flat-bottomed holes	Stepped diameters	Parallel faces
	Counterbored holes	Tapered diameters	Angular faces
	Countersinking	Drilled holes	Steps/shoulders
	Reaming	Bored holes	Open-ended slots
	Tapping	Reamed holes	Enclosed slots
		Profile forms	Recesses
		Internal threads	Tee slots
		External threads	Drilled holes
		Parting off	Bore holes
		Chamfers	Profile forms
		Knurls	Serrations
		Grooves	Indexed forms
		Undercuts	Rotated forms

Did you know?

Computer numerical control (CNC) is used with complex machine tools to automate turning, milling and drilling operations. Instead of the operator having to move and fit the cutting tools, the computer controls their movement and the tool changes.

Just checking

1 What different tools would you use to drill:

  a a blind hole

  b a flat-bottomed hole?

2 What do you call a series of different diameters on a round workpiece?

3 Describe a tee slot.

Machining parameters

Getting started

How would you go about making a nut and a bolt using a lathe, milling machine or drilling machine? What processes would you use? What tools and work-holding devices? Create a flow chart showing the sequence of operations.

Introduction

To complete this topic you will need to demonstrate that you can use appropriate machining techniques to produce two workpieces, ensuring all features are to the required degree of accuracy.

Remember

You should not work unsupervised until you have had some experience using all the required tools and techniques. Even when you feel confident you should only operate machinery when allowed by your teacher/tutor. You should not undertake any machining techniques until you have learned how to operate machines safely.

A drilling operation – step-by-step:

1. The drill bit is placed into the chuck.

2. The chuck is tightened with a chuck key and the guard is positioned.

3. The workpiece is clamped into a vice underneath the drill bit.

4. The drill is switched on.

5. The handle is slowly pulled down.

6. The drill bit is gradually forced through the material.

7. The lever is raised.

8. The drill is switched off.

Figure 7.4 A step-by-step process for a drilling operation

Using machines to make workpieces

In this topic you will demonstrate the ability to produce finished workpieces. You will need to:

- select the correct machining technique
- select the correct tools
- use the correct work-holding techniques to secure the workpiece
- secure the tools correctly
- set the machine parameters correctly
- work safely to produce the required features
- check the finished part meets the required specification.

Parameters for drilling

There is a step-by-step process to a drilling operation (see Figure 7.4).

Drills range from small-scale models for DIY to large-scale radial drilling machines. However, the most commonly used in engineering are bench or pedestal drills. These are very similar in operation – a bench drill is mounted onto a workbench, while a pedestal drill is free-standing.

Are you familiar with this type of drill?

Drilling machine tool feed

In a pillar or bench-type drilling machine the cutting speed can be adjusted by moving a drive belt on to different pulleys. The speed is adjusted depending upon the:

- finish required
- amount of metal removed
- type and diameter of tool being used
- properties of the tool and workpiece
- power and capability of the machine.

The spindle speed and time taken can be calculated using the following simple formula.

Worked example 7.1

Determine the time taken for a 10-mm drill to cut through a 12-mm thick mild steel plate. The cutting speed is 24 m/min and the drill is being fed at a rate of 0.25 mm/rev.

The formula used to calculate spindle speed is:

$$N = 1{,}000S/\pi D$$

where:

N = spindle speed (rpm)

S = cutting speed (m/min) = 24 m/min

D = diameter (mm) = 10 mm

$$N = (1{,}000 \times 24)/(\pi \times 10)$$
$$N = 764 \text{ rpm (to the nearest rpm)}$$

You can calculate the time taken using the formula:

$$t = 60P/NF$$

where:

t = time in seconds

P = depth of material cut (mm)

N = spindle speed (rpm)

F = feed (mm/rev)

$$t = (60 \times 12)/(764 \times 0.25) = 3.8 \text{ seconds}$$

CONTINUED ▶▶

Parameters for turning

Turning requires a sequence of operations to be carried out – this is often much more complex than drilling, particularly if several features are required as this can mean **tool changes** are needed. See Figure 7.5 for a step-by-step description of a turning process.

Different tools are used for removing large amounts of material (roughing) or producing a precise surface finish (finishing) and also for facing and thread cutting, etc. In order to complete these operations you need to stop the machine, remove the guards, remove the tool and insert a different one, secure the new tool and replace the guards. All of this takes time, but must be done carefully.

Some typical machining operations are described in Table 7.6.

Table 7.6 Typical machining operations

Machining operation	Purpose of machining operation
Facing	When material is removed from the end of a workpiece to leave a flat, square finish.
Parting	Used when a cutting operation is required. Parting allows a deep groove to be formed to allow a workpiece to be cut off. An example would be cutting off the head of a bolt.
Turning	When a workpiece is required to have its diameter reduced.
Drilling	To remove material from inside a workpiece. A drill bit is inserted into the tailstock and then moved into the workpiece.
Screw cutting	Similar to turning but specific tools are used depending on the required thread. The tool is applied to the workpiece at a specific angle to allow a thread to be created.

A turning operation – step-by-step

1. The tool is located in the toolpost, tailstock or other tool-holding device.

2. The workpiece is secured in the chuck, faceplate or other work-holding device.

3. Coolant supply (if required) is switched on and directed onto the workpiece.

4. Appropriate safety checks are undertaken, including ensuring all guards are in place.

5. The tool is brought into contact with the workpiece to produce the desired features.

6. The tool is removed from the workpiece and a safe procedure is followed to shut down the machine.

Figure 7.5 A turning operation – step-by-step

Lathe cutting speeds

Lathes are used for turning and range from small-scale models for DIY to large-scale machining centres. They can be manual or computer-operated. **Cutting speeds** and **feed rates** are adjusted using levers which change the gearing ratios as required.

The speed of operation of a lathe depends upon the:

- finish required
- depth of cut
- type of tool being used
- properties of the tool and workpiece.

The speeds required and the time taken can be calculated using a simple formula.

Key terms

Cutting speed – the speed the workpiece moves relative to the tool.

Feed rate – the distance the tool travels during one revolution of the workpiece.

Worked example 7.2

Determine the spindle speed in rpm when turning a 20 mm diameter bar at a cutting speed of 36 m/min.

The formula we use is:

$$N = 1{,}000S/\pi D$$

where:

N = spindle speed (rpm)

S = cutting speed (m/min) = 36 m/min

D = diameter (mm) = 20 mm

$$N = (1{,}000 \times 36)/(\pi \times 20)$$

$$N = 573 \text{ rpm (to the nearest rpm)}$$

Worked example 7.3

Determine the time taken to turn a 30 mm diameter bar if it is 150 mm long, the cutting speed is 30 m/min and the feed rate is 0.44 mm/rev.

The formula we use is:

$$N = 1{,}000S/\pi D$$

where:

N = spindle speed (rpm)

S = cutting speed (m/min) = 30 m/min

D = diameter (mm) = 30 mm

$$N = (1{,}000 \times 30)/(\pi \times 30)$$

$$N = 318 \text{ rpm (to the nearest rpm)}$$

Rate of feed can be converted into mm/min:

$$0.44 \text{ mm/rev} \times 318 \text{ rpm} = 140 \text{ mm/min (to the nearest mm)}$$

To complete the machining of the 150 mm workpiece:

$$150 \text{ mm}/140 \text{ mm/min} = 1.07 \text{ minutes} \times 60 = 64 \text{ seconds}$$

CONTINUED ▶▶

Key terms

Up-cut – a method of material removal where the cutter rotates in the opposite direction as the table is feeding the work.

Down-cut – a method of material removal where the cutter rotates in the same direction as the table is feeding the work.

Parameters for milling

Milling is a process of removing material in order to produce complex shapes. A milling machine consists of a rotating cutter with teeth, which remove material. The table or machine head can be moved **up/down**, sideways and forwards/backwards to bring the workpiece into contact with the cutter. The speed of the rotating cutter is varied depending upon the type of shaping operation and the material being used.

Milling cutters come in a variety of sizes, shapes and types. The cutter itself can be changed quickly depending upon the particular shaping operation and the material being removed.

- Vertical milling machine – has the cutter mounted into a machine head, which moves up and down. More complex vertical milling machines can work at different angles and can produce chamfered edges on the workpiece.

- Horizontal milling machine – often used if less accuracy is required or a significant amount of material needs removing. The cutter is normally fixed in position and the table adjusted to position the workpiece in line with the cutter.

A milling sequence is often quite complex, depending upon the techniques being used, but Figure 7.6 can be used as a guide:

When you start using a milling operation you will need to consider speeds and feeds. If you try to operate too quickly you can cause damage and produce a poor-quality finish. In an engineering workplace or manufacturing environment, however, it is important to produce a high-quality finish in the quickest time possible, so a balance may have to be struck between efficiency and quality.

A milling operation – step-by-step

1. The tool is located in the chuck or other tool-holding device.

2. The workpiece is secured in the chuck, vice or other work-holding device.

3. If required coolant supply is switched on and directed onto the workpiece.

4. Appropriate safety checks are undertaken, including ensuring all guards are in place.

5. The tool is brought into contact with the workpiece to produce the desired features.

6. The tool is removed from the workpiece and a safe procedure is followed to shut down the machine.

Figure 7.6 A milling operation – step-by-step

Milling machine table feed

In a milling machine the calculations are different as you are moving the table not the tool. The table feed rate is adjusted depending upon the:

- finish required
- amount of metal removed
- type of tool being used and its diameter
- properties of the tool and workpiece
- power and capability of the machine.

You can calculate the table feed rate using a similar formula to that used in Worked example 7.3.

Did you know?

When carrying out machining operations, it is not unusual for a lot of heat to be generated. This can cause damage to cutting tools and affect the workpiece. For this reason, remove the material gradually, a little at a time. It usually takes several cuts, sometimes with different tools, to achieve the final shape and surface finish you require.

Worked example 7.4

Determine the time taken to perform a cutting operation on a workpiece 200 mm long with a 100 mm diameter slab mill with six teeth and a feed/tooth of 0.04 mm. Assume the cutting speed is 42 m/min.

$$N = 1{,}000S/\pi D$$

where:

N = spindle speed (rpm)

S = cutting speed (m/min) = 42 m/min

D = diameter (mm) = 100 mm

$$N = (1{,}000 \times 42)/(\pi \times 100)$$

$$N = 134 \text{ rpm (to the nearest rpm)}$$

Rate of feed can be converted into mm/rev:

$$0.04 \text{ mm/tooth} \times 6 \text{ teeth} = 0.24 \text{ mm/rev}$$

The table feed rate = 0.24 mm/rev × 134 rpm = 32 mm/min (to the nearest mm)

Checks for compliance and accuracy

Introduction

When producing components using machining techniques, it is important to check that they are the correct size. The required sizes and tolerances will usually be given in the specification or engineering drawing.

Key terms

Tolerance – how far above, or below, the required size the finished size is allowed to be to be considered accurate or to specification. Accuracy is expressed in terms of a tolerance. For example, a Φ12 ± 1 mm dimension means a feature should have a diameter of 12 mm with a tolerance so it is compliant if it falls between 11 mm and 13 mm.

Engineering drawings are used to allow the production of correctly sized workpieces. If a feature has to be very accurate it is given a **tolerance**. For example, Φ10 ± 0.05 mm means the maximum size is 10.05 mm and the minimum size is 9.95 mm. This cannot be measured using a rule so accurate measuring instruments have to be used instead.

Measuring instruments

Typical instruments used for checking accuracy include:

- **Engineer's rule** – made from hardened and tempered steel with graduations that mark the measurements scribed accurately into the surface at millimetre intervals.
- **Vernier callipers** – like the engineer's rule, it features a linear calibrated scale, which has a fixed and moveable jaw attached. The moveable jaw is adjusted to fit across a workpiece and the measurement is read off the scale.
- **Vernier height gauge** – works using the same principle as the vernier calliper; however, it is fixed to a stand and used to measure the height of a workpiece.
- **Micrometer** – normally consists of a C-shaped frame. A calibrated screw rotates inside a sleeve passing through one end of the frame and traps the workpiece being measured against the anvil, which is attached to the opposite end of the frame. Accurately scribed markings on the outside of the measuring screw align with markings on the sleeve allowing readings to be taken.
- **Dial Test Indicator (DTI)** – records the displacement of a plunger that is very sensitive to movement. This movement is amplified by a series of gears before a rack and pinion turns the linear movement into rotation of a large pointer.
- **Thread gauges** – a thin steel strip with serrations that match a particular thread size. They usually come in sets which are rotated out of a casing when in use.
- **Engineer's square** – an engineer's square is used to ensure objects/features are at right angles (90°). It is constructed by securing a steel blade into a more substantial steel handle. Both are manufactured to a high standard to ensure accuracy.
- **Surface table and surface plates** – a surface table is a large, heavy, flat table manufactured from self-lubricating cast iron. Being perfectly flat means that workpieces placed on it can also be flat, and levels or heights etc. can be accurately measured. A surface plate is a smaller version of a surface table designed to be used on a workbench.
- **Plug gauges** – used to check hole sizes.
- **Texture gauges** – used to check the roughness or surface finish of a workpiece.

Before you start using a measuring instrument perform a quick visual check to ensure that the workpiece:

- has no minor imperfections
- has no sharp edges or burrs
- is not damaged or contains swarf particles
- has no missing features
- has no scores or marks
- is square and threads are intact
- has no false cuts
- has steps in the sections where they are supposed to be
- has correctly shaped holes in the right position.

Checking for accuracy

A typical sequence for each machining operation would be:

- visually check for false cuts, burrs and ensure there are no sharp edges
- refer to the specification/drawing and use appropriate measuring instruments to check all the sizes, dimensions and **surface finish** are correct according to BS 22768-1 or BS 4500.

In addition, the following specific checks might apply:

- drilling – drilled/reamed holes should be checked against tolerances for holes, e.g. H8. Any screw threads should be checked for fit, e.g. BS medium fit
- turning – reamed or bored holes should be checked against tolerances, e.g. H8. Any screw threads should be checked for fit, e.g. BS medium fit. Angles to be checked to the appropriate accuracy – this can vary according to the required specification, e.g. ± 1.0 degree
- milling – flatness and squareness, e.g. within 0.125 mm per 25 mm. Angles to be checked to the appropriate accuracy – this can vary according to the required specification, e.g. ± 1.0 degree.

Key terms

Surface finish – how smooth the surface is. If you run the tip of your fingernail over a surface you will get an indication of how smooth it is. Imagine a saw blade – the distance between the high point and low point is the measure used for surface finish. Surface finish is measured in μm where 1 μm = 0.000001 m.

Remember

When you are performing machining operations it is important to check each stage as you move along. This way if you make a mistake early in the process you can either rework it or scrap it before you have spent too much time and effort.

Micrometers typically measure to 0.001 mm.

Working safely

Getting started

In a group make a list of all the health and safety hazards that can occur when performing machining techniques in an engineering workshop. You should consider whether these hazards are the same for turning, milling and drilling, or whether each machining technique has different hazards. In your group can you think of a way to prevent each hazard? Next to each hazard write down your method of preventing it from occurring.

Introduction

Engineering can be a dangerous occupation because of the nature of the machinery, equipment, tools and techniques used. It is important to ensure that you are careful to maintain the safety of yourself and others.

General safety awareness

Machining operations usually take place in an engineering workshop. A workshop is a potentially dangerous working environment so safety awareness is critical. A risk assessment of the work area should be carried out before you undertake a machining operation. This ensures all hazards have been considered and appropriate measures have been put in place. In addition, you should seek guidance on the use of drilling, turning or milling techniques. Things you need to be aware of include:

- Moving parts – be alert to which parts are moving and do not touch or approach these parts of a machine.

- Ensure machine guards are in place – guards are designed to protect you from getting trapped in a machine or being hit by parts coming off the machine or workpiece. You should know exactly which guards are required and how they work. Never try to reach over or around a machine guard.

- Use of the emergency stop – designed to quickly stop the machine. Before operating a machine make sure you know the location of all emergency stops and check that they work. Remember the machine guard is often interlocked. This means it will stop the machine if moved during a machining operation.

- Machine isolation – to ensure that the machine is properly switched off (isolated) and cannot be accidentally activated. Make sure you know where all power switches and buttons are located, and check they work.

- Wearing appropriate personal protective equipment (PPE) – you should not enter a workshop unless you have the correct protective equipment. Overalls, safety boots and safety glasses are normally the minimum requirement with other equipment, such as safety goggles or gloves used for specific machining operations.

- Keeping a clean and tidy work area – all tools should be put away after use, swarf should be safely removed and all spills should be quickly cleared to prevent accidents. Never rest tools or workpieces on machines or machine tables – vibration can cause these to fall off causing injury.

- Removing burrs and sharp edges – always use a tool to do this as they can be very sharp and easily cut fingers.

- Identification of hazards, associated risks and their control – this is usually carried out using a **risk assessment** and should happen before any workshop activities are carried out.

Think about it

Risk assessments should be carried out by health and safety representatives or trained persons. A good example of managing risks is the use of coolants. While these are non-toxic, they can be a skin irritant. Machine guards prevent coolant splashing onto the operator and wearing overalls protects clothes. However, you should also apply barrier cream to your hands. This forms a protective layer on the skin as you will be handling workpieces and tools which may have a little coolant on their surface.

Safety and hazards

- Always keep hair tied back and wear barrier cream to protect your hands.
- Do not lean on a machine or place tools on it.
- Do not use machines until you have received instruction and been given permission by your teacher/tutor/assessor.
- Do not lift heavy workpieces without assistance.
- Do not wear rings or bracelets while operating machinery.
- Ensure your overalls are in good condition, fit properly and are buttoned.
- Do not remove swarf with your hands.
- Always wear safety boots, goggles and other necessary PPE.

Safe working practices

As well as general safe practice there are specific things you should consider when using individual machines:

- How to handle tools safely – be very careful of sharp edges when handling drilling/turning and milling tools. For example, milling cutters, twist drills and lathe tools should never be held by the cutting surface – use the smooth shank instead.
- What to do when a tool breaks – make sure there are guards in place to prevent broken cutting tools coming off the machine. You should also ensure you isolate the machine and take great care or seek assistance when removing broken tools.
- How to remove and dispose of swarf – this should be carefully removed using a brush and/or hook, taking care to use an appropriate container to remove and recycle the material. Keep the brush or hook well away from any moving surfaces.
- How to safely handle cutting fluids – they must be applied carefully ensuring they cannot splash onto hands, into eyes or come into contact with any other parts of the body or clothing. Cutting fluids can be a skin irritant and barrier cream should be used on the hands prior to use.
- Being aware of backlash in machine slides – this is a feature of lathes and milling machines caused by a poor fit between a drive screw and nut causing backwards/forward movement. Contaminants between the drive screw and nut can increase the problem causing the machine to lose accuracy, and issues such as vibration and tool/workpiece movement can become a danger.

Remember

General safety awareness covers preparation, as well as actually carrying out an activity.

Discussion

Think about when you carry out a machining activity.

- What safe working practices should you consider?
- What could cause you injury or harm during the process?

CONTINUED ▶▶

Assessment activity 7.2 — Outlining the machining process

2B.P4 | 2B.P5 | 2B.M2 | 2B.D2 | 2B.P6 | 2B.M3 | 2B.P7 | 2B.M4

You are working as a trainee machinist and have been asked to produce a written guide with images to distribute to local schools, outlining the machining process for the components shown in Figure 7.7. You should include a flow chart to describe the procedure used. For each step of the flowchart, you should explain why the techniques, checks and/or safe working practices described are important. You should manufacture the components and take photos at every step to show that you can:

- set up and use/adjust the machines before and during the machining activities
- produce two workpieces with high levels of precision and accuracy using drilling and turning or milling techniques (include photos of before, during and after)
- take appropriate measurements and show why the techniques used ensure high levels of precision and

accuracy (include photos before, during and after as evidence)

- carry out checks on the workpieces for visible defects and to ensure they meet specification at all stages of the process
- assess the level of precision and accuracy and reflect on the machining practices you have demonstrated
- wear appropriate PPE and work safely
- explain the importance of PPE and safe working, and assess your own working practices.

It is important that you include supporting explanations with these photographs. You should include a flowchart to describe the procedure used. At each step of the flowchart, you should explain why techniques, checks and/or safe working practices described are important.

Tips

- Ask a friend or your assessor to take lots of pictures. You don't have to use all of them but it's better to have too many than not enough.
- Add explanations, descriptions and assessments of your own performance. Think about what you did well and what you could improve on.

Figure 7.7 Engineering drawing of two components, a locating pin (left) and a tool clamp (two views, right)

WorkSpace

⊳ Ravi Achtar

Skilled machinist

I work in a specialist workshop that manufactures parts for racing motorbikes. My responsibility is machining parts for the braking systems. Brake discs have to be as light as possible so often have lots of holes drilled in them.

We work as a team and can all use the machining techniques required, although I like to concentrate on milling and turning.

A typical day starts with a briefing about how the racing team is performing and which parts are being tested or raced. We get prepared, putting on our overalls and safety gear – remembering to put barrier cream on our hands, too. Each job is specialist so we use all kinds of work-holding and special tools. It can take quite a long time to set up jobs but being patient is vital as we work to very close tolerances.

It is really exciting to watch the motorbikes racing and know that the workpieces we produce play a part in the winning performances.

Think about it

1   Why do you think Ravi takes so much time setting up his work?
2   What sort of safety gear might be required?
3   What tools might be used to produce very accurate holes in a motorbike brake disc?

Introduction

Imagine what life would be like without a mobile phone, or if you could not use the Internet to find that crucial piece of information. What if there were no MP3 players to listen to, no televisions to watch or games consoles to play on? We have electronic engineers to thank for these powerful devices.

Electronic engineers develop the complex control systems used in household appliances, computers and even spacecraft. Such incredible state-of-the-art technology helps make life more comfortable and safer for us all.

In this unit, you will look at the building blocks of electronic circuits – the inputs, processes and outputs, and how we can join these together to develop circuits to solve problems.

Finally, you will consider the different ways in which circuits can be tested to make sure they work correctly.

Assessment: This unit will be assessed by a series of assignments set by your teacher/tutor.

Learning aims

After completing this unit you should:

A know about electronic systems design

B design and construct electronic circuits using electronic building blocks

C know how to populate circuit boards permanently and construct electronic circuits safely

D test and evaluate electronic circuits.

> When I was doing my work experience at a local electronics shop, I was able to ask customers what they wanted their projects to do. I was able to tell them which devices would be suitable, and also give them ideas about how to make their circuits.
>
> Charlie, *17-year-old engineering apprentice*

Electronic Circuit Design and Construction

Assessment Zone

This table shows you what you must do in order to achieve a **Pass, Merit** or **Distinction** grade, and where you can find activities in this book to help you.

Assessment criteria

Level 1	Level 2 **Pass**	Level 2 **Merit**	Level 2 **Distinction**
Learning aim A: Know about electronic systems design			
1A.1 Describe the function and characteristics of electronic input, process, output and passive components.	**2A.P1** Select and apply appropriate input, process and output, and passive components for a circuit. **See Assessment activity 8.1, page 155**	**2A.M1** Explain reasons for the selection of electronic input, process, output and passive components. **See Assessment activity 8.1, page 155**	**2A.D1** Justify the selection of appropriate input, process and output components in a circuit design to solve a given electronics problem. **See Assessment activity 8.1, page 155**
1A.2 Carry out simple calculations using units of current, resistance, voltage and power.	**2A.P2** Maths Describe the characteristics of power supplies and carry out simple and complex calculations using units of current, resistance, voltage and power in electronic circuits. **See Assessment activity 8.1, page 155**		
Learning aim B: Design and construct electronic circuits using electronic building blocks			
1B.3 Identify components in a given circuit diagram.	**2B.P3** Describe the design features of a simple circuit diagram that uses input, process and output components. **See Assessment activity 8.2, page 160**	**2B.M2** Explain the operation of the circuit in terms of its input, process and output components. **See Assessment activity 8.2, page 160**	**2B.D2** Explain the limits of operation of the circuit in terms of its input, process and output components. **See Assessment activity 8.2, page 160**
Learning aim C: Know how to populate circuit boards permanently and construct electronic circuits safely			
1C.4 Identify the main hazards and people at risk when using soldering equipment.	**2C.P4** Describe the risks associated with identified hazards when using soldering equipment. **See Assessment activity 8.3, page 165**	**2C.M3** Explain, with reference to particular soldering activities, the risks involved and record appropriate control measures. **See Assessment activity 8.3, page 165**	**2C.D3** Using a full risk assessment, evaluate all activities in the production of electronic circuits. **See Assessment activity 8.3, page 165**
1C.5 Identify the main features of a given electronic circuit.	**2C.P5** Describe the main features of an electronic circuit and the construction techniques. **See Assessment activity 8.3, page 165**	**2C.M4** Compare the advantages and disadvantages of different circuit construction techniques. **See Assessment activity 8.3, page 165**	

Assessment criteria

Level 1	Level 2 **Pass**	Level 2 **Merit**	Level 2 **Distinction**
Learning aim D: Test and evaluate electronic circuits			
1D.6 Maths Use a test meter to accurately measure the voltage of a power supply.	**2D.P6** Maths Test voltage levels at specific points in an electronic circuit when in use. **See Assessment activity 8.4, page 167**	**2D.M5** Maths Use a range of measurements to test the performance of an electronic circuit. **See Assessment activity 8.4, page 167**	**2D.D4** Maths Use a range of measurements to evaluate the performance of an electronic circuit. **See Assessment activity 8.4, page 167**
1D.7 Identify basic faults in an electronic circuit.	**2D.P7** Diagnose faults in an electronic circuit. **See Assessment activity 8.4, page 167**		

Maths Opportunity to practise mathematical skills

How you will be assessed

This unit will be assessed by a series of tasks set by your teacher/tutor. You will be expected to show that you understand the inputs, processes and outputs used to design a circuit. You will be expected to design a block diagram for a circuit to solve a given problem, such as a dark-sensing device. You will also need to explain the function of components in a circuit, and identify them from a diagram.

In addition, you will need to demonstrate that you can use tools and equipment correctly and safely to construct a circuit. You will also need to test the circuit to make sure that it works correctly.

Your assessment could take a number of forms including:

- a written report showing your circuit designs, calculations and results

- annotated photographs of your practical work

- a written observation record describing safe working practices in the electronics laboratory.

Input components

Introduction

Our lives are dominated by electronic devices – whether it's an MP3 player or a satellite beaming our favourite television programmes into our homes. All have one thing in common – they are controlled by some form of input device. In this topic you will look at a range of different inputs used in circuits, including types of switches and sensors.

Sensors

Sensors are often used in circuits where there needs to be some kind of reaction to the environment. This could be the temperature or how bright the light is. Sensors are usually linked with a **transistor** and a **variable resistor** to control their sensitivity.

Light dependent resistor (LDR)

A light dependent resistor can be used as a sensor in a circuit because it changes its resistance depending on the amount of light shining on to it.

- When there is a lot of light, the resistance is very small.
- When it is dark, the resistance can be very high.

The change in resistance affects the current flowing, so by using a **potential divider circuit** we can use an LDR in either a light sensor circuit or a darkness sensing circuit. LDRs are often used in night lights, security lights and automated car headlamps.

Thermistor (negative temperature coefficient – NTC)

Another special type of resistor is the thermistor. The most common type is the negative temperature coefficient thermistor. With these, as the temperature increases the resistance decreases. There are many uses for this type of thermistor, including:

- inside car engines to measure the temperature of the oil
- digital thermostats used to control the central heating temperature in a house.

Moisture sensor

A moisture sensor isn't really a sensor because, unlike the thermistor and LDR, the resistance value of the sensor itself never changes. Instead, a moisture sensor has strips of copper separated by narrow gaps of an insulator. When the sensor gets wet, an electrical current can flow through the water – between the copper strips. If there is a lot of liquid, more electricity can flow between the strips and current flow increases.

Piezoelectric sensor

These are sometimes known as strain gauges because they convert small changes of pressure, force or strain into an electrical charge. Many contain materials such as quartz and, when the sensor is squeezed, it deforms and produces an electrical charge. The more the sensor is squeezed, the higher the charge produced.

Switches

We use different types of **switch** every day. There are many similarities between them but it is the differences that make them useful.

Table 8.1 Types of switch

Type of switch	Function	Applications
Toggle	The switch works by moving the lever. When it is turned on, the lever makes a connection between the contacts and completes a circuit.	• Miniature circuit breakers • Guitar amplifiers
Slide	Unlike most other types, a slide switch can have lots of different contacts. A common contact is joined to a range of terminals, making this type very useful.	• Children's toys • Reversing motors • Volume controls
Rocker	This type of switch 'rocks' when it is pressed to turn a circuit on or off. Often they will have 'on' and 'off' printed on the switch.	• Light switches • Household appliances
Push-to-make	One of the simplest switches. When pressed, the circuit is completed and current flows. Normally, as soon as they are released the circuit is broken again.	• Doorbells • Computer keyboards • Lift call buttons
Push-to-break	Unlike most switches, push-to-break switches are constantly on. When the switch is pressed, the circuit is broken, cutting the current.	• Reset switch on a computer • Refrigerator lights
Key	A special key is needed to operate these switches. This is often to prevent equipment being turned on by accident.	• Power isolator • Burglar alarms
Micro	Very sensitive and similar to a push switch, usually with a lever which reacts to very small movements. They can either be open or closed switches.	• Safety cut out for workshop machinery • Microwave door interlock
Tilt	Special switches which have a small drop of mercury inside a glass bulb. When the bulb is tilted, the mercury moves, either joining or separating the contacts. Some tilt switches use a metal bead instead of mercury.	• Car alarms • Robotics (to stop them falling over) • Tilt warning systems for cranes

Just checking

1 Which type of sensor would be best in an alarm to warn of freezing temperatures?

2 What happens to the resistance of a light dependent resistor when it is dark?

3 Why are key switches used on workshop machines?

Process components

Getting started

How does a radio convert the signal it receives into sound and why does a kettle stop boiling when the water is hot enough? Can you think of two or three other household products that do something when a sensor of some type receives a signal?

Key terms

Semiconductor – a material that, in certain conditions, allows electricity to pass through it.

Introduction

Do you ever think about what makes your computer work when you are surfing the Internet? What is going on inside the box to make what you type on the keyboard appear on the screen? How does it communicate with other computers all around the world? In this topic you will be looking at the components that work together to perform these complex processes.

Transistor

A transistor can either be used as a current amplifier or an electronic switch. There are two main types – bipolar transistors and field effect transistors (which you will look at later).

Bipolar transistors are split into two further types – NPN (negative-positive-negative) and PNP (positive-negative-positive) transistors. The letters refer to the positive and negative layers of silicon **semiconductor** material that make up the transistor. In reality, the only difference between the two types is the direction in which a current flows through them.

A transistor has three leads:

- the base (b)
- the collector (c)
- the emitter (e).

When a voltage of more than 0.7V is applied to the base it allows a small current to flow from the base to the emitter. This turns the transistor 'on' letting a larger current flow from the collector to the emitter. This is because the resistance has dropped.

If you then remove the voltage from the base, the resistance between the collector and emitter rises again, and the transistor is turned 'off'.

Transistors are used with input devices to form potential divider circuits to control the trigger point of the sensors.

Figure 8.1 Types of transistors – NPN and PNP

Darlington Pair

When you connect the emitter of one transistor to the collector of another you create a **Darlington Pair**.

This arrangement is much more sensitive than a single transistor, with the second transistor making use of the gain of the first. The total gain of a Darlington Pair circuit is the gain of one transistor multiplied by the gain of the other.

It is possible to buy a single component which is a Darlington Pair in one package – an example being a BCX38 transistor.

Thyristor

A **thyristor** looks very similar to a transistor. Again, it has three leads:

- **anode** (a)
- **cathode** (c)
- gate (g).

In the same way that a transistor is turned 'on' when a voltage is passed through the base, a thyristor is turned 'on' when a voltage is applied to the gate. Unlike a transistor, even if the gate voltage is taken away again, the thyristor will stay 'on' until the power supply to the anode is taken away. This is called **latching** and it is very useful in an alarm circuit.

Field effect transistor

A **field effect transistor** is used where there is a weak signal that needs to be amplified. The current flows through a 'channel' which is a semiconductor. One end of the channel is connected to an electrode called the 'source', the other end to an electrode called the 'drain'. When the voltage at the control electrode (called the 'gate') reaches 2V the transistor is turned fully on. Depending on the voltage, the conductivity of the channel changes. A small change in the gate voltage can make the difference in the current from the source to the drain very large. Field effect transistors tend to be used to control high-current devices such as motors.

Key terms

Darlington Pair – a combination of two transistors where the second one benefits from the gain of the first one.

Thyristor – similar to a transistor, a thyristor will stay switched on once it has been triggered until the power source is removed.

Anode – the terminal connected to the positive power supply.

Cathode – the terminal connected to the negative or ground power supply.

Latching – when a component remains turned on, even after the trigger has been removed, it is said to have latched.

Field effect transistor – a type of transistor that works as an amplifier and has digital properties, meaning it is either turned on or off.

CONTINUED ▶▶

555 timer

A **555 timer IC** is a type of integrated circuit. These are tiny chips of silicone in a plastic case and can contain hundreds of different components.

There are two main types of circuit in which a 555 IC can be used. One is called a **monostable circuit**. This is used to turn something on for a set amount of time, then turn it off again. Circuits like this are often found in security systems where a light will remain lit for a certain length of time after a sensor has been triggered.

The other type of circuit is an **astable circuit** used to switch an output on and off continuously, such as a flashing shop sign.

Figure 8.2 Timer circuit

Key terms

555 timer IC – an integrated circuit chip, often used in timer circuits.

Monostable circuit – a type of circuit that can be used as a timer.

Astable circuit – a type of circuit that can be used to make lights flash.

Operational amplifier (Op-Amp) – an integrated circuit that can be used as both a comparator and invertor.

Gain – the increase in the signal power produced by the transistor.

Feedback – a small proportion of the output is fed back into the system to make sure it works correctly. Negative feedback tends to keep a signal under control, whereas positive feedback increases the output signal constantly.

Peripheral Interface Controllers (PICs) – programmable integrated circuits used in many household products.

Operational amplifier (Op-Amp)

An **operational amplifier (Op-Amp)** has two inputs; one is the inverting input (marked as -) and the other is the non-inverting input (marked +).

Op-Amps can be used for lots of applications, including:

- as a comparator
- as an inverting amplifier.

When an Op-Amp is used as a comparator, it can detect very small changes in voltage between the two inputs and it multiplies the difference between the inputs by the **gain** of the Op-Amp.

- If the non-inverting input is higher than the inverting input, the output is a high voltage.
- If the inverting input is higher than the non-inverting input, the output is a low voltage.

This allows us to use an Op-Amp with an analogue sensor, such as an LDR, and convert the signal so it can be used in a logic circuit.

The other use of an Op-Amp – as an inverting amplifier – uses negative **feedback** in a closed loop circuit to reduce the voltage gain. This makes the Op-Amp more stable and the gain more predictable because some of the output voltage is fed back into the inverting input, with the voltage controlled by a feedback resistor.

Peripheral Interface Controllers (PICs)

Almost all modern appliances such as DVD players, MP3 players, children's toys and even cars have special integrated circuits called **Peripheral Interface Controllers (PICs)**. These are programmed to control output devices in a certain way once they receive a signal from a sensor.

Using PICs allows electronic engineers to design products that can be upgraded easily, simply by reprogramming the PIC.

One way to do this is to use a flow chart. This allows you to create programs that turn an output device on or off depending on the signal from the inputs.

It is possible to create a range of different types of program using flow charts, including ones with loops to make outputs such as LEDs flash, others which can make a buzzer sound for a set amount of time and even counting circuits.

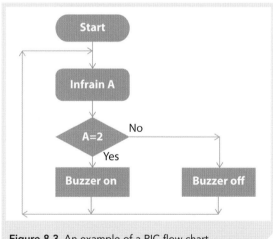

Figure 8.3 An example of a PIC flow chart

Just checking

1 What are the three leads on a transistor?

2 What is the difference between a transistor and a thyristor?

3 Which two types of circuit can be made using a 555 timer chip?

4 If you use an Op-Amp as a comparator, what happens if the inverting voltage is the highest?

Output components

Getting started ▸▸

It's time to get up. Your electronic alarm clock starts to play your favourite music. What different types of outputs does the clock use to make your early mornings more bearable?

Introduction

Do you ever wonder why a computer keyboard has LEDs built into it? Or what makes a mobile phone vibrate? These are just a small selection of devices which either make something move, make a noise or shine a light. They are called output devices. By combining different outputs, an electronic device can become very versatile.

Identification, function and application of output components

Table 8.2 lists output components used in electronic circuits, and outlines their function and examples of where they are applied.

Table 8.2 Output components

Output device	Function	Applications
Lamp/bulb	When electricity passes through the filament of the bulb, it heats up. This makes it glow and give off light. Lamps are not polarised and electricity can flow in both directions.	• Traffic lights • Security light
Buzzer	Although they look simple, buzzers are quite complicated. When connected to a power supply, an electromagnet is turned on. This attracts the arm inside the buzzer. As it moves, the circuit breaks, and the arm goes back to its original position. This happens so fast it creates a buzzing noise.	• Smoke alarm • Personal alarm
Light emitting diode	LEDs give out light when electricity passes through them from the anode (positive) to the cathode (negative). The anode is the longer of the two legs. When you use an LED you need to use a current limiting resistor as an LED only needs around 2V and 20mA to light up.	• Advertising displays • Television screen
Loudspeaker	A loudspeaker works by having a ring-shaped electromagnet. In the hole is a coil of wire attached to a paper cone. The electromagnet makes the coil vibrate. This changes the air pressure allowing us to hear sounds such as music.	• Child's toy • Radio • Mobile phone

Output device	Function	Applications
Motor	A motor uses an electromagnet attached to the rotor. The current in the coil changes direction twice every cycle as it is controlled by a special switch called a commutator. This means that the electromagnet is always pushed and pulled in the same direction by the fixed permanent magnets on the outside of the motor. The higher the voltage or current, the faster the motor turns.	• Digital camera • Remote-controlled car
7-segment display	As its name suggests a 7-segment display is made up of 7 hexagonal LEDs which, when turned on in different combinations, can show numbers from 0 to 9. They have in-built resistors and usually have a common anode or cathode, with signals to the other pins creating the number display.	• Calculator • Digital watch

Activity 8.1   Types of LED

You have probably seen red, yellow and green LEDs in different applications, but how many different colours and sizes are there? Use the Internet to see what other types of LED are available and find out what they are used for.

Just checking   ✓

1 Give an advantage of using an LED instead of a bulb as a visual output.
2 Which type of output device would be most appropriate for a smoke detector?
3 Which output devices are not polarised?
4 Which part of a motor makes sure that it continues turning in one direction?

Passive components

Introduction

Some of the most important components in any electronic device are the ones which seem to do very little. They don't make the flashes of light or the loud noises, nor do they sense what is going on around them. They simply sit on the circuit board and make sure that everything works as it should. These are the passive components.

Fixed resistor

A resistor is used to control the flow of current in a circuit and, in some cases, the voltage flowing through parts of a circuit. Resistance is measured in Ohms (Ω) – a very small unit of measurement. Most resistors are given values such as 5M6, 1K2 or 330R. The M, K and R are multipliers:

- M – multiply by one million (for example, 5M6 = 5,600,000 Ω)
- K – multiply by one thousand (for example, 1K2 = 1,200 Ω)
- R – multiply by one (for example, 330R = 330 Ω).

We write the letter where the decimal point would go; for example, 2.2 kΩ is written 2K2.

We can identify the value of a resistor by the coloured lines printed on the case. This is known as the resistor colour code. In most cases there are four bands, but some resistors have five.

COLOUR	1st BAND	2nd BAND	3rd BAND	MULTIPLIER	TOLERANCE	
Black	0	0	0	1Ω		
Brown	1	1	1	10Ω	± 1%	(F)
Red	2	2	2	100Ω	± 2%	(G)
Orange	3	3	3	1kΩ		
Yellow	4	4	4	10kΩ		
Green	5	5	5	100KΩ	±0.5%	(D)
Blue	6	6	6	1MΩ	±0.25%	(C)
Violet	7	7	7	10MΩ	±0.10%	(B)
Grey	8	8	8	100MΩ	±0.05%	
White	9	9	9	1000MΩ		
Gold				0.1	± 5%	(J)
Silver				00.1	± 10%	(K)

Figure 8.4 The four-band and five-band resistor colour codes.

Variable resistor

Variable resistors also control the current in a circuit, but the value can be changed. This is done by moving a wiper along a resistance track. There are three main types:

- preset potentiometer – usually fitted to a circuit board
- rotary potentiometer – often used for temperature controls
- slide potentiometer – can be used for volume controllers.

Polarised capacitors

A **polarised** capacitor is also known as an electrolytic capacitor. They are used to:

- produce a time delay in a monostable circuit
- set the frequency in a pulse generator circuit
- smooth the input for a power supply.

They are also used to store electrical charge, initially charging quickly but also discharging quickly. A polarised capacitor must be connected into the circuit the right way round otherwise it will not work.

Non-polarised capacitors

It does not matter which way around in a circuit you connect these components. They are usually made from ceramic and are sometimes called ceramic disc capacitors. These have quite small values – usually less than 1µF. They can be used for the same purposes as polarised capacitors.

Diode

Like a one-way street, a diode will only allow electricity to flow through it from the anode (positive) to the cathode (negative). A diode is a polarised component. They are often used to protect transistors and other components from damage which could be caused by a battery being connected the wrong way around.

Relay

A relay is the reason why cars make a 'click – click' noise when the indicators are on. A relay allows one circuit to control another without having an electrical connection. This is useful if you need to control something with a large current from a low power circuit.

When a relay is turned on, an electromagnet moves a lever to switch on a second circuit. When the electromagnet is turned off, the lever moves the other way, opening the circuit again.

> **Key terms**
>
> **Polarised** – components which will only work when they are connected into a circuit in a certain direction. They have different methods of identifying which is the anode and which is the cathode. An LED for example has a long leg for the anode and a flat side on the plastic case for the cathode. Placing a polarised component the wrong way can often be the reason a circuit does not work immediately.

> **Just checking**
>
> 1 What is the difference between an electrolytic capacitor and a ceramic capacitor?
> 2 Give an example of a variable resistor.
> 3 What is the unit of resistance?
> 4 What would the colour code be on a resistor with a value of 3K3?

Power

Getting started

Think about ten items you use everyday. List them under three headings – 'not powered', 'battery powered' and 'mains electricity powered'. Do some of these items fit under more than one heading? Which is the largest group of items?

Introduction

Power. The one thing which is vital for all electronic products. How would our lives be different if there was no electricity? It's hard to imagine a lifestyle without electric lights, television, Internet, cars, trains and telephones. All of these, and much more, need electrical power to make them work, and, in turn, make our life more comfortable.

Power supplies – batteries

There are a number of different types of battery, but all of them do the same thing – provide power to portable devices and appliances.

Table 8.3 Types of battery

Type of battery	Characteristics	Typical applications
Zinc-carbon	• Low cost • Voltage level falls with use	• Projects with low power demand • Torches, radios
Alkaline	• Voltage level doesn't fall as quickly as zinc-carbon • Available in many sizes • Have a high capacity	• MP3 players • TV remote controls • Toys
NiCad rechargeable	• Good voltage retention, but lower capacity than alkaline • Available in common sizes • Can be recharged lots of times	• Cordless tools • Mobile phones • Electric cars
Button cells	• Available as 1.5V or 3V • Provide an almost constant output voltage until they run out • Available in many sizes	• Clocks • Watches • Alarm remote controls

Key terms

NiCad – short for Nickel Cadmium, commonly used in rechargeable batteries.

Low voltage power supply units

In the UK the mains voltage from a socket is 230V. Most of the electronic equipment in our homes only needs a small fraction of this voltage to work properly.

To power devices such as laptops, games consoles and phone chargers, we use a low-voltage power supply unit. These have a transformer inside them to reduce the voltage from 230V to the level needed. They also have a rectifier to convert the current from alternating (AC) to direct (DC).

Solar power

We all know that using fossil fuels causes pollution and that solar power is 'green', but how can we use it with our electronic devices? For many years, calculators have been solar powered, using a silicon solar panel. These charge capacitors to power the calculator.

Similar panels can be used to recharge small products, such as mobile phones or digital cameras.

Units of measurement

Nearly everything we use which has a value also has a unit of measurement. In the same way that time is measured in minutes and length in millimetres, all of the measurements used in electronics have units.

- current (I) – Amp (A)
- resistance (R) – Ohm (Ω)
- voltage (V) – Volt (V)
- power (W) – Watt (W).

Calculations for electronic circuits

When designing circuits, you need to know if the components will work as you expect them to. Some need a higher current than others; some need more voltage. There are a number of different calculations available for use.

Ohm's Law

This is the relationship between the current and potential difference. It states that the current in a conductor is proportional to the potential difference between the ends of the conductor.

In a simple circuit:

potential difference (V) = the current (I) × constant

The constant is the resistance of the conductor, giving us:

potential difference (V) = current (I) × resistance (R)

Or:

$$V = IR.$$

Ohm's Law can be rearranged depending on which values are known (see Figure 8.5).

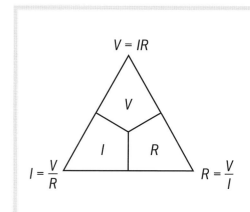

Figure 8.5 Ohm's Law triangle

CONTINUED ▶▶

Resistance

Depending on how resistors are connected together in a circuit, the calculations can be changed. If the resistors are in series – in other words, one after another – you add the resistances together to get a total resistance.

If you look at Figure 8.6 you get the total resistance as:

$$R = R_1 + R_2 + R_3$$

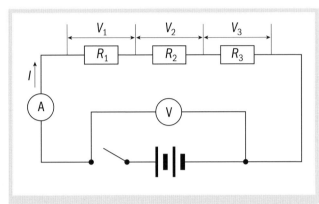

Figure 8.6 Resistors connected in series

This also means that the potential difference across each resistor is different, as the current is the same.

From Ohm's Law you can see that:

$$V_1 = IR_1; \; V_2 = IR_2; \text{ and } V_3 = IR_3$$

And the total potential difference is:

$$V = V_1 + V_2 + V_3$$

Things change when you start to think about resistors being connected in parallel, as each can be thought of as being on a separate circuit.

In Figure 8.7 you can see that the current travels along three different paths. In this case, the potential difference will be the same across the different resistors, but the current will change.

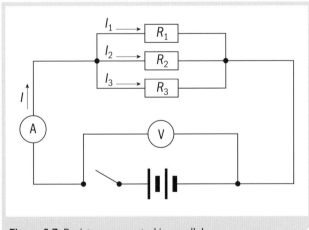

Figure 8.7 Resistors connected in parallel

In this example, the total resistance R can be calculated as:

$$\frac{1}{R} = \frac{1}{R_1} + \frac{1}{R_2} + \frac{1}{R_3}$$

And the current flowing through each resistor can be calculated using

$$I = \frac{V}{R}$$

So $I_1 = \dfrac{V}{R_1}$, etc.

If you only have two resistors on parallel paths in a circuit, you can simplify the formula as follows:

$$R = \frac{R_1 \times R_2}{R_1 + R_2}$$

Time period

The speed at which a capacitor charges is related to its size and also the value of the resistor which limits the current. This is known as the **time constant**.

Time period = Resistance (R) × Capacitance (C).

It takes a capacitor five time periods to fully charge and five to fully discharge. After one time constant, the capacitor will be 60 per cent fully charged and, when discharging, after one time constant it will be 60 per cent discharged.

Power

The rate at which work is done is known as power. In an electronic circuit:

power (W) = current (I) × potential difference (V)

Sometimes, you might not know either the current or the potential difference. In these cases you can use Ohm's Law and generate some alternative formulae:

Power (W) = $V \times I$; Power (W) = I^2R and Power (W) = $\dfrac{V^2}{R}$

Key terms

Time constant – the time taken for a capacitor to fully charge or discharge. Equal to five times the time period ($t = 5CR$).

Worked example 8.1

1 Three resistors are connected into a parallel circuit as shown in Figure 8.7. The values of the resistors are $R_1=3\Omega$; $R_2=8\Omega$ and $R_3=4\Omega$

Calculate the total resistance in the circuit.

$$\frac{1}{R} = \frac{1}{R1} + \frac{1}{R2} + \frac{1}{R3}$$

$$\frac{1}{R} = \frac{1}{3} + \frac{1}{8} + \frac{1}{4}$$

The equation can be simplified by finding the lowest common denominator – in this case 24.

$$\frac{1}{R} = \frac{8}{24} + \frac{3}{24} + \frac{6}{24} = \frac{17}{24}$$

Inversing the equation gives us: $R = \dfrac{V^2}{R} = 1.41\Omega$ or $1R4$

2 Three resistors are connected in a series circuit (as shown in Figure 8.6) and connected to a 12V power supply. The values of the resistors are $R_1 = 6\Omega$; $R_2 = 10\Omega$; $R_3 = 8\Omega$. Calculate:

(a) the resistance of the circuit

(b) the current flowing through each of the resistors

(c) the potential difference across each resistor

(d) the power dissipated in the circuit.

To find the total resistance in the circuit you use: $R = R_1 + R_2 + R_3$

$$R = 6 + 10 + 8$$

$$R = 24\Omega$$

To find the current flowing through the resistors you use Ohm's Law:

$$I = \qquad I =$$

$$I = 0.5A$$

To calculate the potential difference across each resistor you use Ohm's Law:

$$R_1: V = IR = 0.5 \times 6.\ V_1 = 3V$$

$$R_2: V = IR = 0.5 \times 10.\ V_2 = 5V$$

$$R_2: V = IR = 0.5 \times 8.\ V_3 = 4V$$

Finally, check to make sure the answers are correct:

$$V = V_1 + V_2 + V_3 = 3 + 5 + 4 = 12V$$

To calculate the power dissipated you can use Power $= I^2R$

$$\text{Power} = 0.5^2 \times 24 = 0.25 \times 24 = 6W$$

Assessment activity 8.1   An electronic warning   2A.P1 | 2A.M1 | 2A.D1 | 2A.P2

1 You have been asked to produce an outline plan for an electronic system to assist blind people. It will emit a warning sound for a set time period when the water in a bath reaches a set level.

   (a) Produce your outline plan to solve this problem.

   (b) Explain why your chosen input is the best solution.

   (c) Explain why your chosen process is the best solution.

   (d) Explain why your chosen output components are the best solution.

2 The two circuits shown below are powered by 9V low-voltage supplies. Explain the characteristics of this type of power supply and suggest one other type of power source which could be used for the circuits, explaining why it would be suitable. (**2A.P2**)

Tip

- To meet 2A.P1 and 2A.P2, you will need to make sure that you identify appropriate solutions for each part of the system. For example, do not select a light sensor if the problem asks for something to detect changes in temperature. To meet 2A.M1, you need to give reasons for your choice of component. For example, selecting an LDR because the circuit needs to light up in the dark. Finally, to meet 2A.D1, you should justify your choice of output. This could be stating that you have selected an LED to use as a visual indicator because it uses less power than a bulb and it is unlikely to ever need to be replaced.

Circuit design

Key terms

Input – the sensing part of the circuit.

Process – the part of a system which converts the signal from the input into some form of output.

Output – the part of the circuit which either moves, makes a noise or gives off light.

Introduction

The latest aeroplanes being made in both Europe and the USA feature not only modern composite materials, but also cutting-edge computer control systems which control the engines, the in-flight entertainment and, most importantly, all of the devices that keep the aircraft flying.

These systems are not designed at a component level. Instead, the designers create plans for how they want the system to operate by thinking about the inputs and the outputs. This is known as a systems approach and is used to split the circuit design into manageable building blocks.

Design an electronic circuit using input, process and output components

Think of the **inputs**, **processes** and **outputs** of a circuit as building blocks. When you start to combine these blocks, you can produce some complicated circuits.

Figure 8.8 The building blocks of a system

If you think about an alarm system which gives a warning when the temperature is low, you can think about the building blocks like this:

Figure 8.9 Examples of inputs, processes and outputs

More complicated circuits can also be designed in this way, for example, a timer circuit, which can be adapted to do more than one thing (see Figure 8.10).

Figure 8.10 The building blocks of a timer circuit

When you think about the circuit as being made up from building blocks like this, you don't need to think about how the components work individually. Instead, you think about what you want the circuit to do, and select your building blocks to do this.

If you wanted a system that counted the number of people passing through a barrier, you would want some form of display to show the total, with a switch working as the input:

Figure 8.11 The building blocks of a counter circuit

Activity 8.3 Control systems

Find yourself four different control systems. On paper, sketch out the block diagrams with the input, process and output for each of them. Which parts of the systems do they have in common? Can you think of a reason why this could be?

Just checking

1 Which type of input is used to identify changes in temperature?
2 What type of device is an Op-Amp?
3 Which output device needs a protective resistor?
4 Which type of output would be appropriate for an audible fire alarm?

Circuit board construction

Introduction

Imagine what your computer would look like if there was no circuit board inside it holding all of the different parts together. Each individual component would be soldered to a collection of wires, and the whole thing would look like a tangle of wool or a bowl of spaghetti. To make tracing how a circuit works simpler, we can use a number of construction techniques – from those suitable for testing a circuit for a small project through to those appropriate for manufacturing millions of calculators each year.

Types of circuit board

There are three main types of circuit board which you are likely to use in the electronics laboratory. These are breadboard (or prototyping board), stripboard (or veroboard) and printed circuit boards (PCBs).

A breadboard layout

A typical stripboard construction (component side)

A printed circuit board – note the tracks and component layout markings

Table 8.4 Types of board

Type of board	Advantages	Disadvantages	Typical applications
Breadboard (or prototyping board)	• Circuits made quickly • Can make changes easily • Can reuse components	• Not ideal for permanent circuits • Difficult to make complex circuits	• Testing new circuits • Simple school projects
Stripboard (veroboard)	• Low-cost circuit board • Can solder components • Permanent circuit	• Breaks may need to be made in tracks • Tracks are close together	• Prototyping circuits • Simple astable and monostable circuits
Printed circuit board (PCB)	• Layout is designed for the circuit • No need for loose wires • Can be assembled by machinery	• Expensive to initially design and make • Hard to change layout once designed • Hard to replace faulty components	• Computer **motherboard** • Consumer electronics

Mass production, miniaturisation and surface mount technology (SMT)

Mass production

Most of the electronic products we buy are mass produced. They have common components and circuit boards built up like a giant jigsaw to perform their intended functions.

The actual electronics are similar for lots of different brands of the same product, with only the outer casing and body being different. This is a result of mass production, where standardised circuit layouts are designed on computers and produced on automated production lines.

Miniaturisation

If you look at a mobile telephone from the 1980s and compare it to a modern version you would notice one big difference – the size. In a relatively short time advances in technology have allowed us to buy a device which will fit in our pocket, which combines a camera and has other computing functions as powerful as most desktop computers from 30 years ago. This is a result of miniaturisation. Integrated circuits are becoming more powerful as the embedded components become smaller. This means more can fit into the same space.

Surface mount technology (SMT)

With the need to design circuit boards for mass production, the use of surface mount technology becomes more worthwhile. There is no need to have holes in the circuit board for components such as resistors because instead of having leads which are soldered onto the reverse of the board, they have small metal contacts which are tinned and then soldered directly to the board.

The advantage of this is that it simplifies the circuit, the components are smaller, lighter and cheaper, and manufacturing can be completed by automated machines. This means the circuit boards are smaller, they are cheaper to produce and should result in lower prices for consumers.

> **Discussion**
>
> In 1972, an average integrated circuit chip contained around 3,000 transistors per square centimetre. By 2002, this had risen to between 10,000,000 and 100,000,000 transistors per square centimetre. In 1965, the co-founder of a large microchip company, Gordon Moore, predicted that the number of transistors included in an integrated circuit would double every two years – by the end of 2011 his theory was still proving to be correct. Will this continue for the next 40 years?

Just checking

1   Why is a breadboard suitable for testing out designs for circuits?
2   What is the main difference between surface mount components and regular components?
3   Which method of circuit board production is suitable for products such as calculators?
4   Why would it not be easy to construct a computer using stripboard?

CONTINUED ▶▶

Assessment activity 8.2   Investigating a timer circuit   2B.P3 | 2B.M2 | 2B.D2

You have been asked to explain what is going on in this circuit, including:

- the function of each of the components.
- how the circuit works in terms of the input, process and outputs.
- what the limitations of this circuit are.

Tips

- You will need to be able to clearly identify the different components in the circuit diagram. You can do this by drawing the diagram out neatly and labelling individual components.
- When you are explaining how the components work in the circuit, you need to not only describe *what* each component does, but also consider *how* it links to the next component.

WorkSpace

◤ Robert Simons

Autoelectrician

I am a self-employed autoelectrician and hold contracts with a number of different car dealers. I usually work independently, but sometimes I work alongside other technicians, especially when working on accident-damaged vehicles.

Part of my work involves running diagnostic tests on the electrical systems to identify where there are faults. The most interesting part of the job, though, are the little faults which the computerised systems are unable to trace. That is when I need to get the multimeter out and check that electricity is flowing through the right components. This allows me to find out if there are any breaks in the wires – something which happens quite often in older cars.

Sometimes, I will be asked by a customer to do something special for them. It may be that they have bought a car but it doesn't have automatic windscreen wipers or a frost sensor. I will ask them what they want the system to do and what sort of warning they would like to have. I can suggest that it might be nice to have a blue LED light up on the dashboard if the temperature outside is cold enough for ice, but they may prefer a beep to warn them when they start the engine.

These are the more exciting projects, as I can be creative for the customer, but, at the end of the day, making the system always comes down to the same thing. I know what the input is going to be, the customer tells me what they want the output to be and the way in which the two are linked together is through the use of circuits which have PICs programmed to do exactly what the customer wants them to do.

Think about it

1 Why is it important that Robert knows how to test electronic circuits?

2 What are the benefits to Robert of using PICs in his control systems?

3 What skills do you have that could help you carry out a job similar to Robert's?

Circuit soldering techniques

Getting started

There are two methods of soldering components to a circuit – surface mounting and soldering through the holes in a circuit board. Use the Internet to research the similarities and differences between the two different techniques.

Introduction

You have looked at how different components can be used and how you can build a system using the different blocks. You have thought about how you can design a system, but now it is time to actually start to make a circuit that will perform these tasks.

Techniques for soldering components

Constructing a circuit that will consistently work as expected relies on components being permanently joined to the circuit board. In the same way that we use nails to fix pieces of wood together, or weld plates of steel to make a permanent joint, we use soldering in electronics.

Soldering using multi-core, lead-free solder

To construct a successful circuit you need to make sure that your soldering is accurate. There are lots of factors that can have an impact on the quality of your soldering.

- Too much solder – this can leave a ball of solder on the component leads, but they are not connected to the circuit board, and leave a dry joint.
- Not enough solder – the component may be joined to the circuit board, but the contact could be poor and not let enough current through.
- Wrong type of soldering iron tip – tips are designed to be used on certain types of joint. Using the wrong one might not give you enough heat for the joint, or could be too big and melt another joint.
- Dirty soldering iron tip – the tip can get a carbon coating, so it should be kept clean with a damp sponge, and be tinned.

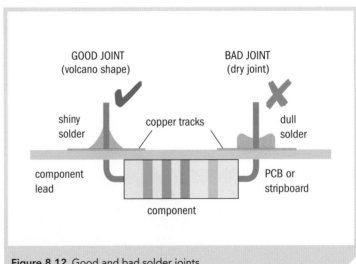

Figure 8.12 Good and bad solder joints

To get a good soldered joint you should use the following technique:

1 Place the tip of the soldering iron against the component lead and the circuit board for 3–4 seconds.

2 Place the solder on the joint between the component and the circuit board. You should not touch the iron with the solder.

3 Let the solder flow onto the circuit board and the component lead. Then take the solder away first, followed by the soldering iron. The joint is complete.

Tinning component legs and multi-strand wire using heat sinks and shunts

When you are working with a circuit board, the holes have a very small diameter of around 1.5 mm. To make it easier to get all of the strands of a multi-core wire through you can tin the exposed strands of wire by covering the exposed strands with solder. This joins them together and allows you to put them through a hole in a PCB much more easily. Some components can be damaged by heat, in which case you can clip a **heat sink** or shunt onto the lead you are soldering. This will absorb the heat from soldering and prevent damage to the component.

Using IC sockets, heat shrink sleeving and insulation tape

In previous sections you have looked at both 555 timer chips and PICs. These are very sensitive – soldering them directly to a circuit board could easily damage the tiny components inside them. It would be almost impossible to change the IC if there was a fault. To overcome this problem you can use a socket which is soldered onto the board. The chip is then placed into the socket. These are sometimes called DIL sockets.

One of the main reasons a circuit will not work is because there is a short circuit – usually caused by component leads touching one another. You can overcome this by using PVC tape called insulation tape. This works in exactly the same way as sticky tape, and you can cut small pieces off and wrap them around exposed component leads. This is usually done after a circuit is made.

Another way to try to prevent short circuits is to use heat shrink sleeving, which is passed over component leads and wires. Once the components are soldered into place, the sleeve can be heated up and it shrinks around the lead, preventing the short circuit.

Key terms

Heat sink – a piece of equipment used to absorb heat when soldering a circuit in order to protect sensitive components.

Discussion

What are the likely problems you could encounter when soldering components onto a piece of stripboard?

Just checking

1 What is the effect of not having enough solder on a joint?

2 Why should you use heat shrink sleeving?

3 Why should you tin the ends of multi-core wire?

4 What is the advantage of using IC sockets?

Risk assessments

Getting started

Select one activity you do every day, for example, lighting a gas fire or riding a bicycle. Write down all of the possible hazards related to that activity. How do you decide whether or not to continue?

Introduction

From getting up in the morning, through to going back to bed at night, our days generally pass without incident. This is despite the fact that we face many hazards throughout the day, many of which could be fatal. We carry out risk assessments in our head every time we cross a road, use a knife to cut a loaf of bread or plug an electrical product into the mains supply.

Risks and control measures

Figure 8.13 shows the five stages of performing a risk assessment. By following these steps, you should be able to spot potential hazards and work out ways to prevent them.

Key terms

Hazard – something that could cause injury or harm.

Risk – the likelihood that there will be some harm done and the severity of the harm from a hazard.

Severity – how serious the harm or injury would be.

Likelihood – the chances of an injury or harm occurring.

1. Identify the hazards	What are the hazards associated with the task?
2. Decide who might be at harm and how they might be harmed	Who could be injured?
3. Evaluate the risks and decide on appropriate control measures	• Are precautions already taken or do you need to do more? • How likely are you to be hurt by the hazard? • How severe could the injury be?
4. Record the findings of the assessment and how it is to be implemented	• The risk assessment should be recorded so it can be used by others. • If it is recorded electronically it is easy to update.
5. Review the assessment and make revisions if necessary	It is a good idea to review risk assessments at the end of an activity to evaluate how successful it has been and decide whether you should change anything in the future.

Figure 8.13 Stages of a risk assessment and factors to consider at each stage

Health and Safety Executive (HSE)

The Health and Safety Executive (HSE) provide guidance for completing risk assessments on their website (visit Pearson hotlinks to access this site). They also publish a downloadable model risk assessment. Their booklet 'Five Steps to Risk Assessment' includes very good guidance about how to carry out a risk assessment.

Just checking

1 What are the five stages of a risk assessment?

2 What is a hazard?

3 What are the likely hazards from soldering a circuit?

4 What control methods should be used when soldering?

Assessment activity 8.3   Carrying out a risk assessment   2C.P4 | 2C.M3 | 2C.D3 | 2C.P5 | 2C.M4

a. There are many potential hazards associated with constructing a PCB. Identify the range of hazards associated with soldering components onto a PCB. Explain the risks involved when soldering a circuit, and explain appropriate control methods to ensure work is completed safely. (**2C.P4, 2C.M3**)

b. Use the Internet to research the different stages of production for manufacturing a printed circuit board. For each of the stages, identify the hazards and associated risks. Suggest control measures and state who is likely to be at risk. Use this information to produce a full risk assessment for producing an electronic circuit using a printed circuit board. (**2C.D3**)

c. There are three main methods of producing circuit boards. Choose one and explain the main features of circuit design using your chosen method and how you construct a circuit using this type of circuit board. (**2C.P5**)

d. There are advantages and disadvantages of using each type of circuit board. Produce a short presentation to compare the advantages and disadvantages of producing a circuit using stripboard rather than using a PCB. (**2C.M4**)

Tips

- Always include as much information as possible in your risk assessments and control measures – just 'PPE' is not good enough, you should name specific items, such as safety glasses.
- To meet the distinction criteria, you will need to consider the **severity** and **likelihood** of the risks, in addition to meeting all the criteria for achieving a pass and merit.

Testing electronic circuits

Getting started

A multimeter can be used for a range of different tasks when checking circuits. Use the Internet to find an example of a mid-range multimeter. List all its different functions, including the range of readings that can be taken.

Introduction

It is annoying when you open a new gadget, put new batteries in and it doesn't work! There are many reasons why this could happen, but it is most likely that there is a fault with the circuit board. This can be an issue for all types of circuit, from the most basic through to those found on high-tech devices. Quality checks need to be carried out to make sure all engineered products work as they should.

Testing and evaluating electronic circuits

There are many different pieces of test equipment which can be used to check for any faults in an electronic circuit.

- Multimeter – can be analogue or digital and is capable of taking many different readings.
- Voltmeter – used for checking voltage across components.
- Ohmmeter – used to check continuity in wires, and identify breaks or bridges in connections.
- Ammeter – used to measure the current in the circuit.
- A logic probe – used to test signals from PICs and other ICs. Unlike the other pieces of test equipment they have two leads and a probe. The red lead is clipped to the positive power supply to the circuit, and the black to the ground. The probe is then touched onto the output connections of components such as transistors and PICs to make sure they are working correctly.

Table 8.5 Test equipment

	Resistance	Current	Voltage
Equipment	• Ohmmeter • Multimeter	• Ammeter • Multimeter	• Voltmeter • Multimeter
Method	Where possible, remove the component to stop false readings from other components.	The meter should be connected in series in the circuit.	The meter is connected in parallel around the component to be tested.

Just checking

1 Which piece of testing equipment should be used for testing outputs from ICs?

2 What is an ammeter used for?

3 Why should components be removed from a circuit to check the resistance?

4 Which type of test should be done in parallel around the component to be tested?

Assessment activity 8.4   Testing electronic circuits   2D.P6 | 2D.M5 | 2D.D4 | 2D.P7

Your teacher/tutor will give you a number of circuits to test. Some of them will have faults, which you will need to find. You may need to use a range of different pieces of test equipment to do this.

You will need to produce a range of different types of evidence for this activity, including:

a. annotated photographs of you testing the voltage levels at different points in the circuit (**2D.P6**)

b. a table of results of the voltage readings at the different points in the circuit (**2D.P6**)

c. a short report which describes the results of the measurements you have taken to test if the circuit performs as you expected it to and an evaluation of the circuit's performance (**2D.M5**, **2D.D4**)

d. a short report describing the faults which you found in circuits and how you identified them (**2D.P7**)

e. an observation record that supports all of the practical tests you performed.

You should record your results in a table, stating readings from the various different tests.

Tip

When testing your circuits it is important to record the results of all the different tests. For example, you can use Ohm's Law to give you the expected current through a resistor, then test the actual current using an ammeter. You need to select test equipment carefully – it must be appropriate for the component being tested or the fault that is being identified.

Introduction

Engineers work with many types of information. For example, when manufacturing an engineered product, a technician will need information about the quantity they should be producing, the materials that will be required, and their precise dimensions. They will also need to know how the parts should be assembled and how the surfaces of the product need to be finished off.

This information can be presented in many different ways; for example, engineers use technical drawings, sketches, circuit diagrams, job sheets and manuals. It is important that the instructions are produced in a clear and standardised way. If mistakes are made these can be expensive.

In this unit you will learn how to interpret drawings and other documentation and how to make effective use of the information when carrying out engineering activities.

Assessment: This unit will be assessed using a paper-based test lasting one hour.

Learning aims

After completing this unit you should:

A know how to interpret drawings and other documentation

B be able to use information from drawings and related documentation.

> I always enjoyed drawing and designing things, but it was only when I had a work placement with a local engineering company that I learned how drawings are used to provide accurate information for engineers. This information looked very confusing to me but the engineers explained what all the symbols and numbers meant and now I use this information all the time.
>
> Eduardo, *16-year-old engineering trainee*

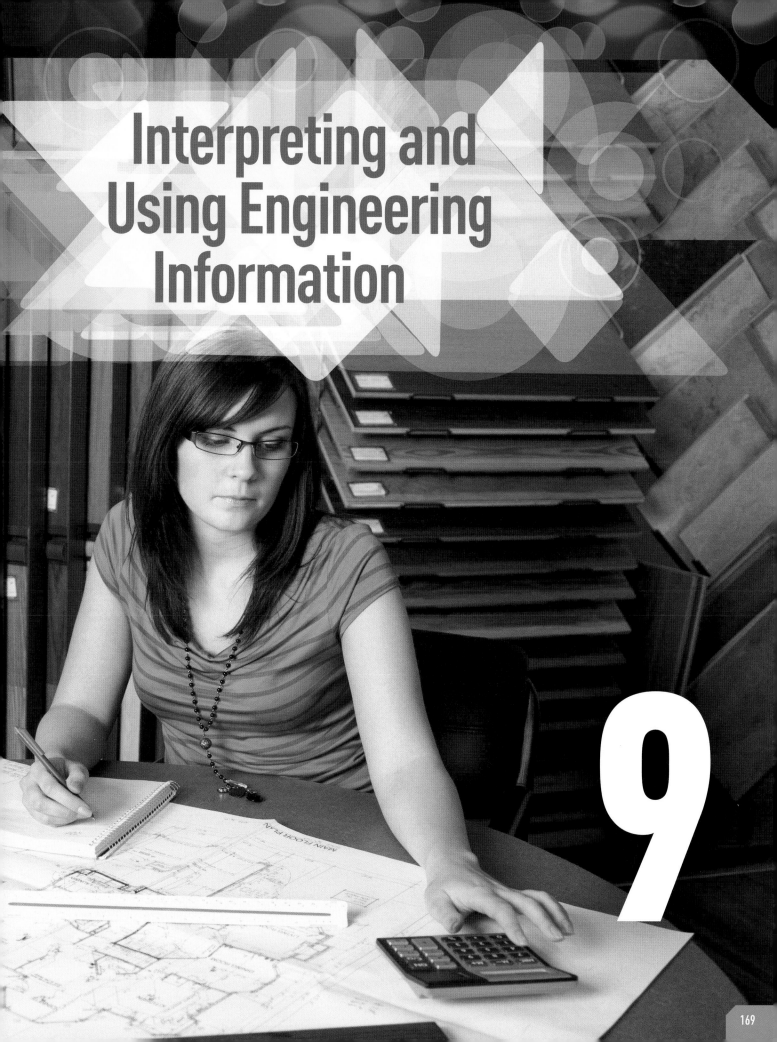

Interpreting and Using Engineering Information

9

Interpreting engineering drawings

Key terms

CAD (computer-aided design) system – computer software that can be used to produce engineering drawings during the design process.

Component – a single part that is sometimes used by itself but is usually assembled with other parts. Fasteners such as nuts and bolts are components, as are complex engineered products such as gears, integrated circuits or filter elements.

Introduction

Working drawings are used to provide engineers with the information they need to manufacture an engineered product. They can be produced by hand using paper and pencil, or in a more sophisticated way with a **computer-aided drawing (CAD) system**. Different types of working drawings are used by engineers depending on the information they require.

Component drawings

A **component** drawing will give us all the information needed to manufacture a component, including:

1 material to be used
2 physical dimensions
3 surface finish
4 specific features such as thread sizes.

The key advantage of this type of drawing is that component sizes and features are easy to understand from the drawing (see Figure 9.1). Component drawings are mainly used in a workshop environment where individual parts are being produced. One of the disadvantages of a component drawing, however, is that it does not show us how parts fit together.

Figure 9.1 Example of a component drawing

Assembly drawings

Assembly drawings are used to show how a series of components are assembled together to form a finished product. They are used by engineers working on a production line or in a manufacturing cell so they can visualise the finished product and assemble it in the correct way (see Figure 9.2).

One disadvantage of an assembly drawing is that it often does not give a good idea of the size and shape of individual components within the assembly. Component drawings are used to show this information.

ITEM	DESCRIPTION	NO OFF
3	GIB-HEAD KEY	1
2	FLYWHEEL	1
1	SHAFT	1

DRAWN BY	DATE	TITLE	DRAWING NO	SCALE	PROJECTION
A N OTHER		ASSEMBLY DRAWING	AE 01	1 :1	

Figure 9.2 An assembly drawing is usually accompanied by a list of the components, called a parts list

There are three other types of assembly drawing:

- Sub-assembly drawings show how several components are assembled together, as part of a larger assembly.
- Fabrication assembly drawings are specific to structures made from sheet materials and show how the materials are joined together by welds, adhesives or mechanical fixings.
- Welding assembly drawings show how parts are joined together by welding.

Repair/modification drawings

These are used to show maintenance technicians how to make a repair or modification to a given component or assembly. Only details of the repair/modification are required as the drawing showing the original part and/or assembly would already have been created.

Installation drawings

These drawings show the overall dimensions of a product and how to install it in its final location. For example, a plumber would use an installation drawing when fitting a boiler; a structural engineer would use an installation drawing when constructing a steel frame for a building.

Wiring/circuit diagrams

Circuit diagrams are used to show how components are connected. A wiring diagram is a specific type of circuit diagram used in electrical systems. These diagrams are useful when engineers are trying to identify and repair faults in electrical and fluid power systems. One disadvantage is that they are often difficult to interpret, because they give no indication of the size and shape of the parts being investigated.

Orthographic projection

When you need to show an object in detail it is common to use an **orthographic projection** technique. This involves showing a three-dimensional object in a two-dimensional way, from different viewpoints. Each system starts with the front view – this is known as the front elevation.

There are two common types of projection, as shown in Figures 9.3 and 9.4.

Figure 9.3 First angle orthographic projection system

Figure 9.4 Third angle orthographic projection system

Orthographic projection is widely used by engineers to represent and manufacture components. The main disadvantage of using this system is that it is not always clear what the final three-dimensional product will look like.

Isometric and oblique drawings

Isometric and oblique drawings are both ways of representing an object in three dimensions (3D), as shown in Figure 9.5. This allows you to get a good idea of the shape of the object you are looking at.

- An **isometric** view is a 2D drawing of a 3D object constructed using lines on a three-axis system. This can be done using special paper, or by using a CAD system. Lines are drawn to scale, with vertical lines and lines at an angle of 30° to the horizontal.

- An **oblique** view shows the front view of an object, drawn using horizontal and vertical lines at the correct scale. Additional parallel lines are added to indicate a 3D view, usually at 45°. Unlike in an isometric drawing, these additional lines are not drawn to scale, producing a less realistic view of the 3D object than an isometric drawing.

Key terms

Isometric projection – a 3D representation of a 2D object.

Oblique projection – a method of taking a 2D view of an object and adding lines to give a 3D impression of the object.

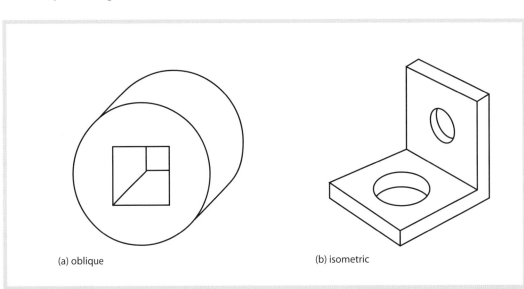

(a) oblique   (b) isometric

Figure 9.5 Examples of a view in (a) oblique and (b) isometric

Drawing standards

British Standards (BS) are technical documents and specifications, which show engineers how to present engineering drawings. These include details such as how to use first and third angle projection systems, how to present dimensions and text on drawings, what size paper you should use, what line types are used, what symbols should be used to represent electrical, pneumatic and hydraulic components, and so on. Engineering drawings are often very complex technical documents and without the use of these standards it would be very difficult for engineers to understand what information is being represented.

Did you know?

BS is short for British Standards.

ISO means International Organization for Standardization.

ANSI is short for American National Standards Institute.

Company standardised layouts

When companies produce drawings it is important that all the people within the organisation can understand the information being presented. Individual companies will often use a standard template for their technical drawings to ensure key information is always given in the same place.

Title block

This is a standard feature for all templates, holding information such as the name and scale of the drawing and the date is was produced or modified. Sometimes a title block is company-specific, with information such as the details of the people who have checked and approved the drawing, the division or department of the company that created the drawing, the weight, material, testing required, etc.

Company logo

Engineering drawings are often shared with other organisations, contractors and customers. By including the company logo, as well as the website address and phone number, the company has the opportunity to promote itself to any person who looks at the drawing.

Assessment activity 9.1

1 Figure 9.6 shows a working drawing of a part used in a racing bicycle. Which of the three sectional lines, shown on the plan view, has been used to create the sectional elevation? [1]

  a X-X   b Y-Y   c Z-Z

2 Figure 9.7 shows an aerospace component manufactured by Freeair Limited. Produce a three-view representation of the part using first angle projection. [3]

Plan view   Sectional elevation

Figure 9.6 A part used in a racing bicycle

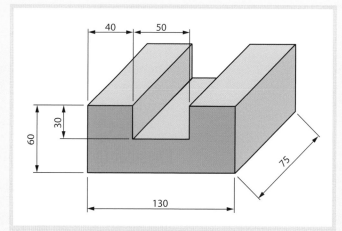

Figure 9.7 An aerospace component

Graphical representations

Introduction

Engineers communicate through the use of a range of graphical techniques. In this section we will explore five different types of graphical representation.

Sketches

These are used as a relatively quick way to communicate information about a component or assembly, particularly if accompanied by notes. They do not contain all the features of a full working drawing. They are often used to manufacture or modify a component quickly, when a part is urgently required.

Schematic diagrams

A schematic diagram is a visual representation of a system, using symbols rather than realistic representations. Colour is often used to allow quick and easy identification. The London Underground map is a good example of a schematic diagram.

Flow charts

A flow chart shows how several individual actions are linked (see Figure 9.8). For example, a flow chart could be used to show the steps required to download and install an application or piece of software from the Internet. Flow charts use standard symbols: the most common ones are an oblong for start/finish, a rectangle for an action/event, and a diamond for a yes/no decision.

Physical layout diagrams

Another name for this is a plan. For example, a physical layout diagram might be produced to show the arrangement of machines in a workshop or the way that a network of heating or ventilation might be arranged around a building (see Figure 9.9).

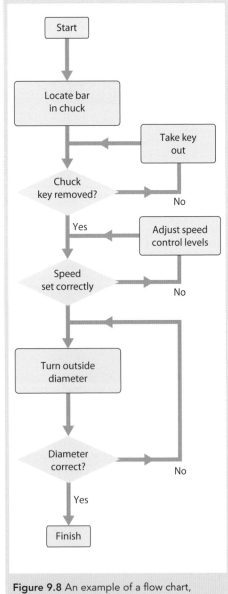

Figure 9.8 An example of a flow chart, for turning a diameter on a lathe

Figure 9.9 A physical layout drawing of a piping arrangement

Illustrations from manufacturers' manuals

These are printed or electronic (e.g. online) documents that contain exploded diagrams and images of products. A designer will refer to this type of manual when deciding which component or part to use for a particular situation. For example, when selecting a hydraulic pump for a given task, the tables of data in a manufacturer's manual help you decide the capacity, flow rate and pressure characteristics. A diagram is often provided to allow the purchaser to understand how connections can be made, what the overall sizes are and how the pump can be fitted/secured.

Activity 9.1   Researching graphical representations

Using the Internet or material provided by your tutor, research examples of:

a flow charts

b physical layout diagrams

c illustrations from manufacturers' manuals.

For each example you identify, explain the reason for the form of graphical representation used.

Assessment activity 9.2

1 Look back at Figure 9.8. The diamond shape is a:

  a Yes/No decision   c Action symbol

  b Start/stop decision   d Event symbol   [1]

2 Look back again at Figure 9.8. The oblong shape is a:

  a Yes/No decision   c Action symbol

  b Start/stop decision   d Event symbol   [1]

3 Explain one advantage of a flow diagram. [2]

Interpreting drawing information

Introduction

Working drawings contain a great deal of important information for engineers. For example, they include information about dimensions which allow us to produce components at the correct size. In this section we will look at how information in engineering drawings is interpreted and used.

Materials or components

Engineering parts are often referred to as being male or female. This generally refers to threaded components. For example, a bolt would have an external thread (a thread on the outside), which is known as a 'male' part. The bolt is often assembled to a nut – this is known as a 'female' part because it has an internal thread (a thread on the inside).

Working drawings show us how these parts are connected. Hydraulic components are often connected with male and female threaded components to prevent fluid escaping and help the flow of fluid within the circuit. Circuit diagrams often indicate the pressure that these parts will need to withstand and the flow rate of fluids travelling through them. In a similar way an electrical/electronic circuit diagram often shows the current or voltage that components should be able to cope with; it is important for engineers to consider this when using these circuits.

Dimensional detail

Engineering drawings include information about the dimensions of a feature or fit so that the final product is produced at the required size. Dimensions always indicate the true size of an object, even if the drawing is not at full size – in other words, drawn to scale. Dimensions are shown just once for each part; they are not repeated. Engineers use different types of line when presenting this information on a drawing (see Figure 9.10):

- Dimension line – used to indicate size; there should be a small arrow (or occasionally a tick mark) at each end.
- Extension line – a line that projects from the edge of the component; there should be a small gap between the line and the part.
- Leader line – a line that points to a feature of the part; there should be an arrow on the end of this line.

Dimensioning rules

- Shorter lines should be placed closer to the object to prevent dimension lines crossing.
- Extension lines should always have the same size gap between the start of the line and the object.
- Dimensions should always appear away from the object, not on top of it.
- Dimensions should be grouped together wherever possible.
- Hidden lines should not be dimensioned.
- Horizontal dimension lines feature the dimension text above the line.
- Vertical dimensions have the text on the left-hand side of the dimension line and in line with it – as though the horizontal dimension and text have been rotated together.

Figure 9.10 Dimensioning examples including radii, diameters, centres, tolerances, surface texture, leader lines and text

Linear tolerances

It is often very expensive to make parts to a very high degree of accuracy so we have to decide whether this expense is necessary. All sizes have **tolerances** applied: this is how we determine the accuracy of a measurement. Tolerance is expressed in a number of ways; however, there are two very common methods:

- 100 ± 10 mm – this means the size is required to be 100 mm but can be bigger by up to 10 mm or smaller by up to 10 mm.
- $\frac{110}{90}$ mm – this means that the size must fall between a minimum of 90 mm and a maximum of 110 mm.

�Manufacturing/production detail

Manufacturing or production details help engineers understand any specific requirements a part or assembly might have; these details are often indicated by notes or annotations on drawings. For example, a metal part might need to be very hard: a note on the drawing would indicate the heat treatment method required to achieve this. An assembly diagram might include a note specifying how adhesive should be applied to components before assembly. A fabrication drawing might note the specific **torque** required when assembling threaded components (or when reassembling components after making repairs or modifications).

◤ Symbols and abbreviations

To save time and space on a drawing we often shorten words, giving an abbreviation instead, or use recognised symbols.

Electrical/electronic

Circuit diagrams are used by engineers to show how a range of components are put together to build a circuit. Standard symbols (see Figure 11.4 on page 242 for some of the more common ones) are used to allow a quick and easy representation of the parts required.

Circuit diagrams will have values written next to many of the components to indicate the required size or capacity.

Mechanical components

Drawings used by mechanical engineers often use standard conventions to allow features to be drawn quickly and consistently. But how can you determine, for example, whether a bolt has a hexagon head (to allow a spanner to secure it) or whether it should be a cap head bolt (requiring the use of a hexagon head key)? Recognising different features from engineering drawings is a very important requirement for all engineers.

- Nuts – used to secure threaded components; a variety of types are available, such as the standard nut, square nut and locking nut.
- Bolts – used to connect and secure components, bolts are used with nuts and take different forms, such as the hexagon head bolt, cap head bolt and coach/carriage bolt.
- Screws – used to secure components, screws are threaded and locate into threaded holes in parts; different designs include the countersunk head screw, cheese head screw and cap head screw.
- Springs – used to retain and control movement; coiled steel wire is often used, although springs can be made from rubber or other metals; they can be used in compression and/or tension.
- Pins – another way to secure components, pins are usually inserted through a hole in a larger component such as a bolt; typical examples include the split pin, cotter pin and dowel pin.
- Clips – a way of securing parts that may need to be removed later; spring pressure is exerted to secure them in a groove; typical examples include internal and external circlips.
- Keys – a key is a small wedge or rectangle of metal that is placed in a key way and locks into another groove, allowing two parts to rotate together; if one of the parts were to stop rotating the key might break – but this would prevent more serious damage to the assembly.
- Drive mechanisms – although a key is often used to allow drive to be transferred between two components, other methods include splines, serrations and couplings.

Weld symbols

Weld symbols, as shown in Table 9.1, are used on drawings to indicate the type and size of weld being applied to a particular assembly or feature.

Table 9.1 BS welding symbols and descriptions

Appearance of weld	Symbol	Description
	‖	Square butt
	V	Single v butt
	V	Single bevel butt
	⌣	Backing run
	◺	Fillet
	⊓	Plug
	◯	Spot

Linear and geometrical tolerances

We have explored the use of **linear tolerances** in the section on dimensions, above. **Geometrical tolerances** are different because they describe the shape or geometry of a part. British standard symbols are used to indicate when a particular geometrical tolerance is required, as shown in Figure 9.11.

Abbreviations

Engineering drawings often have a language all of their own – designers use a special kind of shorthand to abbreviate well-known expressions. Many of these are shown in Table 9.2.

Line types

Engineers use different types of line in drawings. There is a standard for this so that all engineers can understand what is meant by each line. Table 9.3 shows some of the different types of lines and how to interpret them.

Figure 9.11 Geometrical tolerance symbols and descriptions

Symbol	Description	Symbol	Description
—	Straightness	⊕	Position
▱	Flatness	⌖	Orientation of Position
○	Circularity	◎	Concentricity
⌭	Cylindricity	=	Symmetry
⌒	Profile of Line	//	Parallelism
⌓	Orientation of Profile	⊥	Perpendicity
⌓	Profile of Surface	∠	Angularity
⌔	Orientation of any Profile Surface	↗	Run-out
		⌰	Total Run-out

Table 9.3 Line types used in engineering drawing

Type of line	Appearance	Where used
▬▬▬▬▬	Continuous thick line	Visible outlines and edges
————	Continuous thin line	Dimension and extension lines
– – – – –	Dashed thin lines	Hidden outlines and edges
—·—·—·—	Chain thin lines	Centre lines
⌐_	Chain thin lines thick at the edges and changes of direction	Section cutting planes

Activity 9.2 — Measuring a component

With a partner, use a ruler to measure a component. How long is it? How close do you think you can measure to? Write down your answer and suggest how accurate you think you are. What measuring tool would make your answer more accurate?

Assessment activity 9.3

1 A component has the dimension 15 mm ± 0.2.
   a What is the maximum size of the component? [1]
   b What is the minimum size of the component? [1]
2 An engineering drawing uses the symbol shown in Figure 9.12. Which of the following does the symbol represent? [1]

   Figure 9.12

   a roundness   b concentricity   c parallelism   d squareness

3 Explain why it is often difficult to see where spot welds have been used on assembled components. [2]

Table 9.2 Abbreviations used in engineering drawing

CSK	countersink
CBORE	counterbore
CHAM	chamfer
R	radius
RAD	radius
Ø	diameter
DIA	diameter
CL	centreline
INT	internal
EXT	external
PCD	pitch circle diameter

Interpreting tasks and other information

Introduction

Suppose you are working in industry as a technician and at the start of each week you are given a schedule of jobs to carry out. These are tasks which need to be completed to an agreed standard. You may well have all the drawings and documentation you need, but there can be other specialised information that you will need to refer to.

Manufacturing or process operations

Engineers involved in manufacturing or processing often follow specific instructions.

Product manufacture or modification

Engineers often work closely with suppliers of parts or components to ensure that the application being considered meets with the supplier's recommendations and specifications.

Equipment installation or repair

Manufacturers provide information outlining how equipment should be installed and giving details on maintenance and repair, including the details of spare parts.

System or service planning

Engineers also use reference manuals or instructions for service or system planning. For example, when a technician is preparing to service a car, they will refer to the service manual for that vehicle to establish the replacement parts required at that service interval.

Tasks

When carrying out specific engineering tasks, you will need to refer to very specific information to ensure they are carried out to agreed standards.

Electronic component pin configuration specifications

When assembling any kind of circuit, it is important that all components are connected correctly. Electronic circuits often contain components, such as integrated circuits, which have multiple pins. Published specifications are used to indicate the function of each pin, allowing you to design a circuit using some or all of these appropriately.

Standard reference charts for limits and fits

Parts that fit together have varying degrees of fit. There are generally three types of fits used in engineering, depending on how a round object (shaft) fits through a hole.

- Clearance fit – for example, when a shaft is smaller than a hole so it can be put together and taken apart easily (often used for nuts and bolts).
- Interference fit – where a shaft is bigger than a hole and often requires some deformation to allow the parts to be assembled together, producing a very tight fit (often used for assembling bearings on to drive shafts).
- Transition – a compromise between clearance and interference.

BS 4500 is the UK standard covering limits (tolerances) and fits. Engineers refer to its reference chart when specifying the dimensions for parts that need to fit together.

Tapping drill reference charts

Lots of components have holes that are screw-threaded so that fixing bolts can be screwed into them. Engineers use taps to produce an internal thread in a component. It is very important to drill the correct diameter hole before cutting the thread. If the hole is too small, the threading tool will jam up and snap. If the hole is too big, the thread will be weak, and may strip out. By referring to a standard reference chart you can determine the correct size drill for the thread being produced.

Bend allowances

Before bending a piece of sheet metal it has to be marked out and extra length added – this is called the bend allowance, and will depend on the metal thickness, bend radius and angle of the bend. Engineers use tables/charts to ensure that the initial size of the material is correct, so that the finished component will be the required size.

Material specifications

Engineers often need to know how a material may behave and what properties it has. For example, a spring needs to be elastic in order to deform easily and return to its original position, but you would not want a hammerhead to deform easily in use. Using material specifications allows us to judge the properties of materials and select the appropriate material for the particular application.

Manufacturers' data for the use of welding rods/bonding/finishing materials

Engineers involved in fabrication techniques often need to refer to manufacturers' manuals, which list the properties and performance characteristics of the products being considered. These manuals will indicate how the products will behave in terms of their performance and their environmental characteristics. For example, welding rods come in different sizes and compositions for different applications.

Data sheets and books

Data sheets and reference books are often used in engineering.

- Resistor colour codes – Resistors have colour coded bands that allow engineers to determine their values. (see page 148).
- Data sheets for components – Manufacturers will often supply standard data sheets for mass-produced products such as resistors, fuses, nuts, bolts, oils and so on.
- Zeus charts – Many engineers working in mechanical workshops will have a small pocket book containing charts that indicate standard drill sizes and decimal equivalents, tapping drills and clearances for metric and imperial threads, hardness comparisons, jig boring co-ordinates for equally spaced holes, allowances for sheet metal bending and so on. Zeus books contain all these charts in one convenient reference book.
- Machinery handbook – A reference book that is used by design engineers, toolmakers and workshop technicians. As well as containing the sort of reference information contained with the Zeus book, it has chapters on mathematics, mechanics, materials and so on.

> **? Did you know?**
>
> A car body panel is usually formed from a thin sheet of metal; it gains its strength and shape from being bent into shape. The size of the sheet metal changes as the overall shape of the sheet reduces during this forming process.

> **Link**
>
> For more information about material properties, see *Unit 5 Engineering Materials*.

Interpreting health and safety information

Getting started

With a partner, produce sketches or take photos of the health and safety signage within your school/college/workplace. You should ensure that you have permission and have been briefed on health and safety before carrying out this activity. Using the photographs/sketches, put the signs into categories based on their shape and colour. See if you can decide what each sign represents.

Key terms

Mandatory – an action that must be taken.

Did you know?

HSE is short for the Health and Safety Executive. This is a government body in the UK that is responsible for ensuring that employers, employees and others meet their legal obligations to prevent death, injuries or ill health in the workplace.

Introduction

Health and safety is a very important consideration for engineers as there are many hazards associated with engineering activities. When you enter an engineering workshop you will see signs on the machinery and displayed on the walls and notice boards. Many of these will refer to health and safety and you should ensure both that you understand what these signs mean and that you follow their requirements. These signs are presented in a specific way, with different shapes and colours (based on a standard used across Europe) indicating the category of the sign. The signs should be the same wherever they are used.

Mandatory signs

Mandatory means you have to do something, so when you see a mandatory sign you should ensure that you are complying with the given requirement. A mandatory sign is always displayed as a white picture on a blue background, as shown in Figure 9.13. Mandatory signs are used to indicate the following:

- Eye protection – Safety glasses should be worn in any part of the workshop where this sign is displayed.

- Ear protection – Ear protection should be worn: the type of ear protection depends on the general level of background noise, the time that you are exposed to this noise and the noise level of specific loud noises, such as gunfire.

- Protective footwear – When you are working in an engineering workshop you will be expected to wear steel toecap boots to protect your toes against falling objects. These boots are also made of a special material that can withstand oil and chemical attack. In some workshops, such as foundries, more substantial safety boots are required specific to the activity you are engaged in.

- Use of guard – The picture on these signs varies depending on the type of guard, which can be fixed or adjustable. Guards can also be interlocked, meaning the machine cannot be operated without the guard being in place. You should not rely on this, however – the sign means you must check before using the machine or equipment.

- Protective gloves – Where this sign is displayed, protective gloves must be worn to protect hands from sharp edges or when handling chemicals.

- Face protection – Although goggles or safety glasses can be worn to protect the eyes, a full face mask should be used where there may be a risk of sparks or liquid splashes to protect all of the face from danger.

- Switch off instructions – This type of sign is posted as a reminder to operators that a machine must be switched off when not in use.

Figure 9.13 A mandatory sign

Safe condition signs

Safe condition signs are rectangular, with white graphics on a green background, as shown in Figure 9.14. They are presented in green because they are signs you should look for in order to prevent danger or take action to stay safe.

- Emergency exit – A sign that indicates the location of an exit point, such as a door or window, that should be used only in an emergency and should be kept closed and clear for this purpose.
- Fire exit – A sign that indicates where to exit a room or building in case of danger/fire.
- First aid station – A sign that indicates the location of first aid equipment or first aid kit.
- First aid – A sign that indicates first aid information and equipment, such as who the first aid personnel are, where the first aid box is located and so on.
- Emergency eye wash – A sign that indicates the location of eye wash to assist in flushing foreign objects from people's eyes.
- Emergency telephone – A sign that indicates the location of an emergency telephone.
- Assembly point – A sign that indicates the point or place where people should gather in case of an emergency such as a fire evacuation.

Figure 9.14 A safe condition sign

Warning signs

Warning signs indicate that there is a potentially dangerous hazard in the vicinity. Signs are triangular with black graphics on a yellow background, as shown in Figure 9.15.

- Danger of death – A sign that indicates a hazard that could be deadly; often seen on electricity pylons, for example.
- Caution – A sign that indicates care should be taken; an exclamation point is used with a specific indication of what hazard should be considered.
- Caution trip hazard – A sign that indicates a tripping hazard such as steps or trailing leads.
- Slippery surfaces – A sign that indicates that a surface could cause slipping; often seen when cleaning operations are taking place.
- Highly flammable – A sign that indicates that material could easily catch fire; this sign is often seen where petrol is used or stored.
- High voltage – A sign that indicates an electrical source that uses or transmits high-voltage electricity.
- Biohazard – A sign that indicates that biological substances that can cause harm are nearby. These signs are typically used in health care environments where viruses and bacteria are present.
- Irritant – A sign that indicates a substance that may cause itching or irritation if you come into contact with it.
- Harmful – A sign that indicates the presence of a harmful substance; usually a note indicates the precise nature of the potential hazard.

Key terms

Safe condition – a sign that indicates a safety action.

Warning signs – signs that reminds people of dangers in the area.

- Poison – A sign that indicates the presence of a poisonous substance; often seen on vehicles transporting dangerous chemicals.
- Risk of explosion – A sign that indicates a volatile gas or liquid that can explode if not carefully contained and controlled.

Figure 9.15 Standard health and safety signs

Assessment activity 9.4

1 What kind of sign features a white graphic on a blue background? [1]

  a Mandatory   c Warning

  b Safety   d Emergency

2 Which of the following is a safe condition sign? [1]

  a Poison   c Biohazard

  b Emergency stop   d High voltage

3 What shape and colour are warning signs? [2]

WorkSpace

▶ Frank Jones

Technical illustrator

I work in a general purpose workshop where we manufacture parts for a range of products, from agricultural machinery to parts for the oil industry. Because we have constant variety in our jobs, it never gets boring. We have to use different sources of information all the time. This means we have many charts, reference books and tables in the office as well as working from engineering drawings. Sometimes we have to take things apart to repair them. Exploded drawings help here, although we have to use assembly drawings as well.

Because of the variety of jobs we are involved in, we are all multi-skilled; this means we use all the machines in the workshop, although obviously some are used more than others. Fortunately there are safety signs everywhere reminding us of the dangers and safety precautions for each machine. 'Safety first' is our motto.

Think about it

1 What are the benefits to Frank of using charts and tables?
2 What sort of data do you think Frank uses an engineering drawing for?
3 Why do you think there need to be safety signs everywhere in the workshop?

Using work output and production documentation

Introduction

Engineering tasks will usually require expert knowledge on the part of the person carrying them out. An expert will often refer to information sources, because it can be quite difficult to hold all the information they need in their head.

In order to ensure that operations are being carried out effectively in working environments (for example, a brewery or a chemical works), it is important that information related to manufacturing, testing and maintenance is referred to and adhered to.

Work output documentation

Manufacturing documentation

When manufacturing a component, it is important that standard operating procedures (SOPs), assembly instructions, machine settings and so on are referred to regularly. This information is often displayed on machines or posters and can also be found on engineering drawings, in guidance documents, on visual display boards and so on.

Process documentation

When engineers are undertaking complex processes, they use a range of different drawings and design documents to ensure these are carried out correctly. Typical examples of the documentation required might include:

- block flow diagrams
- process flow diagrams
- piping and instrumentation diagrams
- specifications.

Maintenance planning

Engineers involved in carrying out the maintenance of plant and equipment will also need to refer to documentation. For example, if you had to maintain a complex nuclear or chemical processing plant, it would be important to refer to documentation to ensure you sequence and control the shutting down and opening up of the valves and pumps in the correct way.

Production documentation

When an engineer requires a task to be carried out – whether it is a maintenance operation, an engineering operation or a workshop operation – they often complete a **job card** (see Figure 9.16). A job card can indicate the number of people required to carry out the task, the area where the task is carried out, what tools are required and so on.

If the job is a test of some kind – for example, checking the performance of a component or measuring the parameters of a process – a **test report** is completed.

If the check being made is a quality check, such as testing a car before it rolls off the production line, then quality control information is used and **quality control documents** are completed.

Works Order No:			
Part no: **Description:**		**Sales order no:**	
Customer name:		**Customer standards apply:**	
Customer acc no:		**Certificate of conformity required:**	
Customer ref:		**Check issue:**	
Quantity:		**Check drawing:**	
Required by:			
Scheduled for:		**Issued by:**	
Scheduled completion:		**Signature:**	

Materials:
Req qty   Item code   Product description

Mat spec   Issued qty   Batch no   Initials

Figure 9.16 An engineering job card

Assessment activity 9.5

1 What does SOP stand for? [1]

  a Standard operating procedure

  b Safety operating process

  c Standard opening procedure

  d Safe orientation process

2 Which of the following is used when a maintenance activity is required on a production line? [1]

  a Quality control documentation

  b Job card

  c Test report

3 Explain how quality control documentation is used in a production environment. [2]

Using related documentation

Getting started

Place the following in what you consider to be the correct sequence for the production of a machined component:

- Quality control check.
- Select the work piece.
- Clamp the work piece.
- Select the tool.
- Clamp the tool.
- Switch the machine off.
- Remove the workpiece.
- Switch on the machine.
- Carry out the machining operation.

Introduction

In cases where an individual part is to be produced, such as a part for a helicopter rotor assembly or a circuit for the navigation system on a submarine, it is unlikely that documentation similar to that used in mass production would be used. This is because a one-off or small-volume production requires something less complex than assembly instructions or a standard operating procedure.

Working instructions

Working instructions are often used to show how a part might be manufactured, repaired or serviced. This can take the form of a job card or operation sheet showing the individual steps one by one.

When this involves fabricated structures, weld procedure documents describe the preparation and welding procedures required.

Similarly, repair and maintenance often require reference to manufacturers' manuals to ensure the correct assembly, testing and installation sequence is followed.

Production plans

When a component is being manufactured, typically in an engineering workshop, a production plan is often used to ensure that a product is manufactured correctly.

This breaks the process down into a series of operations, with a description for each one, and includes the following types of information to aid the operator:

- feed/speeds for machines
- the required materials and components
- the required tools and equipment
- the required quality control checks
- timings for each operation.

Schedule for manufacture

When large-scale projects are undertaken, a complex plan is often required to ensure that all parts of the project link to each other in the correct sequence.

Gantt charts

Planning documents often indicate the sequence of operations graphically using a Gantt chart, as shown in Figure 9.17.

A Gantt chart breaks the whole project down into individual activities and gives times for each of these activities and an indication of which activities are dependent on others. For example, if you were building a house you could not build the walls until the foundations were complete, but the driveway could be prepared before the roof was put on.

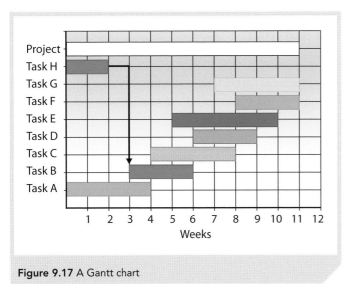

Figure 9.17 A Gantt chart

The Gantt chart shows important dates/times as milestones.

Network diagram

Another way of presenting key events or milestones along with project activities is to use a project network diagram (see Figure 9.18).

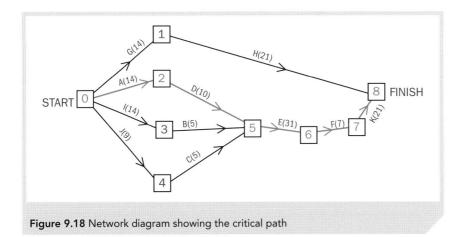

Figure 9.18 Network diagram showing the critical path

To construct a network diagram the following steps should be followed:

- Determine each activity.
- Indicate the sequence of the chosen activities.
- Draw the diagram.
- Suggest the time needed to complete each activity.
- Indicate the longest path through the network (the critical path).

The critical path allows you to determine when an activity can begin (earliest and latest start times) and end (earliest and latest finish times) without having an effect on the time for the whole project.

◤ Quality control information

When products are manufactured it is important that they are produced to meet customer requirements. Products are manufactured to meet a specification. Engineers should check their work against this specification and engineering drawings throughout the process.

Where an individual product or small batches of products are produced, each component or assembly can be checked for size, weight, capacity and so on.

In the case of volume production, it is not possible to check every product so sampling takes place instead as part of the quality control process. Reference tables and charts are referred to, to check that processes and products are within their requirements. The sampled sizes, weights and capacities of finished components are often recorded using statistical methods such as:

- Control charts – These show whether a manufacturing process is within its specified limits (see Figure 9.19). These charts can also be used to predict whether a process is going to stay within the desired limits over time.

Figure 9.19 A control chart

- Statistical process control – This is the use of data to ensure a process remains effective and within specified limits. Data is plotted against expected values to predict whether the part or component being considered can be manufactured to meet its specification over time.
- Pareto charts – A Pareto chart is a combination of a bar chart and a line graph and is used to highlight the most important issues to address in a manufacturing process or operation, with the highest bar representing the biggest problem (see Figure 9.20).

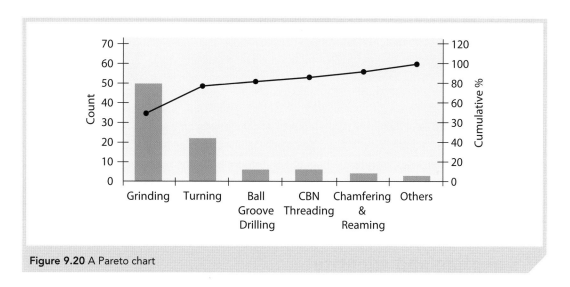

Figure 9.20 A Pareto chart

Assessment activity 9.6

1 When preparing to machine a part, the feed and speed to use would be indicated on a… [1]

   a production plan

   b engineering drawing

   c spares list

   d test report

2 A colour-coded graphical sequence of operations is known as …. [1]

   a an engineering drawing

   b a Gantt chart

   c a network diagram

   d a job card

3 Explain the importance of the critical path in project planning. [2]

Using drawing and document care and control

Key terms

Change note – when a change to a technical document or drawing is made a change note is often issued; this is an official note that is circulated to all key departments where it is signed to confirm that staff are aware of the changes and previous copies of the drawing/document have been discarded.

Introduction

Drawings and technical documents are used by organisations on a regular basis. They are often confidential because they include prototype designs or information that a company might not want their competitors to know about (for example, the ingredients of a soft drink). These documents have to be carefully controlled to ensure the correct version is used. If the wrong version is used this could cause problems in production or maintenance.

Location and security

Documents, drawings, manuals and other key information should be stored in ways that allow authorised people to access them easily. Engineering organisations often keep a document library. There is often a member of staff responsible for storing, archiving and lending this key information, and they will ensure that booking in/out procedures are followed and that the most up-to-date version of any drawing or document is maintained and others destroyed. Typical locations for drawings and documents include:

- ICT systems – These are typically password protected and are often accessible using an intranet, a web-based system that is accessible only within an organisation.
- Computer servers – Back-up copies of computer files are often stored in fireproof or remote locations. This is to ensure that, if a computer system were to fail due to a natural disaster, computer breakdown or computer virus, key files such as CAD drawings could be retrieved and reinstalled.
- Filing cabinets – These are usually lockable and allow key documents to be organised and filed in alphabetical or number order. They are often metal cabinets, which have some resistance to damage, flooding and fire.

Where issues are found with documents or drawings, whether through production of work pieces, production of prototypes or other issues, the use of **change notes** provides an audit trail to show the process of updating and records any changes made.

Drawings produced using computer software

Drawings produced on CAD systems and documents produced using computer software can have electronic master copies. Print-outs of these can be used in office and workshop environments, allowing any mark-ups to be made on the copies. Where hand-drawn drawings are used, the original is often produced using drawing film and this original should not be circulated – once again only paper copies should be used.

Physical handling

Cleanliness

Engineering drawings contain key information, such as dimensions, that need to be easy to see. A dirty fingerprint or drop of oil could easily cause a problem so cleanliness is important with drawing use.

Folding methods

Engineering drawings can often be very large and, just like with large maps, it is important to fold them in a certain way to make them easy to store and reuse. The trick is to fold them so that the drawing number is visible, making it easier to find the drawing you are looking for.

Damage and effects of graffiti

When working drawings become damaged or torn, new copies should be printed. However, if drawings have been amended or marked up in any way, these annotations should be reported as they may necessitate a change to the original drawing. These annotations and amendments are often called graffiti, as they are not authorised amendments.

Document control

Drawings and other documents often require amendments. This can be due to changes in production methods, changes in materials, customer requests and so on. Part of the title block for a drawing should always contain the version of the drawing. When a change is made, the date it took place is added, the issue number is updated and a confirmation signature (or initial) is added. This provides an audit trail, which can be used to back track to the original documentation if the change proves to be flawed.

Engineers use the following system, as shown in Figure 9.21:

- Version A, B, C, etc. in pre-production when designs are being developed.
- Version 1, 2, 3, etc. as the design is manufactured and changes occur.

It is very important that when a drawing change is made all previous version of the drawing are destroyed/archived and the current drawing is used by all departments in an organisation, as well as by suppliers and customers.

Annotations

Engineers use the following annotations on drawings to help guide users:

- Drawing one of two – A second drawing with further detail should be used in conjunction with this drawing.
- Part numbers – On assembly drawings the part numbers or drawing numbers of the parts being put together allows them to be easily located and ensures the correct parts are used.
- Pattern numbers – Patterns are templates used in processes such as casting and indicating them on drawings allows the correct tool or die to be located.

Reporting of loss/damage

As part of a document control system an organisation should have a procedure allowing you to report the loss of or damage to a drawing. Without an accurate drawing a design cannot be accurately reproduced. The organisation should have a master copy of each drawing, which is kept secure and from which additional copies can be made.

? Did you know?

Engineering drawings, like maps, should be folded in a specific way. The technique used allows one corner of the drawing to be folded over to reveal the drawing title and drawing number for quick reference.

Initial prototype drawing of pump produced – Issue A

Testing of prototype pump indicates problems with leaking

Amendments made to design – Issue B

Tests meet customer requirements without leaking

Customer places order

Drawing checked and released for production – Issue 1

Changes made to drawing to allow mass production to be made easier – Issue 2

Pumps manufactured using Issue 2 of the drawing

Figure 9.21 A typical drawing issue procedure for a hydraulic pump manufacturer

Assessment Zone

This section has been written to help you to do your best when you take the examination. Read through it carefully and ask your teacher/tutor if there is anything that you are still not sure about.

How you will be assessed

You will sit for a one-hour written examination. The examination paper will have a maximum of 50 marks, and will be set and marked by the examination board. The number of marks available for each question will be shown in brackets, e.g. [2].

There will be different types of question in the examination.

A Questions where the answers are available and you have to choose the answer(s) that fit. *Tip: Always make sure that you read the instructions carefully. Sometimes you may need to identify more than one correct answer.*

Examples:

The drawing opposite is an example of an engineering drawing.

What type of drawing is shown? [1]

A Isometric ☐

B Perspective ☐

C Oblique ☐

D Orthographic ☐

Answer: D

The images below show two symbols for electronic components. Draw a line between each symbol and its meaning. [2]

LDR
Buzzer
Speaker
Diode
LED

Answer:

LED

Buzzer

B Questions where you are asked to give a short answer worth 1–2 marks

Tip: Look carefully at how the question is laid out to see how many points you will need to give.

Examples:

What is the meaning of the symbol shown below? [1]

Answer: Irritant

Explain **one** advantage of an electronic circuit diagram. [2]

Answer: An electronic circuit diagram uses standard symbols to represent the different components. This means that a drawing is clearer to read than if it were drawn as it looks.

C Questions where you are asked to give a longer answer – these can be worth up to 8 marks *Tips: Ensure you answer **all** parts of the question in order to achieve full marks. Remember to check your answer once you have finished.*

Example:

Discuss how an engineer would use a circuit diagram and an assembly drawing, rather than other drawings such as block diagrams and isometric drawings, during the manufacture of a mobile phone. [8]

Answer:

An engineer would need to use a circuit diagram to show how the different components in the mobile phone are linked together. This is used instead of a block diagram, because a block diagram would only show how the phone is expected to work. The circuit diagram should show the values of the components, such as resistor values and how the pins of integrated circuits will be connected within the circuit.

The circuit diagram would be used with an assembly drawing – this shows how all of the parts of the product need to be joined together. All connections will be shown, with the fittings to be used. The assembly drawing is drawn to scale so it gives an accurate view of the product. If the drawing was not all drawn to scale, it would not be possible for an engineer to easily interpret the information and mistakes could occur when putting the parts together.

If the engineer used an isometric drawing, it would be difficult to be able to see all of the different parts that come together to make the product as each item would be placed one on top of the other. The assembly drawing separates these from each other and shows how everything lines up.

How to improve your answer

Read the two student answers below, together with the feedback. Try to use what you learn here to improve your answers in your examination.

Question

Describe **two** ways in which engineering drawings can become damaged when they are used on a regular basis. [4]

Student 1's answer

> 1: They get dirty.
>
> 2: The drawing will have marks on it.

Feedback

Answer 1: The student has identified that drawings will get dirty when they are used, which would gain them one mark. They have not provided any extension for this point, so they will not gain any further marks for this part of the answer.

Answer 2: The student has repeated their point from answer 1, using different words. This will not gain them any additional marks, therefore no marks will be given for this answer.

Overall, the student has gained one mark for their answers.

Student 2's answer

> 1: The drawing may become dirty over time because people might not clean their hands and will leave dirty fingerprints on the drawings.
>
> 2: The edges of the drawing will get torn and ripped if the drawing is being used regularly, as these parts of the drawing are likely to get caught on things.

Feedback

Answer 1: The student has identified that drawings will become dirty when they are used, which gains them one mark. They then continue to describe why and how the drawing will become dirty. Since the student has extended their answer, they will gain two marks.

Answer 2: The student has correctly identified that the drawing may become ripped and damaged on the edges. This will gain them one mark. They then described the reason why this damage will occur, gaining them a second mark.

In total, student 2 will gain four marks for their answer, as they have covered two points and given extensions to each.

Assess yourself

1. Which welding feature is indicated by the symbol to the right? [1]

2. Describe two features of a safe condition sign. [2]

3. Engineering companies will use a production plan when they start a project. Explain two reasons why a production plan is needed. [4]

4. A number of drawing types are used to explain electronic circuits. Explain the features of circuit diagrams. [4]

5. Sketch the line types that are used to indicate: hidden detail, centre lines and outlines. [3]

For further practice, see the assessment practice questions on pages 173, 175, 179, 184, 187 and 191.

Answers can be found on page 275.

Hints and tips

Before the start of the exam. Make sure that you have got everything you will need. Check that your pen works. Try to make yourself feel comfortable and relaxed.

Keep an eye on the time. The examination will last one hour, and you should be able to see the clock in the examination room so that you will know how long you have got left to complete the paper. As a rough guide, allow one minute for every mark on the paper. This means that a question worth five marks should take you around five minutes to complete.

Read the questions fully. Make sure you read the question through enough times to understand what you are being asked to do. It is easy to misread a question and then write an answer that is wrong. Check you are doing what you are being asked to do. This is where many students can lose marks.

Plan your answers. For longer questions, it is worth spending a minute or two writing down the key points that you want to include in your answer. If you are being asked to evaluate, you will need to think about positive and negative points. Using a plan will allow you to make sure you include both in your answer.

Read through longer answers. Read through your longer answers to make sure your answer makes sense, and you have answered the question fully.

Check your answers. Once you have answered all of the questions on the paper, you will probably have a few minutes to spare. Use this time to check your answers and maybe fill in any parts that you have left blank. You should try to answer every question on the paper.

Make sure you have completed the front of the paper. Once the examination has ended, check that you have written your name and candidate number on the front of the paper. This is important so that you will gain the marks for your work.

Introduction

To become an engineer you will need to be able to solve engineering problems on a day-to-day basis. For instance, you might be asked to estimate the amount of material required for a product, or calculate the stress in a component when loaded.

Mathematics is a tool that will help you to do this. In this unit you will learn about the basic rules of arithmetic and algebra and how to apply these when solving engineering problems. You will also learn how to calculate areas and volumes, and how to apply the basic rules of trigonometry to calculate angles and find missing dimensions.

You will need to equip yourself with a scientific electronic calculator, and as you progress you will learn how to use it correctly. Think of mathematics as being a language: you will learn it a little at a time, and in the same way as a language can make it easier to travel abroad, a basic knowledge of mathematics will help you to progress in engineering.

Assessment: This unit will be assessed by a series of assignments set by your teacher/tutor.

Learning aims

After completing this unit you should:

A be able to use arithmetic, algebraic and graphical methods in engineering contexts

B be able to use mensuration and trigonometry in engineering contexts.

> I didn't think that I would be doing any maths on my work placement but I soon found out that engineers and technicians use it all the time. I spent some time with a technician who I helped to work out how long a maintenance operation was going to take and how much it would cost. I can now see why we do maths at school and how important it will be afterwards.
>
> James, *15-year-old learner*

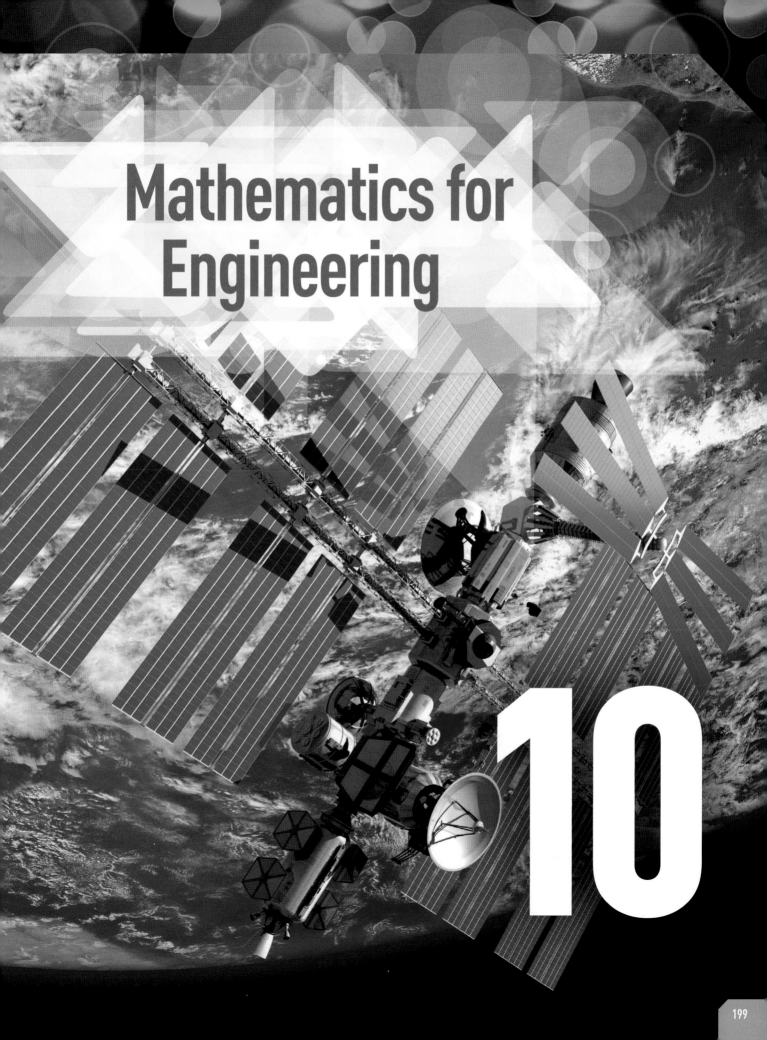

Mathematics for Engineering

10

This table shows what you must do in order to achieve a **Pass**, **Merit** or **Distinction** grade and where you can find activities in this book to help you.

Assessment and grading criteria

Level 1	Level 2 Pass	Level 2 Merit	Level 2 Distinction
Learning aim A: Be able to use arithmetic, algebraic and graphical methods in engineering contexts			
1A.1 Maths Using a scientific calculator, add, subtract, multiply and divide whole and decimal numbers, and calculate a percentage.	**2A.P1** Maths With the aid of a scientific calculator, use arithmetic methods to evaluate data in two engineering contexts. **See Assessment activity 10.1, page 221**		
1A.2 Maths Solve two linear equations and evaluate two simple formulae.	**2A.P2** Maths Use algebraic methods to transpose and solve two linear equations and evaluate two simple formulae in engineering contexts. **See Assessment activity 10.1, page 221**	**2A.M1** Maths Transpose and evaluate complex engineering formulae in engineering contexts. **See Assessment activity 10.1, page 221**	**2A.D1** Maths Carry out chained calculations using a scientific calculator, justifying the sequence of arithmetic precedence in an engineering context. **See Assessment activity 10.1, page 221**
1A.3 Maths Plot a linear relationship using given data.	**2A.P3** Maths Using given engineering data, plot linear graphs and establish gradient, intercept and the law connecting the variables in an engineering context. **See Assessment activity 10.1, page 221**	**2A.M2** Maths Using engineering data, plot a non-linear graph and establish its gradient at a given point in an engineering context. **See Assessment activity 10.1, page 221**	
Learning aim B: Be able to use mensuration and trigonometry in engineering contexts			
1B.4 Maths Find the areas of rectangles and triangles from given data.	**2B.P4** Maths Find the areas of three simple and compound shapes from given data in an engineering context. **See Assessment activity 10.2, page 232**		
1B.5 Maths Find the volumes of rectangular prisms from given data.	**2B.P5** Maths Find the volumes of regular objects from given data in an engineering context. **See Assessment activity 10.2, page 232**	**2B.M3** Maths Find the volumes of compound objects in an engineering context. **See Assessment activity 10.2, page 232**	**2B.D2** Maths Systematically carry out area and volume calculations to a high degree of accuracy in an engineering context. **See Assessment activity 10.2, page 232**
1B.6 Maths Find the hypotenuse lengths of right-angled triangles using Pythagoras' theorem.	**2B.P6** Maths Use Pythagoras' theorem to find the missing lengths of right-angled triangles in an engineering context. **See Assessment activity 10.2, page 232**	**2B.M4** Maths Use trigonometry to find the dimensions and angles of right-angled triangles in an engineering context. **See Assessment activity 10.2, page 232**	**2B.D3** Maths Use trigonometry to find the dimensions and angles of complex engineering shapes and non-right-angled triangles in an engineering context. **See Assessment activity 10.2, page 232**

Maths Opportunity to practise mathematical skills

How you will be assessed

This unit will be assessed through a series of tasks set by your teacher/tutor. To achieve the learning aims, you will need to show that you can use arithmetic methods to solve engineering problems and present experimental data in the form of graphs. You will also need to show that you can calculate areas and volumes, and solve right angle triangles using basic trigonometry. Throughout the assessment, you will need to demonstrate the correct use of your scientific electronic calculator and present answers to the specified degree of accuracy.

Arithmetic methods

Introduction

In this topic you will learn about **arithmetic** and the way that numbers are used when solving engineering problems.

Use of a basic calculator

The basic calculator contains keys for addition [+], subtraction [−], multiplication [×] and division [÷]. There is also an equals key [=] for giving the answer to a calculation. You can use the basic calculator for adding up columns of numbers such as the prices on a components list. You can also use it to take numbers away from each other. You might use this when finding out how much money is left in your bank account after paying a bill.

Sometimes the price of timber is given as the cost per metre. You may need to multiply this by the number of metres wanted to work out the cost.

The division key is useful if you want to divide something up into a number of equal parts. You can also use it to work out the average speed for a journey by dividing the distance travelled by the time taken.

Addition, subtraction, multiplication and division of whole numbers

Whole numbers can be positive (+) or negative (−). You can think of money in a savings account as being positive. If you spend it your account will fall to zero and if you carry on spending it will become negative and need to be repaid. We always put the (−) sign before negative numbers but we do not always put the (+) sign before positive numbers. If a number does not have a sign before it you can assume that it is positive.

When you add and subtract or multiply and divide numbers, there are four basic rules that you must follow.

1 When adding two positive numbers add their **absolute values** together. Sometimes we prefix the answer with a (+) sign, but more often we leave it out.

   For example: $1 + 5 + 6 = 12$ (or sometimes $+12$)

   When adding two negative numbers add their absolute values together and prefix the answer with a (−) sign.

   For example: $(-4) + (-3) + (-1) = -8$

   The brackets help us to show clearly that the numbers are negative.

2 To find the sum of a mixture of positive and negative numbers, add together the absolute values of the positive numbers, then add together the absolute values of the negative numbers. Now subtract the smaller total from the larger one and prefix your answer with the sign of the larger number.

   For example: $2 + (-3) + 5 + (-1) = 7 + (-4) = +(7 - 4) = +3$
   For example: $6 + (-7) + 4 + (-8) = 10 + (-15) = -(15 - 10) = -5$

3 When you multiply or divide numbers with like signs, the answer will always be positive.

For example: $6 \times 3 = +18$ and $14 \div 2 = +7$

For example: $(-4) \times (-5) = +20$ and $(-15) \div (-3) = +5$

Remember – multiplying or dividing two negative numbers always gives a positive answer.

4 When you multiply or divide numbers with unlike signs, the answer will always be negative.

For example: $5 \times (-6) = -30$ and $(-12) \div 3 = -4$

For example: $(-8) \times 3 = -24$ and $20 \div (-4) = -5$

Fractions and percentages

Fractions

If a value lies between two whole numbers we can express it in the form of a **fraction** or a **decimal**. For instance, halfway between 2 and 3 is $2\frac{1}{2}$ or 2.5. In decimal numbers the interval between whole numbers is split up into 10 and these can be further subdivided into 10 depending on the degree of accuracy required. Since adopting the **metric system** of measurement, the use of decimal numbers in the UK has become almost universal in science and engineering.

Percentages

A **percentage** (%) is a fraction that has been converted to hundredths. To do this, simply take your fraction or decimal number and multiply it by 100.

For example, express $\frac{1}{4}$ as a percentage: $\frac{1}{4} \times 100 = 25\%$ which means 25 hundredths

For example, express 0.35 as a percentage: $0.35 \times 100 = 35\%$ which means 35 hundredths

Some common fractions and their equivalent decimal numbers and percentages are shown in Table 10.1. You will see that each of the decimal numbers have been multiplied by 100 to express them as percentages.

Key terms

Fraction – part of a whole expressed in the form of a ratio.

Decimal – part of a whole expressed as the sum of tenths, hundredths, thousands and so on.

Metric system – a system of measurement made up of multiples and submultiples of 10.

Percentage – a fraction that is expressed as the number of parts in 100.

Table 10.1 Fractions, decimals and percentages

Fraction	Decimal	Percentage
$\frac{1}{10}$	0.1	10%
$\frac{1}{8}$	0.125	12.5%
$\frac{1}{4}$	0.25	25%
$\frac{1}{2}$	0.5	50%
$\frac{3}{4}$	0.75	75%
$\frac{1}{16}$	0.0625	6.25%
$\frac{1}{100}$	0.01	1%
$\frac{1}{1000}$	0.001	0.1%

Worked example 10.1

The scale on an analogue voltmeter reads from zero to 30 volts. When a test voltage of 8 V is applied, the meter reading is 8.24 V. Calculate a) the error, b) the error as a percentage of the true reading, c) the error as a percentage of full scale deflection.

a) Finding error in reading:

Error = $8.24 - 8 = +0.24$ V

b) Finding error as a percentage of the true reading:

Percentage error = $+\dfrac{0.24}{8} \times 100 = +3\%$

c) Finding error as a percentage of full scale deflection:

Percentage error = $+\dfrac{0.24}{30} \times 100 = +0.8\%$

A scientific calculator

Use of scientific calculator

The addition, subtraction, multiplication and division of whole and decimal numbers can be done very quickly using a scientific electronic calculator.

In addition to the plus [+], minus [−], multiply [×], divide [÷] and equals [=] keys, you also need the keys marked [EXP] or [10ˣ] and [ENG] and the keys for solving problems in trigonometry that are marked [sin], [cos] and [tan].

Also useful are the keys marked [(] and [)] for opening and closing brackets. You will find out what these and some other keys are used for as you progress with your maths.

Lengthy calculations and the 'BODMAS' rule

When you carrying out a lengthy calculation involving addition, subtraction, multiplication, division, and possibly powers and roots, it is essential that you do it in the following order.

1 Work out any terms that are in **B**rackets.
2 Work out any powers or roots. (Sometimes called '**O**rder'.)
3 Work out any **D**ivisions.
4 Work out any **M**ultiplications.
5 Work out any **A**dditions.
6 Work out any **S**ubtractions.

This is sometimes called the **BODMAS** rule and it is the procedure that your scientific electronic calculator is programmed to follow. This order of working is sometimes called **precedence**.

Look at the following calculation: $4 - 2 \times 6 + 9 \div 3$

If you work through it in the order it is written the answer comes to 7 but if you do the same on you calculator it comes to −5. This is quite a big difference but your calculator is correct. There are no brackets, powers or roots so, following the BODMAS rule, the multiplication and division should be done first:

$$4 - 2 \times 6 + 9 \div 3 = 4 - 12 + 3 = -5$$

Powers and roots

When a number has been multiplied by itself a number of times we say that it has been raised to a **power**. When a number is multiplied by itself we say that it has been **squared** and if it is multiplied by itself again we say that it has been **cubed**. Taking the number 2 as an example, we write it as:

$2^2 = 2 \times 2 = 4$
$2^3 = 2 \times 2 \times 2 = 8$

We can carry on doing this; for example:

$2^4 = 2 \times 2 \times 2 \times 2 = 16$

Here we say that we have raised the number 2 to the power of 4. When we write 2^4, the number two is called the **base** and the number 4 is called the **index**. The plural of index is indices. When the index is 1, this just means the number itself, i.e. $2^1 = 2$ and $3^1 = 3$ and so on. When the index is zero, it does not matter what number the base is, the answer is always 1, e.g. $2^0 = 1$, $3^0 = 1$, $4^0 = 1$ and so on.

Key terms

BODMAS – **B**rackets, **O**rder, **D**ivision, **M**ultiplication, **A**ddition, **S**ubtraction.

Precedence – the order in which you should carry out arithmetical calculations.

Power – the number of times that a number has been multiplied by itself.

Squared – a number multiplied by itself.

Cubed – a number multiplied by itself twice.

Base – a number that is to be raised to a power.

Index – the power a number is to be raised to.

When we add together or subtract different numbers that have to be raised to a power, we apply the BODMAS rule. We raise each one separately and then do the addition or multiplication.

For example: $3^3 + 4^2 = (3 \times 3 \times 3) + (4 \times 4) = 27 + 16 = 43$

For example: $6^2 - 5^3 = (6 \times 6) - (5 \times 5 \times 5) = 36 - 125 = -89$

The same applies if we are multiplying or dividing different numbers that are raised to a power.

For example: $2^3 \times 4^2 = (2 \times 2 \times 2) \times (4 \times 4) = 8 \times 16 = 128$

For example: $3^3 \div 2^2 = (3 \times 3 \times 3) \div (2 \times 2) = 27 \div 4 = 6.75$

If, however, we have to multiply powers of the same number (same base) we can add the indices together and then raise the number to this power.

For example: $3^3 \times 3^2 = 3^{(3+2)} = 3^5 = 3 \times 3 \times 3 \times 3 \times 3 = 243$

For example: $4^3 \times 4 = 4^{(3+1)} = 4^4 = 4 \times 4 \times 4 \times 4 = 256$

Note that 4 is taken to be 4^1 in this last example.

When we are dividing powers of the same number we can subtract the indices before raising the number to this power.

For example: $3^5 \div 3^2 = 3^{(5-2)} = 3^3 = 3 \times 3 \times 3 = 27$

For example: $4^4 \div 4^3 = 4^{(4-3)} = 4^1 = 4$

It is quite possible to have negative indices. The reciprocal of a number always has the index -1.

For example: $\dfrac{1}{3} = \dfrac{1}{3^1} = 3^{-1}, \dfrac{1}{5} = \dfrac{1}{5^1} = 5^{-1}, \dfrac{1}{10} = \dfrac{1}{10^1} = 10^{-1}$ and so on.

We can do the same with reciprocals of numbers that are raised to a power that is greater than 1.

For example: $\dfrac{1}{3^2} = 3^{-2}, \dfrac{1}{6^4} = 6^{-4}, \dfrac{1}{9^3} = 9^{-3}$ and so on.

When you went to add, subtract, multiply or divide numbers with negative indices, you need to change them back to reciprocal form before carrying out the operations.

For example: $3^{-3} + 5^{-2} = \dfrac{1}{3^3} + \dfrac{1}{5^2} = \dfrac{1}{3 \times 3 \times 3} + \dfrac{1}{5 \times 5} = \dfrac{1}{27} + \dfrac{1}{25}$
$= 0.037 + 0.04 = 0.077$ (to 3 sf)

For example: $4^{-2} \times 2^{-4} = \dfrac{1}{4^2} \times \dfrac{1}{2^4} = \dfrac{1}{4 \times 4} \times \dfrac{1}{2 \times 2 \times 2 \times 2}$
$= \dfrac{1}{16} \times \dfrac{1}{16} = \dfrac{1}{256} = 0.003\ 91$ (to 3 sf)

The square root of a number is a value that when multiplied by itself equals that number. Because $2 \times 2 = 4$, the square root of 4 is 2. But it could also be (-2) because you will recall that $(-2) \times (-2) = 4$. The square root is often written as $\sqrt{4}$ or $4^{\frac{1}{2}}$ and as you can see there are two possibilities for the square root of any number. A number such as 4 is called a **perfect square** because its square root is a whole number. Other perfect squares are 9, 16, 25, 36, 49 and so on.

You can of course have cube roots and roots to higher powers. Whatever the case, the index is always written as a fraction.

For example: $27^{\frac{1}{3}}$ is the cube root of 27 which is 3.

i.e. $3 \times 3 \times 3 = 27$

 Key terms

Perfect square – a number whose square root is a whole number.

For example: $16^{\frac{1}{4}}$ is the 4th root of 16 which is ±2.

i.e. $2 \times 2 \times 2 \times 2 = 16$ and also $(-2) \times (-2) \times (-2) \times (-2) = 16$

You should note that roots to an uneven power are positive but roots to an even power can be positive or negative.

Worked example 10.2

Carry out the following calculations showing the correct order of precedence and check your answers using a scientific calculator.

a) $(6 + 2) + 4^2 \times (5 - 3) - 18 \div 3$

1st the brackets $\quad 8 + 4^2 \times 2 - 18 \div 3$

2nd the powers and roots $\quad 8 + 16 \times 2 - 18 \div 3$

3rd the multiplication $\quad 8 + 32 - 18 \div 3$

4th the division $\quad 8 + 32 - 6$

5th the addition $\quad 40 - 6$

6th the subtraction $\quad 34$

The answer is 34 and this checks out using the scientific calculator.

b) $2^3 - (10+6)^{\frac{1}{2}} \times (13 - 4) + 15 \div 5$

1st the brackets $\quad 2^3 - 16^{\frac{1}{2}} \times 9 + 15 \div 5$

2nd the powers and roots $\quad 8 - 4 \times 9 + 15 \div 5$

3rd the multiplication $\quad\quad 8 - 36 + 15 \div 5$

4th the division $\quad 8 - 36 + 3$

5th the addition $\quad 8 - 33$ (Be careful, this is $-36 + 3 = 33$)

6th the subtraction $\quad -25$

The answer is −25 and this checks out using the scientific calculator.

Key terms

Standard form – a very large or very small number converted to one with a single digit between 1 and 10 before the decimal point (the mantissa) and multiplied by a power of 10 (the exponent) to give it the same value.

Scientific notation – same as standard form.

Standard form and engineering notation

A number such as 13,579 can be written as 1.3579×10^4. To do this you move the decimal point back to just after the first digit. In the above example it has been moved back through 4 places and this is the power of 10 that the new number must be multiplied by to give the same value. It is then said to be written in **standard form**, which is also sometimes called **scientific notation**. The number 1.3579 is called the mantissa and the 10^4 is called the exponent.

For example: $156.5 \times 210 = 32\,865$ or 3.2865×10^4 in standard form

We can do the same with decimal fractions such as 0.01357. This time the decimal point must be moved forwards to just after the first digit, which is 1. It has been moved forward through 2 decimal places, so in standard form the number is written as 1.357×10^{-2}. The exponent is now given a minus sign.

For example: $5.26 \div 1250 = 0.004208$ or 4.208×10^{-3} in standard form

You are sometimes asked to give your answer correct to a number of decimal places. The above answer is correct to 6 decimal places, that is, 6 places after the decimal point. More often in engineering you are asked to give your answer correct to 3 significant figures, which is considered to be a sufficient degree of accuracy. This includes the digits before the decimal point. To 3 significant figures, the answer above would be 4.21×10^{-3}. If the 4th significant figure is 5 or above, the 3rd significant figure is rounded up.

For example: $76 \times 821 = 62{,}396$ or 6.24×10^4

You should note that for answers that are less than 1, the first significant figure is the first figure after the decimal points that is not zero. The units that we use in engineering, such as millimetres, metres and kilometres, rise in multiples of 1,000, which is 10^3. It is the same with electric current, where we have millivolts (mV), volts (V) and kilovolts (kV). Engineering notation is similar to standard form except that the mantissa can be between 1 and 999 and the index is always a multiple of 3. This helps us to identify units when solving engineering problems.

For example: $250 \text{ mm} \times 325 = 81{,}250 \text{ mm}$ or $81.3 \times 10^3 \text{ mm}$ or 81.3 m

For example: $7.25 \text{ V} \div 450 = 0.01\,611 \text{ V}$ or $16.1 \times 10^{-3} \text{ V}$ or 16.1 mV

On your scientific calculator you will find a key that is very helpful when entering numbers in engineering notation. It is the one that is sometimes marked [EXP], which is short for exponent, or more often marked [10^x]. There is another useful key marked [ENG]. We use this for converting our answers into engineering notation.

Worked example 10.3

Use your scientific electronic calculator to evaluate the following expressions. Give your answer in standard form correct to 3 decimal places and in engineering notation correct to 3 significant figures.

a) $\dfrac{201 \times 154}{0.65}$ b) $\dfrac{221 \times 10^3 \times 255}{3.3}$ c) $\dfrac{452 \times 10^{-3} \times 12 \times 10^9}{25 \times 10^3}$

a) $\dfrac{201 \times 154}{0.65} = 47{,}622$

In standard form $47{,}622 = 4.762 \times 10^4$ correct to 3 decimal places

To convert your answer to engineering notation, keep the answer on your display and press the [ENG] key.

In engineering notation $47{,}622 = 47.6 \times 10^3$ correct to 3 significant figures

b) $\dfrac{221 \times 10^3 \times 255}{3.3} = 17{,}077{,}273$

To enter 221×10^3 key in [2] [2] [1] [EXP] [3] and then multiply and divide by the other numbers as normal.

In standard form $17{,}077{,}273 = 1.708 \times 10^7$ correct to 3 decimal places

To convert your answer to engineering notation, press the [ENG] key.

In engineering notation $17{,}077{,}273 = 17.1 \times 10^6$ correct to 3 significant figures

c) $\dfrac{452 \times 10^{-3} \times 12 \times 10^9}{25 \times 10^3} = 216{,}960$

To enter 452×10^{-3} key in [4] [5] [2] [EXP] [3] [+/−] and then key in the other numbers to multiply and divide.

In standard form $216{,}960 = 2.170 \times 10^5$ correct to 3 decimal places

To convert your answer to engineering notation, press the [ENG] key.

In engineering notation $216{,}960 = 217 \times 10^3$ correct to 3 significant figures

Substituting numerical values into simple engineering formulae

There are lots of standard formulae that engineers use to calculate things such as surface area, volume, expansion, stress, electrical resistance, power rating and so on. When using an electronic calculator to evaluate these formulae it is important to enter the numbers correctly and use the correct order of working.

Worked example 10.4

Calculate the tensile stress in a tie rod of 50 mm diameter cross-section when carrying a load of 1.5 kN using the formula:

$$\text{Tensile stress} = \frac{\text{Tensile load } (W)}{\text{Cross-sectional area } (A)}$$

State your answer in kPa, correct to 3 significant figures

First we need to calculate the cross-sectional area, A, in square metres.

$$A = \frac{\pi d^2}{4} = \frac{\pi \times (50 \times 10^{-3})^2}{4}$$

$$A = 1.96 \times 10^{-3} \text{ m}^2$$

To enter π directly on your calculator use the 2nd function of the [10^x] key.

Now calculate the tensile stress.

$$\text{Tensile stress} = \frac{W}{A} = \frac{1.5 \times 10^3}{1.96 \times 10^{-3}}$$

Tensile stress = 765×10^3 Pa or 765 kPA

Reasonable answers and approximations

Sometimes we need to make a quick estimate of an amount of material that will be required or the time that a particular task will take. You can do this by rounding decimal numbers up or down to the nearest whole number and making a rough mental calculation. It is sometimes called a 'ball-park figure'. It is also useful to do this when solving problems, so that if the value you obtain from your calculator turns out to be very different, you will know to recheck your calculation.

Worked example 10.5

An automated machine produces a component in 1 minute 28 seconds at a cost of 48p. What will be a) the approximate hourly production rate, b) the approximate cost of making a batch of 72, c) the percentage error in the hourly rate and in the cost due to the approximations?

a) Finding approximate hourly production rate if time is rounded up to 1.5 min per component

Approximate hourly rate $= 60 \div 1.5 = 60 \times \dfrac{2}{3} = 40$ components per hour

b) Finding the approximate cost of batch if cost is rounded up to 50p or £0.5 per component and the batch size is rounded down to 70

Approximate cost $= 0.5 \times 70 = £35$

c) Finding actual hourly production rate

Time per component $= \dfrac{60 + 28}{60} = 1.47$ min

Actual hourly rate $= 60 \div 1.47 = 40.8$ components per hour

Finding % error

% error $= \dfrac{(40.8 - 40) \times 100}{40.8} = +1.96\%$

Finding actual cost per batch

Actual cost $= 0.48 \times 72 = £34.56$

Finding % error

% error $= \dfrac{(34.56 - 35) \times 100}{34.56} = -1.27\%$

As you can see, there is not much between the two but the 'ball-park figures' can be arrived at quickly without the use of a calculator.

Just checking

1 What does the [ENG] key on your calculator do to a number?

2 What do you use the [EXP] or [10^x] key on your calculator for?

3 What do we mean by a 'ball-park figure'?

4 What does BODMAS stand for?

Algebraic methods

Key terms

Transposition – manipulation of a mathematical or engineering formula to make the quantity you require the subject of the formula.

Introduction

Algebra is a branch of mathematics that uses a mixture of numbers and letters. The letters represent numbers whose values we do not know and are trying to find. We often use letters to represent scientific quantities – for instance, F for force, L for length and V for voltage. The letters we use most often to represent unknown quantities are x and y and we have special ways of finding their values.

Linear equations and engineering formulae

Transposing linear equations

We often express scientific laws and principles as mathematical formulae, also known as equations. They give us the relationship between different physical quantities. Depending on which of the physical quantities we require to solve a problem, a formula or equation may need to be changed round to make that quantity the subject. The process is called **transposition**.

In some formulae the quantities may be multiplied or divided and there may be roots and powers present. In others the quantities may be added or subtracted.

The general rule with formulae in which the quantities are multiplied and/or divided is that they may be transposed by multiplying or dividing each side by the quantity that needs to be moved. It is rather like balancing the kitchen scales.

For example: Make v the subject of the formula:

$$s = vt$$

To get v on its own, divide each side by t so that it can be cancelled on the right-hand side.

$$\frac{s}{t} = \frac{v\cancel{t}}{\cancel{t}}$$

This leaves $\frac{s}{t} = v$ or $v = \frac{s}{t}$

For example: Make R the subject of the formula:

$$I = \frac{V}{R}$$

To get R on its own, begin multiplying each side by R so that it can be cancelled on the right-hand side.

$$IR = \frac{V\cancel{R}}{\cancel{R}}$$

This leaves $IR = V$

Now divide each side by I so that it can be cancelled on the left-hand side.

$$\frac{\cancel{I}R}{\cancel{I}} = \frac{V}{I}$$

This leaves $R = \frac{V}{I}$

The general rule with formulae in which the quantities are added and/or subtracted is that they may be transposed by adding or subtracting from each side the quantity that needs to be moved.

For example: Make a the subject of the formula:

$v = u + at$

Begin by subtracting u from each side so that at is left by itself on the right-hand side.

$v - u = \cancel{u} + at - \cancel{u}$

This leaves $v - u = at$

Now divide both sides by t so that it can be cancelled on the right-hand side.

$$\frac{v-u}{t} = \frac{a\cancel{t}}{\cancel{t}}$$

This leaves $a = \dfrac{v-u}{t}$

Solving linear equations

Using these transposition methods we will now be able to solve some simple linear equations of the form you might find in engineering, to find the value of the unknown quantity. Remember, equations are like the kitchen scales. Whatever you do to one side, you must do to the other to make them balance.

Worked example 10.6

Find the value of the unknown quantity, x, in the following equation:

$x + 3 = 8$

Begin by subtracting 3 from each side.

$x + 3 - 3 = 8 - 3$

This gives $x = 5$

Worked example 10.7

Find the value of the unknown quantity, m, in the equation:

$6m + 11 = 35 - m$

Begin by adding m to both sides so that it only appears on one side of the equation.

$6m + 11 + m = 35 - \cancel{m} + \cancel{m}$

The values of m cancel out on the right-hand side, leaving:

$7m + 11 = 35$

Now subtract *11* from each side.

$7m + 11 - 11 = 35 - 11$

This gives $7m = 24$

Finally, divide each side by 7 to obtain the value of m.

$$\frac{\cancel{7}m}{\cancel{7}} = \frac{24}{7}$$

This gives $m = 3.43$ (correct to 3 significant figures)

Worked example 10.8

Find the value of t in the equation:

$$\frac{4}{t} = \frac{2}{3}$$

Begin by multiplying both sides by t.

$$\frac{4}{\cancel{t}} \times \cancel{t} = \frac{2}{3} \times t$$

This gives $4 = \dfrac{2t}{3}$

Now multiply each side by 3.

$$4 \times 3 = \frac{2t \times \cancel{3}}{\cancel{3}}$$

This gives $12 = 2t$

Finally, divide each side by 2.

$$\frac{12}{2} = \frac{\cancel{2}t}{\cancel{2}}$$

This gives $6 = t$ or $t = 6$

Worked example 10.9

Find the value of x in the equation:

$3x = 7(8 - 2x)$

Begin by multiplying the bracketed terms by 7.

$3x = 56 - 14x$

Now add $14x$ to each side.

$3x + 14x = 56 - 14x + 14x$

This gives $17x = 56$

Finally, divide each side by 17.

$\dfrac{\cancel{17}x}{\cancel{17}} = \dfrac{56}{17}$

This gives $x = 3.29$ (correct to 3 significant figures)

Simple engineering formulae

There are quite a lot of simple linear equations and formulae that we use in engineering. Very often we have to transpose them to make the unknown quantity the subject.

We can then put in the known values and calculate the value of the unknown quantity.

Worked example 10.10

Transpose the electrical formula $V = IR$ to make the current I amps the subject. Calculate its value if the voltage $V = 12$ volts and the resistance $R = 7.5$ ohms.

Transposing the formula

Begin by dividing both sides of the equation by R to make I the subject.

$\dfrac{V}{R} = \dfrac{I\cancel{R}}{\cancel{R}}$

This gives $\dfrac{V}{R} = I$ or $I = \dfrac{V}{R}$

Calculating the current

Now put in the values $V = 12$ volts and $R = 7.5$ ohms.

$I = \dfrac{12}{7.5} = 1.6$ amps

Worked example 10.11

Transpose the uniform motion formula $s = \dfrac{1}{2}(u+v)t$ to make velocity, u, the subject. Determine the value of u given that $s = 125$ m, $v = 10.5$ ms^{-1} and $t = 18$ s.

Transposing the formula

Begin by multiplying each side by 2.

$2 \times s = 2 \times \dfrac{1}{2}(u+v)t$

This leaves $2s = (u + v)t$

Now divide each side by t.

$\dfrac{2s}{t} = \dfrac{(u+v)\cancel{t}}{\cancel{t}}$

This leaves $\dfrac{2s}{t} = u + v$

Finally, subtract v from each side.

$\dfrac{2s}{t} - v = u + \cancel{v} - \cancel{v}$

This leaves $\dfrac{2s}{t} - v = u$ or $u = \dfrac{2s}{t} - v$

Evaluating u when $s = 125$ m, $v = 10.5$ ms^{-1} and $t = 18$ s

$u = \dfrac{2 \times 125}{18} - 10.5$

$u = 3.39$ ms^{-1}

Complex engineering formulae

More complex formulae may contain powers and roots. Where these occur you may have to raise both sides of the formula to a power or take the root of each side as a step to isolating the required subject.

Worked example 10.12

Transpose the electrical formula to make the capacitance C farads the subject.

$$\frac{1}{2}\,QV = \frac{1}{2}\,CV^2$$

Find the value of C when stored charge $Q = 0.015$ coulombs and the voltage $V = 120$ volts.

Transposing the formula

Begin by multiplying both sides of the equation by 2.

$$\not{2} \times \frac{1}{\not{2}}\,QV = \not{2} \times \frac{1}{\not{2}}\,CV^2$$

This leaves $QV = CV^2$

Now divide both sides by V^2.

$$\frac{Q\not{V}}{V^{\not{2}}} = \frac{C\not{V}^{\not{2}}}{\not{V}^{\not{2}}}$$

This gives $\dfrac{Q}{V} = C$ or $C = \dfrac{Q}{V}$

Evaluating C when $Q = 0.015$ coulombs and $V = 120$ volts

$$C = \frac{0.015}{120} = 1.25 \times 10^{-4} \text{ farads}$$

Changing this to engineering notation gives
$C = 125 \times 10^{-6}$ farads or 125 microfarads

Worked example 10.13

Transpose the mechanical formula $v^2 = u^2 + 2as$ to make the starting velocity u ms^{-1} the subject and find its value when the final velocity $v = 12$ ms^{-1}, the acceleration $a = 1.5$ ms^{-2} and the distance travelled $s = 40$ m.

Transposing the formula

Begin by subtracting $2as$ from each side so that u^2 is left by itself on the right-hand side.

$$v^2 - 2as = u^2 + 2as - 2as$$

This leaves $v^2 - 2as = u^2$

Now take the square root of each side.

$$\sqrt{v^2 - 2as} = \sqrt{u^2}$$

This gives $u = \sqrt{v^2 - 2as}$

Evaluating u when $v = 12$ ms^{-1}, $a = 1.5$ ms^{-2} and $s = 40$ m

$$u = \sqrt{12^2 - (2 \times 1.5 \times 40)}$$

$u = 4.90$ ms^{-1} (correct to 3 significant figures)

Worked example 10.14

Transpose the conservation of energy formula $\dfrac{1}{2}\,mv^2 = mgh$ to make the velocity, v, the subject. Determine the value of v given that the acceleration due to gravity $g = 9.81$ ms^{-2} and the height fallen $h = 5.1$ m.

Transposing the formula

Begin by dividing both sides by m.

$$\frac{1}{2}\frac{\not{m}v^2}{\not{m}} = \frac{\not{m}gh}{\not{m}}$$

This leaves $\dfrac{v^2}{2} = gh$

Now multiply each side by 2 to isolate v^2 on the left-hand side.

$$\not{2} \times \frac{v^2}{\not{2}} = gh \times 2$$

This leaves $v^2 = 2gh$

Finally, take the square root of each side.

$$\sqrt{v^2} = \sqrt{2gh}$$

This leaves $v = \sqrt{2gh}$

Evaluating v when $g = 9.81$ ms^{-2} and $h = 5.1$ m

$$v = \sqrt{2 \times 9.81 \times 5.1}$$

$v = 10.0$ ms^{-1} (correct to 3 significant figures)

Chained calculations

Chained calculations are calculations which involve performing a number of operations on your scientific electronic calculator on the way to an answer. They might contain powers and roots: the key marked $[x^n]$ and its second function $[\sqrt[n]{x}]$ will help you with these.

Worked example 10.15

Evaluate the following calculation:

$$(3.25 + 52.75)^5 \times (1025 - 375)^{\frac{1}{3}}$$

Follow the BODMAS rule and begin by working out the brackets and removing them.

$$56^5 \times 650^{\frac{1}{3}}$$

Now work out 56^5 using the following sequence of keys. Your value will be in engineering notation.

[5] [6] $[x^n]$ [5] [=] [ENG]

The value shown on your calculator will be 551×10^6.

Now work out $650^{\frac{1}{3}}$ using the following sequence of keys. Your value will again be in engineering notation.

[6] [5] [0] $[x^n]$ [INV] [3] [=] [ENG]

The value shown on your calculator will be 8.66

You can now complete the calculation by multiplying these values together, making use of the $[10^x]$ key.

$$551 \times 10^6 \times 8.66 = 4.77 \times 10^9$$

Worked example 10.16

Evaluate the following calculation:

$$\frac{(0.25 \times 37.2)^{\frac{1}{4}}}{(52.1 - 15.5)^3}$$

Follow the BODMAS rule and begin by working out the brackets and removing them.

$$\frac{9.3^{\frac{1}{4}}}{36.6^3}$$

Now work out $9.3^{\frac{1}{4}}$ using the following sequence of keys. Your value will be in engineering notation.

[9] [.] [3] $[x^n]$ [INV] [4] [=] [ENG]

The value shown on your calculator will be 1.75

Now work out 36.6^3 using the following sequence of keys. Your value will again be in engineering notation.

[3] [6] [.] [6] $[x^n]$ [3] [=] [ENG]

The value shown on your calculator will be 49.0×10^3.

You can now complete the calculation by dividing. Make use of the $[10^x]$ and [ENG] keys.

$$\frac{1.75}{49.0 \times 10^3} = 35.7 \times 10^{-6}$$

Engineering calculations

Some of the calculations that we have carried out are the sort you might encounter in engineering. We are now going to do some more of the kind that you might soon encounter in your engineering science studies.

Just checking

1 What is transposition of a formula?

2 What is the basic rule of transposition?

3 What do you use the $[10^x]$ key for on your calculator?

4 What do you use the $[x^n]$ key for on your calculator?

Worked example 10.17

Making use of the formula $V = IR$, calculate the current, I, in the series circuit shown in Figure 10.1. Calculate also the potential differences V_1 and V_2 across each of the resistances.

Figure 10.1 A series circuit

Calculating the current I

Begin by finding the total resistance, R, of the circuit.

$R = R_1 + R_2 = 5 + 8$

$R = 13\Omega$

Next calculate the current, I amps.

$V = IR$

Dividing each side by R gives

$\dfrac{V}{R} = I$ or $I = \dfrac{V}{R}$

$I = \dfrac{20}{13} = 1.54$ amps

Using the current to find the voltages V_1 and V_2.

$V_1 = IR_1$

$V_1 = 1.54 \times 5 = 7.7$ volts

$V_2 = IR_2$

$V_2 = 1.54 \times 8 = 12.3$ volts

Check to show that these add up to the supply voltage.

$7.7 + 12.3 = 20$ and so the values are correct

Worked example 10.18

A gas at a pressure of 100 kPa and volume 1.5 m^3 is compressed into a volume of 0.25 m^3. During the process its temperature rises from 300 K to 750 K. Calculate its final pressure using the formula

$\dfrac{p_1 V_1}{T_1} = \dfrac{p_2 V_2}{T_2}$.

To make p_2 the subject of the formula, multiply each side by T_2 and divide each side by V_2.

$\dfrac{p_1 V_1 T_2}{T_1 V_2} = p_2$ or $p_2 = \dfrac{p_1 V_1 T_2}{T_1 V_2}$

$p_2 = \dfrac{100 \times 10^3 \times 1.5 \times 750}{300 \times 0.25}$

$p_2 = 1.5 \times 10^6$ Pa or 1.5 MPa

Worked example 10.19

A car of mass 900 kg is travelling at a speed of 12 ms^{-1} on a level road when the brakes are applied and it is slowed down smoothly to a speed of 3 ms^{-1} over a distance of 15 m. Calculate the force applied by the brakes.

Begin by calculating the work done, W, during the braking process. This is equal to the change in kinetic energy given by the formula:

$W = \dfrac{1}{2} m(v_1^2 - v_2^2)$

$W = \dfrac{1}{2} \times 900(12^2 - 3^2)$

$W = 60.8 \times 10^3$ J or 60.8 kJ

The work done is also the braking force, F, multiplied by the distance travelled, s.

$W = Fs$

Divide both sides by s.

$\dfrac{W}{s} = F$ or $F = \dfrac{W}{s}$

$F = \dfrac{60.8 \times 10^3}{15}$

$F = 4.05 \times 10^3$ N or 4.05 kN

Graphical methods

Key terms

Variable – a quantity with changing values.

Graph – a means of displaying the changes in value of the two variables.

Dependent variable – a variable whose changing values we can control.

Independent variable – a second variable that changes as a result of change in the dependant variable.

Scale – the distance on a graph that represents an increase or decrease of 1 unit of a variable.

Introduction

There are a number of different ways in which numerical information can be displayed. It can be listed in the form of a table. It can also be shown on a bar chart, where the heights of the columns might show production figures for succeeding months. Sometimes a pie chart is used, with the different 'slices' showing at a glance, say, how much money is being spent in the different departments of a company. It can also be displayed in the form of a graph – this is the method we shall now be looking at.

Sometimes, when two things are related, it is useful to plot a graph that shows how they affect each other as they change. We can picture the way that two **variable** quantities are related by plotting their values on a **graph**. We often do this with data gathered during an experiment. The quantity whose change we can control is called the **dependent variable** and the quantity that is changing with it is called the **independent variable**.

Plotting points on a graph

We usually plot the dependent variable on the horizontal **scale** (the x-axis) and the independent variable on the vertical scale (the y-axis), as shown in Figure 10.2. This is not a hard and fast rule and if one of the variables is time, this is generally plotted on the horizontal scale.

The points on your graph should be carefully plotted and marked using pencil, with a small cross or a dot surrounded by a small circle. You may find that the points do not quite lie on a straight line or a smooth curve. Check that you have plotted them correctly if any of them seem to be widely displaced. Some scatter may be due to errors in recording equipment or human error when taking readings. When you are satisfied that the points have been correctly plotted, draw a line or curve of best fit that passes through or as close to as many points as possible.

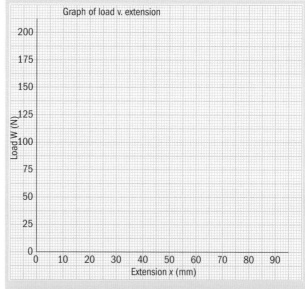

Figure 10.2 You should choose the scale to make the best use of the graph paper so that the points are not clustered together in one corner. The axes of your graph should be clearly labelled with the names of the variables and their units. It should also have a title that states exactly what has been plotted.

Plotting a proportional relationship

When a graph is a straight line passing through the origin we say that there is a **proportional relationship** between the variables and the law or equation connecting them is of the form $y = mx$.

The term m is called the **gradient** or slope of the graph. For a relationship such as this it is also called the **constant of proportionality** that connects the two variables. To find the gradient, draw a large triangle on the graph and, using the scales, write on the values a and b of the vertical and horizontal sides (see Figure 10.3). You can then find the gradient, m, using the formula $m = \dfrac{a}{b}$.

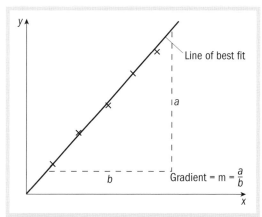

Figure 10.3 Graph showing a proportional relationship

Plotting a linear relationship

When a graph is a straight line that does not pass through the origin we say that there is a **linear relationship** between the two variables. The law or equation connecting them is now of the form $y = mx + c$.

The gradient, m, is found in the same way (see Figure 10.4). c is the value of the intercept on the vertical or y-axis. In addition to showing how the two variables are related you can sometimes find extra information from the area between the graph and the horizontal or x-axis. For example, if you are plotting force exerted against distance moved by an object, the area under the graph is the work done. If you are plotting velocity against time, the area under the graph gives the distance travelled.

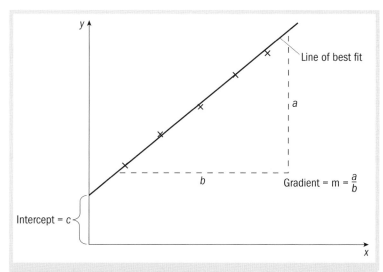

Figure 10.4 Graph showing a linear relationship

Worked example 10.20

Table 10.2 shows readings of load applied, F, and extension, x, produced during a test on a helical spring.

Table 10.2 Load v. extension

Load (Newtons)	50	75	100	125	150	175	200
Extension (mm)	6	20	34	48	62	76	90

Plot a graph of the two variables and from it determine the stiffness of the spring measured in Nmm⁻¹ and the law connecting them.

continued

The graph (Figure 10.5) is a straight line of the form $W = mx + c$.

The intercept $c = 40$ N. This shows that the spring is close-coiled and a load of 40 N is required before the coils start to separate.

The gradient $m = \dfrac{a}{b} = \dfrac{125}{70} = 1.79$ Nmm^{-1}. This is the stiffness of the spring.

The law connecting the two variables is $W = 1.79x + 40$

Figure 10.5 Graph of load v. extension

Plotting a non-linear relationship

We sometimes find that quantities are **inversely proportional**. This means that as one of them increases, the other one decreases by a proportional amount. In such cases the quantities are related by a law of the form $xy = c$, where c is a constant.

When a graph is plotted for quantities that vary inversely, the result is a curve as shown in Figure 10.6.

A gas that obeys Boyle's law behaves in this way. With such a gas an increase in its absolute pressure, p, causes its volume, V, to decrease in inverse proportion, provided its temperature remains constant. Pressure and volume are connected by the law $pV = c$, where c is a constant that depends on the particular gas and its mass. The curve that results when quantities such as these are plotted has a special name. It is called a **rectangular hyperbola**.

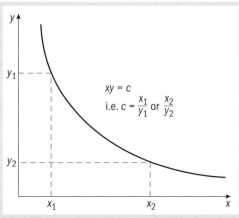

Figure 10.6 Graph showing an inversely proportional relationship

Worked example 10.21

Table 10.3 shows readings of absolute pressure, p, of a gas and its volume, V, produced during a test carried out at a constant temperature.

Table 10.3 Pressure v. volume

Pressure (kPa)	1.0	1.5	2.0	2.5	3.0	3.5	4.0	4.5	5.0
Volume (m³)	2.5	1.67	1.25	1.0	0.83	0.71	0.63	0.56	0.50

continued

Plot a graph of the two variables and from it determine the law that connects them.

From point (1) on Figure 10.7, $p_1 = 4.25$ kPa and $V_1 = 0.59$ m^3

   and so $p_1V_1 = 4.25 \times 0.59 = 2.5$ kPam^{-3}

From point (2) on Figure 10.7, $p_2 = 1.25$ kPa and $V_2 = 2.0$ m^3

   and so $p_2V_2 = 1.25 \times 2.0 = 2.5$ kPam^{-3}

Since $p_1V_1 = p_2V_2 = 2.5$ the law that connects the two variables is $pV = 2.5$ kPam^{-3}.

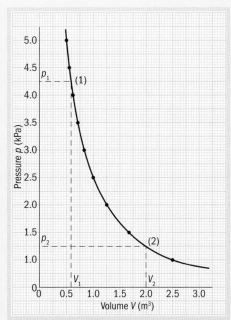

Figure 10.7 Graph of pressure v. volume

Key terms

Square law – a relationship where one variable increases in proportion to the square of the other.

Another example of a non-linear relationship is quantities that vary according to a **square law**. That is to say that one quantity is proportional to the square of the other. The law is of the form $y = ax^2$, where a is a constant. The curve appears as shown in Figure 10.8.

A typical example of this kind of behaviour is the power consumption in an electric circuit given by the formula $P = I^2R$. Here, I is the current and R, the circuit resistance, is the constant. Another example is the kinetic energy of a moving body given by the formula $E = \frac{1}{2} mv^2$. Here, v is the velocity and the $\frac{1}{2} m$, which is half the mass of the body, is the constant.

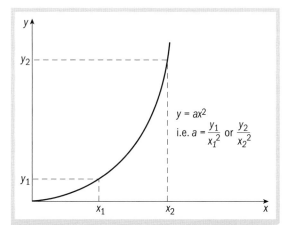

Figure 10.8 Graph of a square law relationship

Worked example 10.22

Table 10.4 shows readings of current flowing in a circuit and its power consumption P.

Table 10.4 Power v. current

Current (Amps)	0.2	0.4	0.6	0.7	0.8	0.9	1.0	1.2
Power (Watts)	0.4	1.6	3.6	4.9	6.4	8.1	10.0	14.4

Plot a graph of the two variables and show that they are connected by a square law of the form $P = I^2R$.

continued

If the square law is of the form $P = I^3 R$
then $\dfrac{P}{I^2} = R$.

From point (1) on Figure 10.9, $P_1 = 2$ W
and $I_1 = 0.445$ A

and so $\dfrac{P_1}{I_1^2} = \dfrac{2}{0.445^2} = 10\ \Omega$

From point (2) on Figure 10.9, $P_2 = 12$ W
and $I_2 = 1.095$ A

and so $\dfrac{P_2}{I_2^2} = \dfrac{12}{1.095^2} = 10\ \Omega$

Since $\dfrac{P_1}{I_1^2} = \dfrac{P_2}{I_2^2} = 10\ \Omega$, the law that

connects the two variables is $P = 10I^2$.

Figure 10.9 Graph of power v. current

Exponential growth – increase at an ever faster rate, as seen in the world's population.

Exponential decay – decrease at an ever-faster rate.

Natural growth and decay – a form of exponential growth and decay.

When regular increments in one variable produce increasingly large increments in the other we say that we have **exponential growth**. Alternatively, when regular decrements in one variable produce ever smaller decrements in the other, we say that we have **exponential decay**. We get examples of this in electrical and mechanical systems and also in nature.

For instance, the human population of the world has risen exponentially over the centuries, apart from a few hiccups due to wars, plagues and famine. At the same time we have seen an exponential decay in the population of some animals, such as the Asian tiger and giant panda, which are threatened with extinction. When the figures are plotted on graphs we call them **natural growth and decay** curves. They appear as shown in Figure 10.10.

Natural growth and decay curves have characteristic equations that relate the two variables. They are $y = ae^x$ and $y = ae^{-x}$. The constant a can have any positive or negative value but the constant e is special and always has the value 2.718. Just like π = 3.142 is a constant peculiar to the circular measurement, so e = 2.718 is a constant peculiar to natural growth and decay graphs.

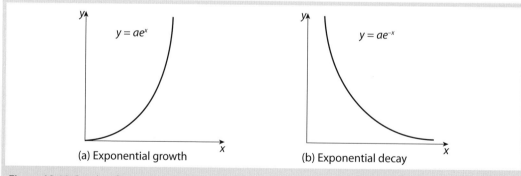

Figure 10.10 Graphs of natural growth and decay

Assessment activity 10.1

1 a) A diesel engine cylinder contains 0.125 m³ of air at the start of its compression stroke. If this is compressed into a volume of 7.35×10^{-3} m³ at the end of the stroke, calculate its compression ratio correct to 3 significant figures.

   b) An engineering component costs £2.25 and a buyer requires a batch of 110. What will be the cost if a discount of 15% is allowed for this quantity.? Give your answer correct to 2 decimal places.

2 A gantry crane moving at 1.0 ms⁻¹ accelerates uniformly to a velocity of 2.75 ms⁻¹ in a time of 12 s. What is its acceleration? Give your answer correct to 3 significant figures.

3 A vehicle travelling at a steady speed starts to accelerate. Its velocity is recorded at one-second intervals and the readings are shown in the following table.

Velocity v (ms⁻¹)	2.5	3.7	4.9	6.0	7.2	6.4	9.6	10.8
Time t (seconds)	1	2	3	4	5	6	7	8

Plot a graph of velocity v, against time t. From the graph, determine the velocity of the vehicle as it started to accelerate, the acceleration of the vehicle and the law that connects the two variables, v and t.

4 For different lengths of the cantilever shown in Figure 10.11, the load at the point of failure is shown in the following table.

Figure 10.11 Cantilever

Length, L (m)	0.5	1.0	1.5	2.0	2.5	3.0	3.5
Load, W (kN)	1.21	0.59	0.40	0.29	0.24	0.21	0.17

Plot a graph of length, L, against load-carrying capacity, W, and determine the law that connects the two.

Tips

- Set out your calculations clearly and begin each step by stating what it is you are doing.
- Show clearly all the steps when transposing a formula.
- Choose scales that make best use of your graph paper.
- Clearly label the two axes, stating the units of the variables.
- Draw a curve or line of best fit through the points you have plotted.
- Show clearly that you have determined the law connecting the variables.

Areas of regular and compound shapes

Key terms

Mensuration – the branch of mathematics dealing with measurement.

Introduction

Engineers very often need to calculate the area of sheet material required for a product, and then use the area to work out the cost. They also need to know the cross-sectional area of loaded components so that they can calculate the stress in the material. The calculation of floor area is very important when designing workshop and office space where regulations state how much space each person should have at their work station.

◤ Measurement of area

Mensuration is the branch of mathematics dealing with measurement, in particular the measurement of areas and volumes. In engineering we may be required to calculate the area of sheet metal required for a product or the volume of a containing vessel such as a storage tank or a boiler. The shapes that we have to deal with may be simple or complex. However, it is often possible to break a mensuration problem down into a number of simple shapes or volumes. These can then be calculated and totalled up to solve the problem.

Areas are generally measured in square metres (m²) except for very small areas where we may use square centimetres (cm²) or square millimetres (mm²) and very large areas of land that are measured in hectares (ha). A hectare is 10,000 or 10^4 square metres.

Regular shapes

By regular shapes we mean squares, rectangles, triangles and circles. The formulae for finding their areas are shown in Figure 10.12.

Compound shapes

Other shapes may be split up into their elements. For instance, a rhombus and parallelogram can be rearranged into a square and rectangle as shown in Figure 10.13.

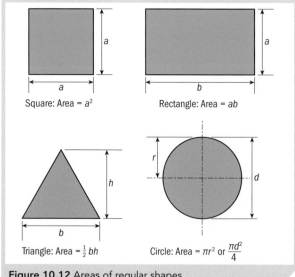

Figure 10.12 Areas of regular shapes

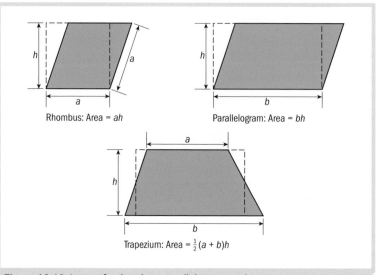

Figure 10.13 Areas of a rhombus, parallelogram and trapezium

As can be seen, a rhombus and a parallelogram are rather like a distorted square and rectangle. If the triangular area shown by the dotted line is removed from the right-hand side and attached to the left-hand side, this converts both shapes into rectangles. Their areas can then be found by multiplying the base by the perpendicular height.

A trapezium is a four-sided figure with two sides that are parallel and two that are not. The vertical dotted lines intersect the sloping sides at their mid-points. If the triangular corner sections are removed and reattached to the upper side, this results in a rectangle whose length is the average of the two parallel sides. The area is found by multiplying the average length by the distance between the parallel sides.

The cross-section of an I-section beam can be split into three rectangles whose separate areas can be added together, as shown in Worked example 10.23. Other complex shapes are regularly encountered in sheet metal work. The panels that are used to make washing machines, ovens and cookers regularly contain holes, triangular off-cuts and curves.

Worked example 10.23

Calculate the cross-sectional area of the I-section beam shown in Figure 10.14. All the dimensions are in millimetres.

Finding the total area of rectangles A

  Total of Areas A = 2 × 75 × 20 = 3,000 mm²

Finding the total area of rectangle B

  Area B = 80 × 25 = 2,000 mm²

Finding the total area of the I-section

  Total area = 3,000 + 2,000 = 5,000 mm²

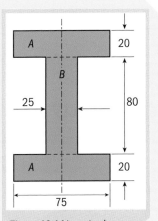

Figure 10.14 I-section beam

Worked example 10.24

Figure 10.15 shows the floor plan of a workshop. Calculate its floor area.

Figure 10.15 Floor plan of a workshop

Finding area of triangle C

  Area of C = $\frac{1}{2}$ Base × Height

Area of C = $\frac{1}{2}$ × (20 – 11.5) × (18 – 13.2)

Area of C = 20.4 m²

Finding floor area of A

  Area of A = Area of rectangle – Area of triangle C

  Area of A = (20 × 18) – 20.4

  Area of A = 339.6 m²

Finding area of semi-circular floor area B

  Area of B = $\frac{1}{2}$ ≠ r² = $\frac{1}{2}$ × ≠ × 9²

  Area of B = 127.2 m²

Finding total floor area

  Total floor area = Area of A + Area of B

  Total floor area = 339.6 + 127.2

  Total floor area = 466.8 m²

Volumes of regular and compound three-dimensional objects

Introduction

The volume of a body is the amount of space it occupies. We also sometimes call it cubic capacity. In the case of a storage tank it is the volume of fluid required to fill it completely. Engineers often have to make this kind of calculation and also calculate the volume of molten metal required to make castings.

Measurement of volume for solving engineering problems

Large volumes are generally measured in cubic metres (m^3). For smaller volumes we may use litres and for still smaller volumes we may use cubic centimetres (cm^3).

- $1\ m^3 = 1{,}000$ litres (10^3 l)
- 1 litre $= 1{,}000\ cm^3$ ($10^3\ cm^3$)
- $1\ m^3 = 1{,}000{,}000\ cm^3$ ($10^6\ cm^3$)

Regular objects

By regular objects we mean rectangular prisms, cylinders, cones and spheres. The formulae for finding their volumes are shown in Figure 10.16.

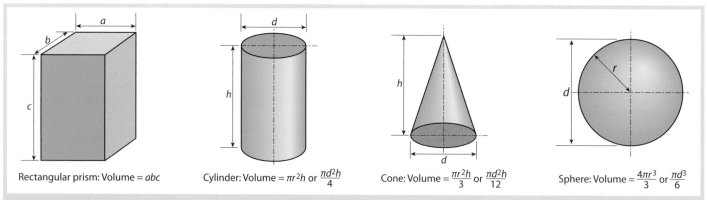

Rectangular prism: Volume $= abc$ Cylinder: Volume $= \pi r^2 h$ or $\dfrac{\pi d^2 h}{4}$ Cone: Volume $= \dfrac{\pi r^2 h}{3}$ or $\dfrac{\pi d^2 h}{12}$ Sphere: Volume $= \dfrac{4\pi r^3}{3}$ or $\dfrac{\pi d^3}{6}$

Figure 10.16 Volumes of regular solid bodies

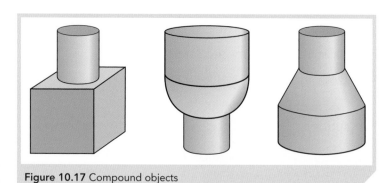

Figure 10.17 Compound objects

Compound objects

Compound objects are most often made up from a number of regular objects. Some of these are shown in Figure 10.17.

Separating compound objects into the cylindrical, conical and spherical parts of which they are made, and calculating their separate volumes, enables the total volume to be found.

Worked example 10.25

Figure 10.18 shows a cross-section through a concrete beam whose length is 2.5 m. Calculate the volume of concrete in cubic metres required to cast the beam.

Figure 10.18 Concrete beam

Finding cross-sectional area of beam in square metres

Area of cross-section = Area of outer square − Area of two semicircles (equal to a full circle)

Area of cross-section = $(0.45 \times 0.45) - (\frac{1}{4} \times \pi \times 0.25^2)$

Area of cross-section = 0.2025 − 0.0491

Area of cross-section = 0.1534 m²

Finding volume of concrete required

Volume required = Cross-sectional area × Length

Volume required = 0.1534 × 2.5

Volume required = 0.384 m³ (to 3 significant figures)

Worked example 10.26

Figure 10.19 Pressure vessel

The pressure vessel shown in Figure 10.19 has a cylindrical centre section and hemispherical ends. Calculate its volume.

Finding volume of central cylindrical section

Volume of centre cylindrical section = $\frac{\pi d^2 l}{4} = \frac{\pi \times 1.5^2 \times 2.1}{4}$

Volume of centre cylindrical section = 3.71 m³

Finding volume of hemispherical ends (equal to that of a sphere)

Volume of hemispherical ends = $\frac{\pi d^3}{6} = \frac{\pi \times 1.5^3}{6}$

Volume of hemispherical ends = 1.77 m³

Finding total volume of pressure vessel

Total volume = Volume of centre section + Volume of ends

Total volume = 3.71 + 1.77 = 5.5 m³

Just checking

1 What is the cubic capacity of a container?

2 What is the formula for the volume of a cylinder of diameter d, and height h?

3 What is the formula for the volume of a sphere of radius r?

4 How many litres are there in a cubic metre?

Trigonometry

Getting started

You have probably seen an Ordnance Survey (OS) map. These were originally drawn by government surveyors who divided the county up into large triangles and set about the task of calculating the distances along their sides. The corners of the triangles had a special name: 'triangulation points', or 'trig' points for short. Small concrete columns were positioned at these points and most of them are still in evidence today. Have a close look at an OS map of your local area, find out the symbol for trig points from the key, and see if you can find the one nearest to you.

Key terms

Trigonometry – study of the relationship between the sides and angles of triangles.

Hypotenuse – the longest side of a right-angled triangle that is opposite the right angle.

Opposite – the side that is opposite one of its other angles.

Adjacent – the side that lies next to one of the other angles and, together with the opposite side, forms the right-angled corner.

Pythagoras' theorem – the square on the hypotenuse of a right-angled triangle is equal to the sum of the squares on the other two sides.

Introduction

Trigonometry is the study of the relationship between the sides and angles of triangles. It is at least 2,000 years old, its name coming from two Greek words meaning 'angle measurement'. Over the centuries it has been used by astronomers and scientists, and for navigation at sea. It is an important tool of engineers and we shall be looking at some of its applications.

We use **trigonometry** quite a lot in engineering design to calculate dimensions and angles. Building and land surveyors also use it to calculate distances and heights. Some triangles have special names, as shown in Figure 10.20.

In an equilateral triangle the sides are all of the same length and all of the angles are equal. An isosceles triangle has two sides the same length and two of its angles are equal. In a scalene triangle the sides are all unequal. We shall mostly be dealing with right-angled triangles as shown in Figure 10.20(a).

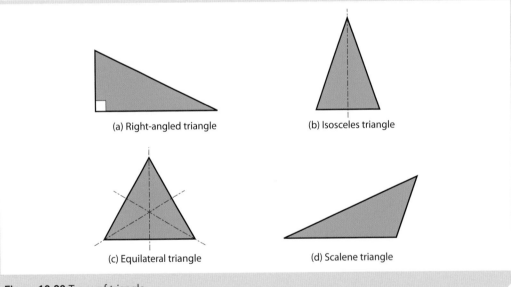

(a) Right-angled triangle

(b) Isosceles triangle

(c) Equilateral triangle

(d) Scalene triangle

Figure 10.20 Types of triangle

As you probably know, the circumference of a circle can be divided up into 360 degrees (360°). Whatever the kind of triangle, the internal angles always add up to 180°. In the right-angled triangle we have one angle that is 90° and so the other two internal angles must also add up to 90°.

We often use the Greek letter θ (theta) to identify an angle, as in Figure 10.21. The longest side of the triangle is called the **hypotenuse**. The side away from the angle θ is called the **opposite** side and the other side next to the angle θ is called the **adjacent** side.

Figure 10.21 Right-angled triangle

Pythagoras' theorem

Over 2,000 years ago and living in ancient Greece, Pythagoras discovered the relationship between the sides of a right-angled triangle. He discovered that if you make each side of the triangle the side of a square, as in Figure 10.22, the area of the square on the hypotenuse is equal to the sum of the areas of the squares on the other two sides.

This means that $c^2 = a^2 + b^2$

or $c = \sqrt{a^2 + b^2}$

Pythagoras' theorem comes in very useful for finding out the length of a side of a right-angled triangle when we know the length of the other two sides.

An easy way to construct a right-angled triangle on paper is to use the 3, 4, 5 method. Note that $3^2 + 4^2 = 5^2$ so the sides of your triangle will be in these relative lengths.

Begin by drawing the hypotenuse 5 units long, then set your compasses to 4 units and strike an arc from one end of the hypotenuse. Now set your compasses to 3 units and strike another arc from the other end of the hypotenuse. Where the two arcs intersect, you have the point of the right angle and can draw in the two remaining sides.

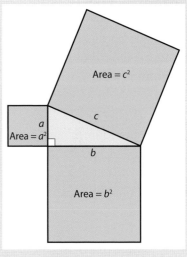

Figure 10.22 Pythagoras' theorem

Trigonometric functions

An **acute angle** is one that is less than 90°. The angles at *A* and *B* in Figure 10.23 are acute angles. Angle *C* is 90° and the sides opposite the angles *A*, *B* and *C* are lettered *a*, *b* and *c*.

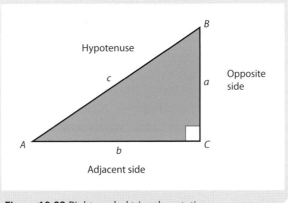

Figure 10.23 Right-angled triangle notation

Tangent of an angle

The ratio of the side *a*, opposite the angle *A*, to side *b*, adjacent to the angle *A*, is known as the tangent of the angle. It is usually written as tan *A* for short.

$$\tan A = \frac{\text{opposite side}}{\text{adjacent side}}$$

$$\tan A = \frac{a}{b}$$

You can find the tangent of any angle on your electronic calculator by entering the number of degrees and pressing the [tan] key. If you know the angle and either of the sides *a* or *b*, you can find the other one. Alternatively, if you know both the opposite and adjacent sides you can calculate the tangent of the angle *A* and obtain its value in degrees by pressing [shift] [tan].

Worked example 10.27

In the triangle *ABC* shown in Figure 10.24, calculate the angle at *A*, the angle at *B* and the length of the hypotenuse, *c*.

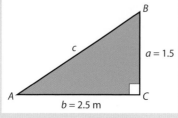

Figure 10.24 Triangle ABC

Finding tangent of angle at *A*

$$\tan A = \frac{a}{b} = \frac{1.5}{2.5}$$

$$\tan A = 0.6$$

Finding value of angle (by pressing [shift] [tan])

$$A = 30.96°$$

Finding angle at *B*

$$A + B + C = 180°$$

$$B = 180° - C - A = 180° - 90° - 30.96°$$

$$B = 59.04°$$

Finding value of hypotenuse, *c*, using Pythagoras' theorem

$$c = \sqrt{a^2 + b^2} = \sqrt{1.5^2 + 2.5^2}$$

$$c = 2.92 \text{ m}$$

Sine of an angle

The ratio of the side *a*, opposite the angle *A*, to side *c*, the hypotenuse, is known as the sine of the angle. It is usually written as sin *A* for short.

$$\sin A = \frac{\text{opposite side}}{\text{hypotenuse}}$$

$$\sin A = \frac{a}{c}$$

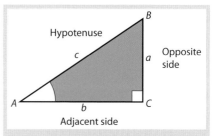

Figure 10.25 Right-angled triangle notation

You can find the sine of any angle on your electronic calculator by entering the number of degrees and pressing the [sin] key. If you know the angle and either of the sides *a* or *c*, you can find the other one. Alternatively, if you know both the opposite side and the hypotenuse you can calculate the sine of the angle *A*, and obtain its value in degrees by pressing [shift] [sin].

Worked example 10.28

In the triangle *ABC* shown in Figure 10.26, calculate the length of the sides *b* and *c* and the angle at *B*.

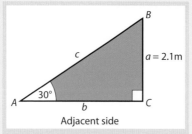

Figure 10.26 Triangle ABC

Finding side *c*

$$\sin A = \frac{a}{c}$$

$$c = \frac{a}{\sin A} = \frac{2.1}{\sin 30°}$$

$$c = \frac{2.1}{0.5} = 4.2 \text{ m}$$

Finding side *b*

$$\tan A = \frac{a}{b}$$

$$b = \frac{a}{\tan A} = \frac{2.1}{\tan 30°}$$

$$b = \frac{2.1}{0.577} = 3.64 \text{ m}$$

Checking the answers using Pythagoras' theorem

$$c = \sqrt{a^2 + b^2} = \sqrt{2.1^2 + 3.64^2}$$

$$c = 4.2 \text{ m, i.e. the answers check out}$$

Finding angle at *B*

$$A + B + C = 180°$$

$$B = 180° - A - C = 180° - 30° - 90°$$

$$B = 60°$$

A triangle such as this is known as a 60°–30° triangle. You should note that with such a triangle the hypotenuse is always twice the length of the shortest side.

Cosine of an angle

The ratio of the side b, adjacent to the angle A, to side c, the hypotenuse, is known as the cosine of the angle. It is usually written as cos A for short.

$$\cos A = \frac{\text{adjacent side}}{\text{hypotenuse}}$$

$$\cos A = \frac{b}{c}$$

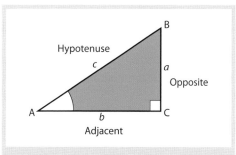

Figure 10.27 Right-angled triangle notation

You can find the cosine of any angle on your electronic calculator by entering the number of degrees and pressing the [cos] key. If you know the angle A and either of the sides b or c, you can find the other one. Alternatively, if you know both the adjacent side and the hypotenuse you can calculate the cosine of the angle A, and obtain its value in degrees by pressing [shift] [cos].

Worked example 10.29

In the triangle ABC shown in Figure 10.28, calculate the length of the sides b and c and the angle at B.

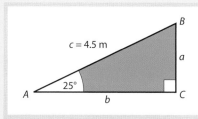

Figure 10.28 Triangle ABC

Finding side b

$$\cos A = \frac{b}{c}$$
$$b = c \cos A = 4.5 \cos 25°$$
$$b = 4.5 \times 0.906 = 4.08 \text{ m}$$

Finding side a

$$\sin A = \frac{a}{c}$$
$$a = c \sin A = 4.5 \sin 25°$$
$$a = 4.5 \times 0.423 = 1.90 \text{ m}$$

Checking the answers using Pythagoras' theorem

$$c = \sqrt{a^2 + b^2} = \sqrt{1.90^2 + 4.08^2}$$
$$c = 4.5 \text{ m, i.e. the answers check out}$$

Finding angle at B

$$A + B + C = 180°$$
$$B = 180° - A - C = 180° - 25° - 90°$$
$$B = 65°$$

◤ Trigonometric relationship

As you now know, the tangent, sine and cosine of the angle at A are calculated as follows.

$$\tan A = \frac{a}{b} \qquad \sin A = \frac{a}{c} \qquad \cos A = \frac{b}{c}$$

Dividing sin A by cos A gives:

$$\frac{\sin A}{\cos A} = \frac{a}{c} \div \frac{b}{c} = \frac{a}{\cancel{c}} \times \frac{\cancel{c}}{b}$$

$$\frac{\sin A}{\cos A} = \frac{a}{b}$$

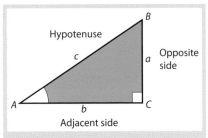

Figure 10.29 Right-angled triangle notation

This is the same as tan A, and so we have the relationship:

$$\tan A = \frac{\sin A}{\cos A}$$

You will not make much practical use of this relationship immediately, but you may find that it comes in useful in future studies.

Worked example 10.30

Figure 10.30 shows a triangular sheet metal panel. Calculate the angle at C and the lengths of each of its sides.

Finding angle at C

$A + B + C = 180°$

$C = 180° - A - B = 180° - 20° - 30°$

$C = 130°$

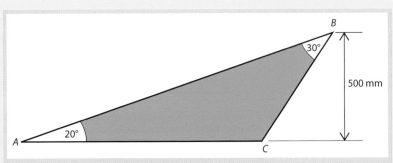

Figure 10.30 Triangular sheet metal panel

Drawing in the dotted lines to D gives two right-angled triangles, ABD and CBD, as shown in Figure 10.31.

Finding distance AD

$$\tan 20° = \frac{BD}{AD}$$

$$AD = \frac{BD}{\tan 20°} = \frac{500}{\tan 20°}$$

$$AD = 1,374 \text{ mm}$$

Finding distance CD

$$\tan 50° = \frac{BD}{CD}$$

$$CD = \frac{BD}{\tan 50°} = \frac{500}{\tan 50°}$$

$$CD = 420 \text{ mm}$$

Finding length of side AC

$$AC = AD - CD = 1,374 - 420$$

$$AC = 954 \text{ mm}$$

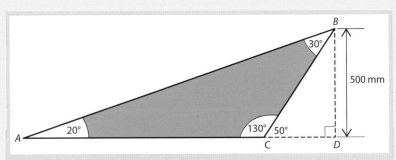

Figure 10.31 Triangular sheet metal panel with dotted lines to D drawn

Finding length of side AB

$$\sin 20° = \frac{BD}{AB}$$

$$AB = \frac{BD}{\sin 20°} = \frac{500}{\sin 20°}$$

$$AB = 1,462 \text{ mm}$$

Finding length of side BC

$$\sin 50° = \frac{BD}{BC}$$

$$BC = \frac{BD}{\sin 50°} = \frac{500}{\sin 50°}$$

$$BC = 653 \text{ mm}$$

Worked example 10.31

Figure 10.32 shows a roof truss. Calculate the lengths of the outer members *AB*, *BC* and *AC* and the inner members *ED* and *DF*.

Consider triangle *ABD* to find the length of member *AB* and distance *AD* (ignore member *ED*).

Figure 10.32 Roof truss

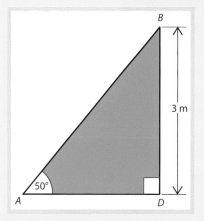

$$\sin A = \frac{DB}{AB} \quad \therefore AB = \frac{DB}{\sin A} = \frac{3}{\sin 50°}$$

$$AB = 3.92 \text{ m}$$

$$\tan A = \frac{BD}{AD} \quad \therefore AD = \frac{BD}{\tan A} = \frac{3}{\tan 50°}$$

$$AD = 2.52 \text{ m}$$

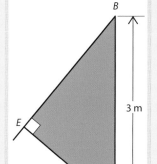

Consider triangle *EDB* to find length of internal member *ED*.

$$\cos D = \frac{ED}{DB} \quad \therefore ED = DB \cos D = 3 \cos 50°$$

$$ED = 1.93 \text{ m}$$

Consider triangle *DBC* to find length of member *BC* and distance *DC* (ignore member *DF*).

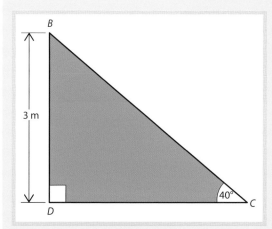

$$\sin C = \frac{DB}{BC} \quad \therefore BC = \frac{DB}{\sin C} = \frac{3}{\sin 40°}$$

$$BC = 4.67 \text{ m}$$

$$\tan C = \frac{DB}{DC} \quad \therefore DC = \frac{DB}{\tan A} = \frac{3}{\tan 40°}$$

$$DC = 3.58 \text{ m}$$

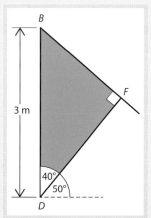

Consider triangle *DFB* to find length of internal member *DF*.

$$\cos D = \frac{DF}{DB} \quad \therefore DF = DB \cos D = 3 \cos 40°$$

$$DF = 2.30 \text{ m}$$

The total length of member *AC* can now also be found.

$$AC = AD + DC = 2.52 + 3.58$$

$$AC = 6.10 \text{ m}$$

The outer triangle is a right-angled triangle with the angle *B* being 90°. You can now check that your answers for *AB*, *BC* and *AC* are correct by applying Pythagoras' theorem.

$$AC^2 = AB^2 + BC^2$$

$$AC^2 = 6.10^2 = 37.2$$

$$AB^2 + BC^2 = 3.92^2 + 4.67^2 = 37.2$$

The answers are correct.

Assessment activity 10.2

2B.P4 | 2B.P5 | 2B.M3 | 2B.D2 | 2B.P6 | 2B.M4 | 2B.D2 | 2B.D3

These are examples of the types of activities you could find in an assignment for learning aim B.

1 Calculate the area of the panel shown in Figure 10.33.

Figure 10.33 Panel

2 Calculate the volume of the vessel shown in Figure 10.34.

Figure 10.34 A vessel

3 Calculate the length of each member in the roof truss shown in Figure 10.35.

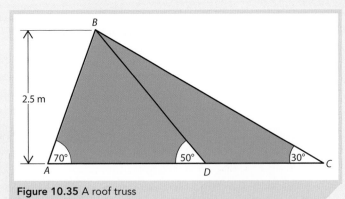

Figure 10.35 A roof truss

Tips

● Draw a neat diagram with the angles accurately measured.

● Clearly label any additions that you make to the diagram to help your working.

● Set out your calculations in an orderly fashion, stating clearly what you are doing.

● Give your answers to three significant figures.

WorkSpace

▶ Andrew Griffin

Air conditioning systems engineer

I am employed by a company that supplies and maintains full air conditioning equipment to office buildings and hospitals. My responsibilities include meeting with customers to identify their needs and suggest to them the most appropriate heating, ventilation and air conditioning systems. We then have further meetings to discuss the estimated cost of the equipment, installation and planned maintenance.

All of the costs have to be totalled up as accurately as possible, making allowances for problems that might arise during installation. As you might imagine, this involves quite a bit of maths. Areas, volumes, installation times, percentages and unit costs all come into it. Quite a bit of this is done on the computer but it can't handle everything and some of the work has to be done by hand using the desk-top calculator. If our tender is accepted we can then draw up detailed production, installation and maintenance schedules, and this involves even more calculations and use of graphics.

I work as part of a team and can always call on their help to solve any tricky problems. I enjoy my work and it gives us all great satisfaction when a customer accepts a new tender.

Think about it

1 What communication skills do you think are required in Andrew's job?

2 What topics that we have covered do you think would be the most important in estimating the cost of a product?

3 Would you enjoy working as part of a highly skilled team of engineers?

4 How can you improve your communication skills?

Introduction

We take it for granted that the cars we drive and the domestic appliances we use will work safely and reliably. For this we can thank the mechanical and electrical engineers who design, manufacture and test the finished products and their component parts. In carrying out these tasks they often need to understand the principles of mechanical and electrical science. This might be to calculate the dimensions of a component so that it is strong enough to carry a load or withstand a force. It might also be to calculate the current in an electric circuit or to calculate the liquid or gas pressure in a container.

In this unit you will be introduced to some of the basic scientific principles that underpin electrical and mechanical engineering and how they are applied to solve engineering problems. They are rather like building blocks and, once they are in place, they will enable you to move on to a higher level of study.

Assessment: This unit will be assessed through a series of assignments set by your teacher/tutor.

Learning aims

After completing this unit you should:

A know about concepts and principles relating to electrical science

B know about concepts and principles relating to mechanical science.

> I work on a chemical plant with a team of instrumentation technicians. Our job is to carry out routine checks on the pressure gauges, temperature sensors and flow measuring equipment. We use special test equipment and any that are faulty we have to replace. We take the faulty items to our workroom and if possible we repair and reset them. I find that the scientific principles that I learned in this unit have helped me to understand how the different kinds of measuring and recording equipment operate.
>
> Oliver, *17-year-old engineering apprentice*

Electrical and Mechanical Science for Engineering

11

Assessment Zone

This table shows what you must do in order to achieve a **Pass**, **Merit** or **Distinction** grade and where you can find activities in this book to help you.

Assessment and grading criteria			
Level 1	Level 2 Pass	Level 2 Merit	Level 2 Distinction
Learning aim A: Know about concepts and principles relating to electrical science			
1A.1 Identify parameters of direct current circuits.	**2A.P1** English Define parameters of direct current circuits. **See Assessment activity 11.1, page 253**		
1A.2 Identify parameters of magnetic fields.	**2A.P2** English Define parameters of magnetic fields. **See Assessment activity 11.1, page 253**		
1A.3 Draw a simple series DC circuit and calculate the total resistance, current and power.	**2A.P3** Maths Draw a series and a parallel DC circuit and determine total resistance, potential difference, current and power for each. **See Assessment activity 11.1, page 253**	**2A.M1** Maths Find total resistance, potential difference, current and power in a combined series/parallel circuit. **See Assessment activity 11.1, page 253**	
1A.4 English Describe the interaction between a current-carrying conductor and a magnetic field.	**2A.P4** Maths Find the force on a current-carrying conductor situated in a magnetic field from given data. **See Assessment activity 11.1, page 253**	**2A.M2** Maths Find the torque produced by the armature of a simple DC motor. **See Assessment activity 11.2, page 269**	**2A.D1** English Compare the construction and operation of two types of electro-magnetic coils in the context of engineered products. **See Assessment activity 11.2, page 269**
Learning aim B: Know about concepts and principles relating to mechanical science			
1B.5 Identify parameters of static and dynamic mechanical systems.	**2B.P5** English Define parameters of static and dynamic mechanical systems. **See Assessment activity 11.2, page 269**		
1B.6 Maths Using a graphical method find the resultant of two concurrent coplanar forces from given data.	**2B.P6** Maths Using a graphical method find the resultant and equilibrant of a system of concurrent coplanar forces from given data. **See Assessment activity 11.2, page 269**		

Assessment and grading criteria

Level 1	Level 2 Pass	Level 2 Merit	Level 2 Distinction
1B.7 Maths	**2B.P7** Maths	**2B.M3** English	**2B.D2** Maths
Produce a velocity/time graph from given data.	Find the uniform acceleration and retardation of a body by plotting and interpreting a velocity/time graph from given data. **See Assessment activity 11.2, page 269**	Describe the conditions required for the static equilibrium of a body. **See Assessment activity 11.2, page 269**	Calculate the work done and power dissipated in moving a body of given mass along a horizontal surface at constant velocity. **See Assessment activity 11.2, page 269**
1B.8	**2B.P8** Maths	**2B.M4** English	
Describe gauge and absolute pressure.	Describe gauge and absolute pressure and calculate the pressure at depth in a fluid from given data. **See Assessment activity 11.2, page 269**	Describe how a U-tube manometer would be used to measure gas pressure. **See Assessment activity 11.2, page 269**	

Maths / Opportunity to practise mathematical skills   English / Opportunity to practise English skills

How you will be assessed

This unit will be assessed through a series of tasks set by your teacher/tutor. You will be expected to use scientific principles to solve engineering problems. You will need to show your full working out and use the correct mathematical techniques. For example, you might be expected to calculate the values of resistance, current, potential difference and power in an electric circuit. You might also be asked to plot a velocity/time graph for a moving vehicle and calculate its acceleration.

Your assessment could be in the form of written work, diagrams and calculations, for example, as part of a written report.

Parameters of direct current circuits

Getting started

Think of the different ways that you use electricity and how different your life would be without it. Think about where you might be able to make savings by using electricity more efficiently.

Introduction

In this topic you will learn how we define current, voltage, resistance, power, electrical charge, electromotive force and potential difference in direct current electrical circuits.

◢ System parameters

Quantities such as current, voltage and resistance are known as system parameters. A parameter is a quantity that:

- affects the way the system operates
- helps to describe the state of the system
- can change and can be measured.

Electrical charge

To understand what makes an electric current you first need to know about electrical charge. The atoms that make up all substances are composed of a nucleus that carries a positive charge and orbiting electrons that carry a negative charge. The basic unit of electrical charge is carried by a single electron. This is extremely small.

The SI unit of charge is the Coulomb (C), where:

1 Coulomb = 6.25×10^{18} electron charges.

Electrical current (I)

When a conductor such as a lamp is attached across the terminals of a battery, a current of electrons is made to flow through it. The flow is continuous in one direction and that is why we call it a direct current.

The SI unit of electric current is the Ampere (A) where:

1 Ampere = 1 Coulomb of charge passing in 1 second.

We use the symbol I for current. An ammeter can be connected to a circuit to record the flowing current.

Electromotive force (E) and potential difference (V)

Electromotive force, or **emf** for short, is the force exerted by a device such as a battery that causes an electric current to flow. In other words, we can say that it is the force available at the battery output terminal before any current is drawn from it. The SI unit of electromotive force is the Volt (V).

Did you know?

Although a lamp lights up immediately when you switch it on, the drift of electrons that form the current is very slow. It is said that for a typical electric torch, no one electron manages to make the complete trip around the circuit during the life of the battery.

Key terms

Electromotive force (emf) – the voltage across the terminals of a battery before anything is connected to it.

When a current flows, the terminal voltage is seen to fall a little and what remains is the **potential difference** across the connected circuit. A voltmeter connected across a circuit, or part of a circuit, records the potential difference that is present.

Electrical resistance (*R*)

The flow of electrons in a conductor is impeded by the stationary atoms around which they must pass. We call this electrical **resistance**. The SI unit of electrical resistance is the Ohm (Ω).

A conductor has a resistance of 1 ohm when a potential difference of 1 volt causes a current of 1 ampere to flow.

Electrical power

When an electric current flows along a conductor, we can say that some work has been done, or that some energy has been transferred. **Electrical power** is that rate of energy transfer. Its SI unit is the Watt (W). It is that rate at which energy is transferred when a potential difference of 1 volt causes a current of 1 ampere to flow. It is calculated by multiplying the potential difference *V* volts by the current *I* amperes.

Electrical power = *VI* (Watts)   (1)

The purpose of an electrical system is to deliver this energy in a useful form. Sometimes it is used to power a motor and in other instances it is used to produce light, heat or sound.

Did you know?

In the 1780s in Bologna, the Italian scientist Alessandro Volta produced the first battery, enabling the flow of direct current to be studied. The unit of potential difference is named after him.

Key terms

Potential difference – the voltage between any two points in an electric circuit.

Resistance – opposition in a conductor to the flow of electric current.

Electrical power – the energy consumed per second by an electric circuit. It is measured in Watts (W). Heat, light and work are forms of energy into which electrical energy is often transferred.

Activity 11.1   Formula for power

You will most likely have a number of plug-in electrical appliances in your home – for example, an electric kettle, electric iron, bedside light, hair dryer. Somewhere on each one will be printed its power rating.

Make a note of these and, using the above formula for power, see if you can calculate the current that each one will consume when connected to the 230 volt mains supply.

Just checking

1   What is the SI unit of electric current and how is it defined in terms of the passage of electrical charge?

2   What is the SI unit of electrical resistance and how is it defined in terms of electric current and potential difference?

Parameters of magnetic fields

Did you know?

When a bar magnet is suspended by a cord at its centre, it will swing round and align itself with the earth's magnetic field. The end that points north is designated a north-seeking pole and the other end is designated a south-seeking pole. Sometimes they are labelled N and S. This is what happens with the magnetised needle of a compass.

Key terms

Magnetic field – a force field produced around a magnet.

Magnetic flux – the imaginary lines of force in a magnetic field.

Introduction

In this topic we will look at the close relationship between magnetic fields and electric current.

Magnetic field

You will be familiar with fridge magnets and probably also with horseshoe magnets and bar magnets. A magnet seems to affect the space around it. We say that it produces a **magnetic field** or force field. We cannot see it but we know it exists because the magnet will attract iron and steel objects. Magnets will also attract or repel each other.

A magnetic field is set up wherever charged particles are in motion. In every kind of material, electrons are in motion around the nucleus of the atoms and each electron produces a small magnetic field. In most cases, however, they orbit in pairs in such a way as to cancel out each other's magnetism. But in some materials, such as iron, nickel and cobalt, there are unpaired electrons where the magnetic fields are not cancelled out. When these electron orbits are aligned in the same direction, a strong magnetic field can be produced. This is what happens when iron and steel becomes magnetised to make a horseshoe magnet or a bar magnet.

Field around a current-carrying conductor

In Topic A.1 we looked at direct electric current and learned that this is the flow of electrons along a conductor – this is the reason why a magnetic field is set up around a current-carrying conductor. When the conductor is in the form of a coil wound around an iron core, the magnetic field can become very strong. This is the principle behind the construction of electro-magnets.

Magnetic flux (Φ)

We say that a magnetic field is made up of lines of force. When you sprinkle iron filings on to a sheet of paper under which there is a bar or horseshoe magnet, they seem to arrange themselves along the lines of force. We call these imaginary lines of force **magnetic flux** and use the Greek letter Φ (phi) as an abbreviation. They are not really present but it is convenient to think of a magnetic field in this way. The SI unit of magnetic flux is the Weber (*Wb*), which you can think of as belonging to a single line of force.

The magnetic flux is assumed to flow out of the north pole of a magnet and flow into the south pole, as shown in Figure 11.1. In the case of a straight current-carrying conductor, the flux encircles it, as shown in Figure 11.2(a). Its direction is said to follow a right-hand screw rule; that is, when the current is flowing away from the observer, the flux is in a clockwise direction.

Figure 11.1 Magnetic field around a bar magnet

The way that we indicate the direction of current flow and the direction of the lines of force is shown in Figure 11.2(b). Imagine the cross (+) as being the head of a wood screw. To screw it into a piece of wood you would turn it clockwise, and that is the direction of the lines of force when the current is flowing away from you. On the far right of Figure 11.2, imagine the point of the screw coming towards you. It will be turning anticlockwise as you see it, and that is the direction of the lines of force when the current is flowing towards you.

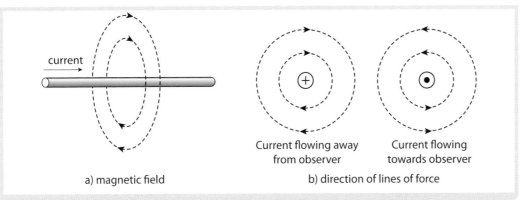

a) magnetic field   b) direction of lines of force

Figure 11.2 Field around a current-carrying conductor

A current-carrying coil produces a magnetic field similar to that of a bar magnet. It is known as a solenoid. The north- and south-pole ends are determined by the direction of the windings and the direction of the current, as shown in Figure 11.3. When the coil is wound around an iron core and the current is switched off, the core is found to have retained some of its magnetism, becoming a bar magnet. Soft iron tends to lose its magnetism fairly quickly but hard steel will keep it for long periods. This is how bar magnets are made.

Did you know?

An iron or steel magnet will lose its magnetism when heated to 770°C, which is known as its Curie temperature.

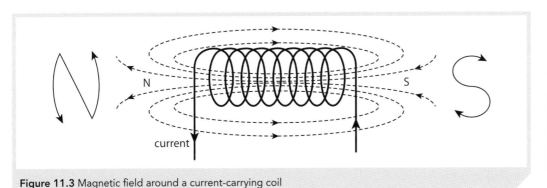

Figure 11.3 Magnetic field around a current-carrying coil

Remember

The direction of the lines of force around a current-carrying conductor is such as to obey a right-hand screw rule (clockwise when the current is flowing away from the observer).

Flux density (*B*)

In a strong magnetic field the lines of force are packed closely together and we measure the intensity of the field by its **flux density** (*B*). This is the number of lines of force (*Wb*) passing at right angles through an area of 1 square metre. The SI unit of flux density is the **Tesla (*T*)**, which is a flux of 1 Weber per square metre.

Key terms

Flux density – the flux passing through an area of 1 m² at right angles to the field.

Just checking

1   What is the direction of the lines of force around a current-carrying conductor when the current is flowing away from the observer?

2   What do we mean by the 'flux density' of a magnetic field?

Direct current electrical circuits

Introduction

In this topic you will learn about electrical circuits, their parameters and their components.

Circuit symbols

An electric circuit consists of a number of components linked together and connected to a source of electromotive force such as a battery.

In order to understand electric circuits, you need to be able to recognise the symbols used for the circuit components. Some of the more common ones are as shown in Figure 11.4.

Figure 11.4 Circuit symbols

Circuit diagram

An electric circuit might contain a number of components connected together and supplied with current from a battery. A typical circuit diagram containing a number of the above components is shown in Figure 11.5. Can you recognise them without looking at Figure 11.4?

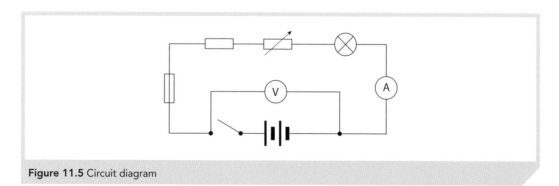

Figure 11.5 Circuit diagram

Combining resistors in series circuits and parallel circuits

When the components in an electric circuit are connected in series, they are connected nose to tail as shown in Figure 11.6. Each component has a resistance R_1, R_2, R_3 and so on, and the total resistance, R, of the circuit is the sum of the separate resistances.

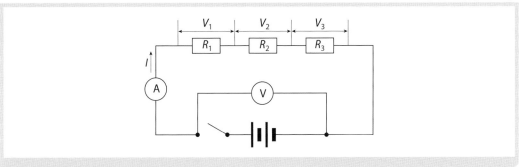

Figure 11.6 Resistances in series

$$R = R1 + R2 + R3 + \dots \quad (2)$$

It is the same current, I, that flows through each resistance and will be recorded on the ammeter. The voltmeter records the total potential difference across the circuit and this is the sum of the separate potential difference values V_1, V_2, V_3 and so on, across each resistance.

$$V = V1 + V2 + V3 + \dots \quad (3)$$

When the components in an electric circuit are connected in parallel, they are connected as shown in Figure 11.7. The components again have the resistance R_1, R_2, R_3 and so on, and the resultant resistance, R, of the circuit is found from the sum of their reciprocals.

Figure 11.7 Resistances in parallel

$$\frac{1}{R} = \frac{1}{R_1} + \frac{1}{R_2} + \frac{1}{R_3} + \dots \quad (4)$$

Now it is the same potential difference, V, across each resistance as recorded on the voltmeter but the current through each one is different. The total current, I, is the sum of the separate currents I_1, I_2, I_3 and so on.

$$I = I_1 + I_2 + I_3 + \dots \quad (5)$$

?   Did you know?

When resistances are connected in parallel, the resulting resistance of the network is always less than the smallest value of resistance. Why do you think that this is so?

Ohm's law and electrical power

Getting started

You now know how to calculate the resistance of a circuit when resistors are connected in series and in parallel. What do you think will happen to the current flowing through each resistor if we increase the supply voltage?

Introduction

Electric circuits are designed to do a particular task. Typical examples are the lighting circuit in your home or the temperature control circuit that turns your central heating on and off. The engineers who design these circuits must be able to calculate the current that will be flowing and the power that they will consume.

Ohm's law gives us the relationship between potential difference and current. We state it as follows.

The current flowing in a conductor is proportional to the potential difference between its ends.

The law assumes that physical conditions such as temperature do not change and that, if they do, the flow of current will not be affected. When Ohm's law is obeyed, a graph of potential difference against current for a conductor or circuit will be a straight line that starts from the origin, as shown in Figure 11.8.

As Ohm's law states, the graph shows that current is proportional to potential difference.

Potential difference = Constant × Current

The constant is the resistance, R, of the conductor and so we can write:

Potential difference = Resistance × Current

$$V = IR \quad (6)$$

This simple formula is the foundation of all electrical calculations. It can be transposed to make either the current, I, or the resistance, R, the subject.

$$I = \frac{V}{R} \quad (7) \qquad R = \frac{V}{I} \quad (8)$$

As can be seen from Figure 11.8, you can also find the resistance of a conductor or circuit from the gradient of the potential difference v. current graph.

You may find it easy to remember these formulae by drawing the triangle shown in Figure 11.9.

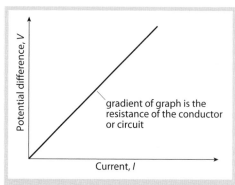

Figure 11.8 Graph of potential difference v. current

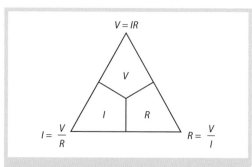

Figure 11.9 Ohm's law triangle

WorkSpace

► Emma Robinson

Instrumentation technician

I am employed at a chemical plant that produces a range of solvents and catalysts that are used in the manufacture of plastics and protective coatings. My day-to-day job includes the routine inspection of pressure-, temperature- and flow-measuring instruments. These are part of the control and recording system that includes programmable logic controllers and data loggers, monitored from a central control room. Our processes work for long periods of production and it is important that there are no interruptions.

I work as part of a team of technicians and we operate a programme of preventative maintenance. We know that if they are left alone, some items of equipment will develop faults, so we check them regularly and replace them after they have been in service for a planned length of time.

Some of the instruments and controllers that we replace can be used again and we take them to our workshop where we repair and recalibrate them. Sometimes we get an alarm signal that part of the plant is not working correctly, and this takes priority over our routine jobs. Some of my time is spent in updating our maintenance records and writing reports. Our records give us a picture of the things that can go wrong and how with planned maintenance we can prevent this from happening.

Think about it

1 Why do you think a knowledge of electric circuits is important in Emma's job?

2 Why is planned maintenance essential to the smooth running of engineering systems?

3 Why is it important to repair, recondition and reuse engineering equipment?

Electrical power – the energy consumed per second by an electric circuit. It is measured in Watts (W). Heat, light and work are forms of energy into which electrical energy is often transferred.

We can use these Ohm's law formulae to give us alternative way of calculating **electrical power**.

From equation 1 (page 239): Electrical power = VI

But $V = IR$, and substituting IR for V gives

Electrical power = IRI

Electrical power = I^2R (9)

Also, $I = \dfrac{V}{R}$, and substituting $\dfrac{V}{R}$ for I gives

Electrical power = $V \times \dfrac{V}{R}$

Electrical power = $\dfrac{V^2}{R}$ (10)

Worked example 11.1

Figure 11.10 Circuit diagram

Figure 11.11 Graph of potential difference v. current

In the circuit shown in Figure 11.10, the variable resistance is used to vary the current flowing through the lamp, causing it to be brighter or dimmer. The voltmeter records the potential difference across the lamp and the readings of current and potential difference are recorded in Table 11.1.

Table 11.1 Current v. potential difference

Current (amps)	0.5	0.8	1.1	1.3	1.6	1.9
Potential difference (volts)	2.0	3.2	4.4	5.2	6.4	7.6

Plot a graph of potential difference against current and use it to find the resistance of the lamp.

When plotted, the graph is a straight line through the origin, as shown in Figure 11.11. This shows that Ohm's law is obeyed; that is, the current flowing through the lamp is proportional to the potential difference across it.

The gradient of the graph, which gives the resistance of the lamp, is found by drawing the triangle shown and dividing the vertical side (7 volts) by the horizontal side (1.75 amps).

Resistance of lamp = Gradient of graph

$$R = \frac{7}{1.75} = 4\ \Omega$$

Worked example 11.2

An ammeter placed in an electric circuit shows that a current of 0.43 A is flowing, and a voltmeter placed across the input terminals to the circuit records a potential difference of 12.6 V. Calculate a) the resistance of the circuit, b) the power dissipated.

Finding resistance of the circuit

$$R = \frac{V}{I} = \frac{12.6}{0.43}$$

$$R = 29.3 \ \Omega$$

Finding power dissipated (the energy transferred per second)

$$\text{Power} = VI = 12.6 \times 0.43$$

$$\text{Power} = 5.42 \ \text{W}$$

Worked example 11.3

The circuit shown in Figure 11.12 contains three resistances in series, which are connected to a 24 V supply. Calculate a) the resistance, R, of the circuit, b) the current, I, flowing through the resistances, c) the potential difference across each of the resistances, d) the power dissipated in the circuit.

Figure 11.12 Circuit diagram

a) Finding total resistance of circuit

$$R = R_1 + R_2 + R_3 = 9 + 8 + 5$$

$$R = 22 \ \Omega$$

b) Finding current flowing in circuit.

$$I = \frac{V}{R} = \frac{24}{22}$$

$$I = 1.09 \ \text{A}$$

c) Finding potential difference V_1 across R_1

Now that we know the current flowing through the resistances we can apply the Ohm's law formula for potential difference to each one in turn.

$$V_1 = IR_1 = 1.09 \times 9$$

$$V_1 = 9.81 \ \text{V}$$

Finding potential difference V_2 across R_2

$$V_2 = IR_2 = 1.09 \times 8$$

$$V_2 = 8.72 \ \text{V}$$

Finding potential difference V_3 across R_3

$$V_3 = IR_3 = 1.09 \times 5$$

$$V_3 = 5.45 \ \text{V}$$

Finally, do a check to see that these all add up to the supply voltage.

$$V = V1 + V2 + V3 = 9.81 + 8.72 + 5.45$$

$$V = 23.98 \ \text{V so the answers are correct (the 0.02}$$
difference is caused by rounding I to 1.09).

d) Finding power dissipated

$$\text{Power} = \frac{V^2}{R} = \frac{24^2}{22}$$

$$\text{Power} = 26.2 \ \text{W}$$

CONTINUED ▸▸

Worked example 11.4

A circuit contains two resistances connected in parallel to a 12 V supply as shown in Figure 11.13. Calculate a) the resistance, R, of the circuit, b) the current, I, flowing in the circuit, c) the current flowing through each of the resistances, d) the power dissipated in the circuit.

Figure 11.13 Circuit diagram

a) Finding resulting resistance R, of circuit

$$\frac{1}{R} = \frac{1}{R_1} + \frac{1}{R_2} = \frac{1}{4} + \frac{1}{10}$$

This is where your electronic calculator comes in handy. Use the $[\frac{1}{x}]$ key to add these reciprocals together as follows.

$[4]\ [\frac{1}{x}]\ [+]\ [10]\ [\frac{1}{x}]\ [=]$

The answer that should appear on your display is:

$$\frac{1}{R} = 0.35$$

You can now press the [1/x] key once again to invert this number, giving you the value of R. That should appear on your display as:

$R = 2.86\ \Omega$

As you can see, this is less than the value of the lower of the two resistances.

b) Finding current, I, flowing in circuit

$$I = \frac{V}{R} = \frac{12}{2.86}$$
$$I = 4.2\ A$$

c) Finding current I_1 flowing through resistance R_1

$$I_1 = \frac{V}{R_1} = \frac{12}{4}$$
$$I = 3.0\ A$$

Finding current I_2 flowing through resistance R_2

$$I_2 = \frac{V}{R_2} = \frac{12}{10}$$
$$I = 1.2\ A$$

Finally, do a check to see that these add up to the total current flowing.

$$I = I_1 + I_2 = 3.0 + 1.2$$
$$I = 4.2\ A \text{ so the answers are correct.}$$

d) Finding power dissipated in circuit

$$Power = \frac{V^2}{R} = \frac{12^2}{2.86}$$
$$Power = 50.3\ W$$

Worked example 11.5

A circuit contains resistors connected in a series–parallel combination as shown in Figure 11.14. If the ammeter in the circuit shows the current to be 3.5 A, calculate a) the combined resistance of the circuit, b) the supply voltage, c) the voltage across each of the resistors, d) the current flowing through each if the resistors in parallel, e) the power dissipated in the circuit.

Figure 11.14 Circuit diagram

a) Finding combined resistance R_{3-4} of parallel resistors R_3 and R_4.

$$\frac{1}{R_{3-4}} = \frac{1}{R_3} + \frac{1}{R_4} = \frac{1}{3} + \frac{1}{6} = \frac{3}{6}$$

$$R_{3-4} = 2\ \Omega$$

Finding total resistance, R, of circuit

$$R = R_1 + R_2 + R_{3-4} = 6 + 4 + 2$$

$$R = 12\ \Omega$$

b) Finding supply voltage, V

$$V = IR = 3.5 \times 12$$

$$V = 42\ V$$

c) Finding voltage across R_1

$$V_1 = IR_1 = 3.5 \times 6$$

$$V = 21\ V$$

Finding voltage across R_2

$$V_2 = IR_2 = 3.5 \times 4$$

$$V = 14\ V$$

Finding voltage across parallel resistors R_3 and R_4

$$V_{3-4} = IR_{3-4} = 3.5 \times 2$$

$$V_{3-4} = 7\ V$$

Check that the separate voltages add up to the supply voltage.

$$V_1 + V_2 + V_{3-4} = 21 + 14 + 7$$

$$V_1 + V_2 + V_{3-4} = 42\ V \text{ so the values are correct.}$$

d) Finding current passing through R_3

$$I_3 = \frac{V_3}{R_3} = \frac{7}{6}$$

$$I_3 = 1.17\ A$$

Finding current passing through R_4

$$I_4 = \frac{V_4}{R_4} = \frac{7}{3}$$

$$I_4 = 2.33\ A$$

Check that the separate currents add up to the supply current.

$$I_3 + I_4 = 1.17 + 2.33$$

$$I_3 + I_4 = 3.5\ A \text{ so the values are correct.}$$

e) Finding power dissipated.

$$\text{Power} = I^2R = 3.5^2 \times 12$$

$$\text{Power} = 147\ W$$

Magnetic circuits

Introduction

When we talk of magnetic circuits, we assume that there is a flow of magnetism in the direction of the imaginary lines of force. The lines of force can pass through the metal of a bar magnet, the iron core of an electro-magnet, through air or even through a vacuum. Let us look at some devices that use the energy in a magnetic field to do useful work for us.

Interaction between a current-carrying conductor and a magnetic field

When a current-carrying conductor passes through a magnetic field, as shown in Figure 11.15, it experiences a force that tries to push it sideways. The reason is that the circular magnetic field produced around the conductor reacts against the field through which it passes. This is shown in Figure 11.16.

The directions of the magnetic field, the current and the force exerted are given by **Fleming's left-hand rule** (see Figure 11.15). When you hold your left hand in the position shown, the direction of the **f**lux is given by the **f**irst finger. The direction of the current, **I**, is given by the m**I**ddle finger and the direction of the **th**rust is given by the **th**umb.

The force, or thrust, acting on the conductor is proportional to three things:

- The flux density (B) of the magnetic field, which is measured in Tesla (T).
- The current (I) flowing in the conductor, which is measured in amps (A).
- The length (L) of the conductor that is in the field, which is measured in metres.

Multiplying these together will give you the value of the force (F) on the conductor, measured in Newtons (N).

$$F = BIL \quad (11)$$

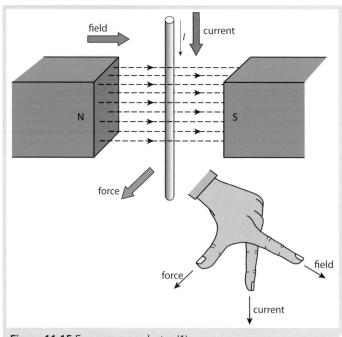

Figure 11.15 Force on a conductor (1)

Figure 11.16 Force on a conductor (2)

Worked example 11.6

a) Calculate the force acting on a conductor which carries a current of 7.5 A and is situated in a magnetic field of flux density 0.25 T at right angles to the flux. The length of the conductor that lies in the field is 1.35 m.

b) Calculate the current needed to increase the force on the conductor to 6N.

a) Finding force on conductor

$$F = BIL = 0.25 \times 7.5 \times 1.35$$

$$F = 2.53 \text{ N}$$

b) Finding current required

$$F = BIL$$

$$I = \frac{F}{BL} = \frac{6}{0.25 \times 1.35}$$

$$I = 17.8 \text{ A}$$

Direct current (DC) motors

Now that we are able to calculate the force on a conductor, we can apply this knowledge to the operation of a simple direct current (DC) motor.

The rotating part of an electric motor is called the **armature**. In the simple case shown in Figure 11.17 it is a rectangular coil which is fed with direct current through the brushes and split slip-ring. This part of the motor is called the **commutator**. In the position shown in Figure 11.17, each long side of the coil experiences a force, F, that causes the armature to rotate. The forces exert a turning moment. We call this the output **torque**, which is the force multiplied by the turning radius, r.

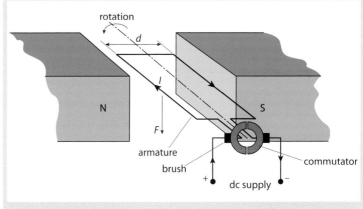

Figure 11.17 DC motor

The torque is a maximum when the coil is in the position shown. As it rotates, the force stays the same, pulling upwards and downwards, but the torque becomes less. When the coil is in the vertical position the force, F, is still upwards and downwards but there is no turning effect and the torque falls to zero.

Because the force, F, acts on each side of the coil, the maximum torque will be:

Max Torque = $2Fr$

But $2r = d$, the width of the coil, so that:

Max Torque = Fd (12)

Now from equation 11, $F = BIL$:

Max Torque = $BILd$

The torque can be increased by having more than one turn of wire on the coil. If it has n turns, the maximum torque will be:

Max Torque = $nBILd$ (13)

The momentum of the coil carries it through the vertical position and the two halves of the slip-ring exchange brushes. This ensures that the current is always in the direction that maintains the rotation and the torque builds up to a maximum again.

Key terms

Armature – the rotating part of an electric motor.

Commutator – that part of the armature through which the electric current is supplied.

Torque – a measure of the turning effect of the force.

Remember

The force on a current-carrying conductor is proportional to the flux density of the magnetic field, the effective length of the conductor and the current flowing through it.

CONTINUED ▶▶

Worked example 11.7

The armature coil of a simple DC motor has 250 turns of wire and the magnetic field between the pole pieces has a flux density of 0.3 T. The effective length of the coil sides is 120 mm and the width of the coil is 80 mm. Calculate a) the force acting on each side of the coil when a direct current of 3.5 A flows through it, b) the maximum torque acting on the coil.

a) Finding force acting on each side of the coil

$F = nBIL$ (where $n = 250$ turns)

$F = 250 \times 0.3 \times 3.5 \times 0.12$

$F = 31.5\,N$

b) Finding maximum torque acting on coil

Max Torque $= Fd$ (where $d = 0.08$ m)

Max Torque $= 31.5 \times 0.08$

Max Torque $= 2.52\,Nm$

Electro-magnetic devices

The solenoid, which is basically a coil of wire wound around an iron core, is put to use in a great many engineering applications. The magnetic field produced is used to open and close electrical switches and also pneumatic and hydraulic valves. We have already described electric motors; moving coils are also to be found in ammeters, voltmeters, microphones and loudspeakers.

Moving coil meters

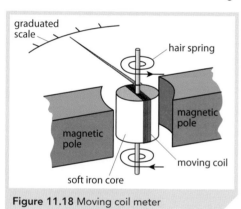

Figure 11.18 Moving coil meter

Analogue voltmeters and ammeters, where a pointer moves over a scale to give a reading, are generally of the moving coil type. Their principle of operation is very similar to that of the DC motor. The coil, which is shown in Figure 11.18, is wound around a soft iron core. The difference is that the coil, to which the pointer is attached, is only allowed to swing through an angle of around 90°.

It is restrained by the two hair springs. They control the swinging of the pointer and are also used to supply current to the coil. The difference between a voltmeter and an ammeter is the resistance that the coil offers to the flow of current. A voltmeter has a high resistance while an ammeter has a low resistance. You will learn the reasons for this when you continue your studies at a higher level.

Relays and contactors

Key terms

Relay – a magnetically operated switch.

Contactor – a heavy-duty relay.

A **relay** is a magnetically operated switch. It enables a small electric current in one circuit to switch on or off a much larger electric current in another circuit. A relay consists of a coil of wire wound on a soft iron core, a yoke and a hinged armature, as shown in Figure 11.19(a).

When you turn the ignition key to start a car engine, you activate a switch similar to that shown schematically in Figure 11.19(a). It is very often referred to as 'the solenoid' but is in fact a relay. It allows a very small current from the battery to switch on a much larger current to the starter motor.

Heavy-duty relays used to switch high-voltage power-supply systems on and off are often called **contactors**. They operate on the same relay principle, but are of much larger and more robust construction.

Figure 11.19 Relays

Solenoid valves

Just as relays are used to control the flow of electric current, solenoid valves are used to control the flow in pneumatic and hydraulic circuits. In these valves the iron core of the solenoid is a cylinder and contains a spring-loaded piston, as shown in Figure 11.20.

Figure 11.20 Solenoid valve

When the solenoid is energised, the magnetic field pushes the piston up the cylinder to compress the spring. As this occurs, the piston releases a diaphragm, allowing the fluid to flow. As can be seen, the diaphragm contains two small holes. The one on the left equalises the pressure above and below it when it is in the closed position. As the piston rises, the hole in the centre allows a little fluid to flow from above it so that the pressure is greater underneath the diaphragm. This causes it to flex upward, allowing the fluid to flow to the exit. The spring returns the piston to its original position when the current to the solenoid is switched off and the flow ceases.

This is just one type of solenoid valve. With other types used in pneumatic and hydraulic actuation circuits, the piston is arranged to cover and uncover ports in the wall of a cylinder. This directs fluid in different directions to operate the different actuators. Automated packaging and machining systems use this type of solenoid valve.

Assessment activity 11.1   2A.P1 | 2A.P2 | 2A.P3 | 2A.M1 | 2A.P4 | 2A.M2 | 2A.D1

You are working for an engineering company that produces a range of electro-mechanical products. You have been asked by the training manager to produce a series of learning documents that will be of help to new electrical/electronic apprentices. You will need to begin by defining the parameters of direct current circuits and magnetic fields. These must include voltage, current, resistance, power, electric charge, electromotive force, potential difference, magnetic field, field around a current-carrying conductor, magnetic flux and flux density. You will also need to draw a DC circuit with a combination of resistances in series and

parallel, and demonstrate the calculation of total resistance, potential difference and power for each one.

Your next task will be to explain and demonstrate the calculation of force on a current-carrying conductor in a magnetic field and the torque produced by the armature of a simple DC motor.

Finally, with the help of suitable diagrams, you will need to compare the construction and operation of two applications of electro-magnetic coils in engineered products.

Tips

- Make sure that you have defined the full range of parameters.
- Illustrate explanation of force on a conductor by means of a diagram showing the directions of current, magnetic flux and force exerted.
- Clearly show the input connections and output motion in diagrams describing the applications of electro-magnetic coils.

Parameters of static and dynamic mechanical systems

Introduction

In this topic you will learn how we define the parameters used in static and dynamic system calculations.

◢ System parameters

First we need to define what we mean by vector quantities and scalar quantities. A vector quantity is a measure of something that has both magnitude (size) and a direction. An example of this is the force acting on an object. As you probably know, its magnitude is measured in Newtons, but just as important is the direction in which it acts. A vector quantity can be represented by a line drawn to a suitable scale on a vector diagram. The length of the line represents the magnitude of the quantity and the way that it points represents its direction.

A scalar quantity is one that has magnitude only. This means it just has a size. An example of this is the mass of an object. As you know, it is measured in kilograms and does not have any direction.

Mass

Mass is a measure of the amount of matter contained in a body. The SI (Système International) unit of mass is the kilogram (abbreviation kg).

The kilogram is the only fundamental SI unit to be defined in terms of an actual object. It is a scalar quantity and defined as the mass of a platinum-iridium cylinder measuring 39.17 mm in both height and diameter which resides at International Bureau for Weights and Measures (BIPM) at Sèvres on the outskirts of Paris.

Density

The density of a substance is its mass per cubic metre. In the case of water, 1 litre has a mass of 1 kg, and because there are 1,000 litres in a cubic metre, its density is 1,000 kgm^{-3}. Density is a scalar quantity. It is represented by the Greek letter ρ, 'rho'.

Relative density

The mild steel that we use as a general engineering material in the workshop has a density of 7,870 kgm^{-3}. This means that it is 7.87 times more dense than water. This figure is called its 'relative density' and sometimes it is also called its 'specific gravity'. Mercury is even more dense than steel. Its density is 13,600 kgm^{-3}. This means that it is 13.6 times heavier than water and so its relative density is 13.6.

Force

Force is measured in Newtons (abbreviation N). A Newton is defined as the force needed to accelerate a mass of 1 kg at the rate of 1 ms^{-2} when there is no friction or other kind of resistance present. If you can imagine a mass of 1 kg floating in space, a steady force of 1 N would cause it to pick up speed at this rate. Force is a vector quantity.

Earth's gravity and weight

In scientific and engineering terms the weight (abbreviation *W*) of an object is the force that the earth's gravity exerts on it. This varies slightly in different regions but its accepted value in calculations is 9.81 Newtons pulling down on each kilogram of mass. It is sometimes referred to as gravitational field strength and is given the symbol *g*. It is numerically the same as the acceleration due to gravity of a freely falling body (that is, $g = 9.81$ Nkg^{-1} or $g = 9.81$ ms^{-1}) and the two are very closely connected. Sometimes we use specific weight in calculations (symbol *w*), which is related to density. It is the weight per cubic metre of a substance ($w = \rho\,g$ Nm^{-3}).

Pressure

Pressure is a measure of how a force is distributed over a surface on which it acts. The SI unit of pressure is the Pascal (Pa), where 1 Pascal is a force of 1 Newton evenly distributed over an area of 1 square metre.

Moment of a force

When a force is applied to a body it sometimes tries to make it rotate. A force acting on the rim of a wheel or pulley will do this, as in Figure 11.21. The moment of a force is a measure of this turning effect. It is the product of the force and the turning radius that is at right angles to it. Its units are Newton-metres (Nm).

Moment of force = Force × Perpendicular turning radius

Moment of force = $\mathbf{F}r$ (Nm)   (14)

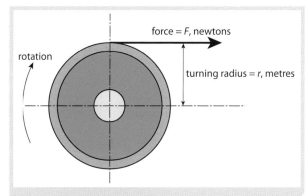

Figure 11.21 Moment of a force

Displacement

Displacement is the distance moved by a body measured in a straight line from the starting point to the finish position. The body might not have moved along this straight line, as shown in Figure 11.22, but its displacement is always the distance from start to finish.

Displacement is a vector quantity because it has direction, and can be represented by a line drawn to scale on a vector diagram as in Figure 11.22.

Figure 11.22 Displacement diagram

Velocity

The velocity of a moving body is its rate of change of displacement and, like displacement, it is a vector quantity. Its magnitude is measured in ms^{-1} or kmh^{-1}, which is its speed. But the body will also be travelling in some given direction. Very often we omit to mention this, especially if it is travelling in a straight line, but a full statement of velocity should include both speed and direction of travel. As with force and displacement, this enables the velocity of a body to be drawn to scale on a vector diagram.

Acceleration and retardation

Acceleration is also a vector quantity. It is the rate of change of velocity and its magnitude is usually measured in ms^{-2} (the change of speed per second). A body can

CONTINUED ▸▸

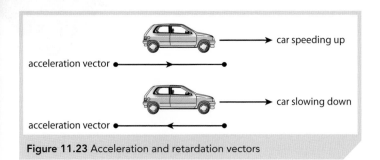

acceleration vector ●————▶●

car speeding up

acceleration vector ●————————▶●

car slowing down

acceleration vector ●————————●
◀————

Figure 11.23 Acceleration and retardation vectors

of course be speeding up or slowing down and this affects the direction in which its acceleration is drawn on a vector diagram. When a body is slowing down this is said to be retardation. If a body is speeding up, we draw its acceleration vector in the direction of travel. If the body is slowing down, however, its retardation vector is drawn in the opposite direction to its travel.

Work

When a force acts on a body and causes it to move, work is done. Work is defined as the force multiplied by the distance moved in the direction in which the force acts. The SI unit of work is the Joule (J). It is defined as the work done when a force of 1 Newton moves a body through a distance of 1 metre along its line of action. Work is a scalar quantity.

applied force, F (Newtons)

distance moved, s

Figure 11.24 Work done

When a force of F Newtons moves through a distance of s metres as in Figure 11.24, the work done is given by the formula:

Work done = Force × Distance moved

Work done = Fs Joules   (15)

Power

Power is a scalar quantity. It is the rate at which work is done. This means it is the work done per second. The SI unit of power is the Watt (W). It is defined as the work done when a force of 1 Newton moves a body through a distance of 1 metre in a time of 1 second. If the time taken to move the body in Figure 11.24 is t seconds, the average power developed will be:

$$\text{Average power} = \frac{\text{Work done}}{\text{Time taken}}$$

$$\text{Average power} = \frac{Fs}{t} \text{ Watts}   (16)$$

The distance, s, divided by the time, t, is the average velocity, v, at which the body shown in Figure 11.24 is travelling and so the average power developed can be calculated using the formula:

Average power = Force × Average velocity

Average power = $Fv_{(avg)}$ Watts   (17)

If the body is speeding up or slowing down, this formula can also be used to calculate the power that is being developed at an instant when the velocity has a value of v ms^{-1}.

Instantaneous power = Force × Instantaneous velocity

Instantaneous power = $Fv_{(inst)}$ Watts   (18)

Limiting coefficient of friction (μ)

Frictional resistance is always present in mechanical systems. Sometimes it is an essential part of the system, such as with friction clutches and brakes. In other instances – for example, in bearings and gear trains – it is wasteful in energy and can lead to overheating and breakdown. Efficient lubrication systems are needed for these components.

Within limits, frictional resistance between dry surfaces in sliding contact is found to be dependent on two things and independent on two others things. The following statements are sometimes known as Coulomb's laws of friction (the same Coulomb that the unit of electric charge is named after).

- Frictional resistance depends on the normal force or pressure between the surfaces. (Here the word 'normal' means perpendicular to, or at right angles to the surfaces.)
- Frictional resistance depends on the roughness of the two surfaces.
- Frictional resistance is independent of the area of contact.
- Frictional resistance is independent of the sliding speed.

We say that these laws apply 'within limits' because if the pressure is too great, the area of contact is very small and the sliding speed is very high, there is a tendency for the surfaces to seize or become welded together.

Consider a body resting on a flat and dry horizontal surface as shown in Figure 11.25.

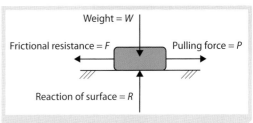

Figure 11.25 Surfaces in sliding contact

In this case the force pressing the surfaces together is the weight of the body. It is called the normal force because it acts at right angles to the surface and the surface pushes back with an equal force that we call its reaction, R. As the pull is gradually increased the frictional resistance increases up to the point where the body starts to move.

The frictional resistance as the body 'unsticks' is called the 'limiting frictional resistance'. As the body is pulled along its value does not increase any more; in fact it usually falls off a little. We find that if we divide the limiting frictional resistance, F, by the reaction, R, it will always come to the same value for a given pair of surfaces. This ratio is called their 'limiting coefficient of friction' which is given as its symbol the Greek letter μ (mu).

$$\text{Limiting coefficient of friction} = \frac{\text{Limiting frictional resistance}}{\text{Normal reaction between surfaces}}$$

$$\mu = \frac{F}{r} \text{ or } F = \mu R \quad (19)$$

The value of μ for the brakes and clutches in cars is around 0.3 to 0.4 and for rubber tyres on dry asphalt it is around 0.7.

 Did you know?

The study of frictional resistance and how it can be made use of, or be reduced by the use of lubricating oils and greases, is called tribology.

Just checking

1 What is the difference between a scalar and a vector quantity?
2 What are the two factors on which the frictional resistance between dry surfaces depends?

Statics

Introduction

In this topic we shall be looking at static force systems. These are systems of forces acting on stationary objects.

When an object is stationary the forces acting on it must be in balance. In cases where they are not balanced the object will move or rotate; we shall be using graphical methods to find the additional force needed to restore balance. Instead of saying 'in balance', we say 'in a state of static equilibrium', which means very much the same thing.

Conditions for static equilibrium

When a body is at completely at rest it is in a state of static equilibrium. There are three possible states of static equilibrium which can be described by considering the different ways in which a cone can be at rest.

Figure 11.26 Vertical and horizontal forces

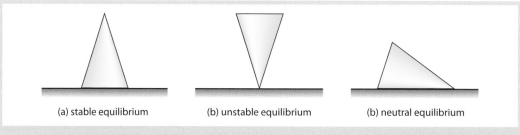

(a) stable equilibrium   (b) unstable equilibrium   (b) neutral equilibrium

Figure 11.27 States of static equilibrium

If the cone in Figure 11.27(a) is tilted slightly and released, it will return to its stable equilibrium position. The cone in Figure 11.27(b) is finely balanced on its apex. It is unstable and the slightest force will cause it to topple. The cone in Figure 11.27(c) is in a state of neutral equilibrium. An applied force will cause it to roll on its side and settle in a new position when the force is removed.

The conditions necessary for all the forms of static equilibrium are illustrated in Figure 11.28.

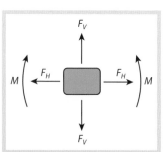

Figure 11.28 Conditions for static equilibrium

- The vertical forces acting on a body must be equal and opposite so that there is no vertical movement.
- The horizontal forces acting on a body must be equal and opposite so that there is no horizontal movement.
- The clockwise and anticlockwise moments acting on a body must be equal so that there is no rotation in any direction.

Concurrent coplanar forces

In this unit we shall only be considering bodies acted upon by 'coplanar forces'. Coplanar forces are forces that all act in the same plane, or two-dimensional force systems. Also the forces will be concurrent; that is to say they will all be acting at, or their lines of action will be passing through, a single point. The forces acting in Figure 11.26 are coplanar, but as you can see they are not all concurrent.

Parallelogram of forces

When two forces act on a body they may try to pull it in different directions as shown in Figure 11.29(a). This is called a **space diagram**. It shows accurately the directions in which the forces act but the forces themselves are not drawn to scale. The combined effect of F_1 and F_2 is called the **resultant**, R, of the system. It can be thought of as the single force that could replace F_1 and F_2 and exert the same pull on the body. For the body to remain stationary, an equal and opposite force called the **equilibrant**, E, must be applied.

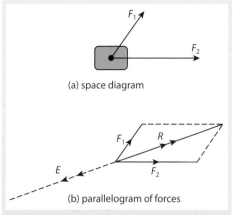

(a) space diagram

(b) parallelogram of forces

Figure 11.29 Parallelogram of forces

The resultant and equilibrant can be found by drawing a force **vector diagram** as in Figure 11.29(b). The two forces F_1 and F_2 are now drawn to a suitable scale from the same point. They are then used to construct the parallelogram whose diagonal gives the magnitude and direction of the resultant. The two arrow-heads on the resultant (and equilibrant) show that it is the combined effect of F_1 and F_2.

Key terms

Space diagram – a labelled diagram that shows a system of coplanar forces acting on a body.

Resultant – the single force that can replace a coplanar system and have the same effect.

Equilibrant – the force equal and opposite the resultant that is required to hold a body in static equilibrium.

Vector diagram – a diagram in which forces are drawn to scale and acting in a given direction.

Worked example 11.8

Find the magnitude and direction of the resultant and equilibrant for each of the systems of forces whose space diagrams are shown in Figure 11.30.

From vector diagram,

   $R = 6.24$ kN and $\theta = 43.9°$

The equilibrant, E, is equal and opposite to the resultant, R.

From vector diagram,

   $R = 7.94$ kN and $\theta = 49.1°$

The equilibrant, E, is equal and opposite to the resultant, R.

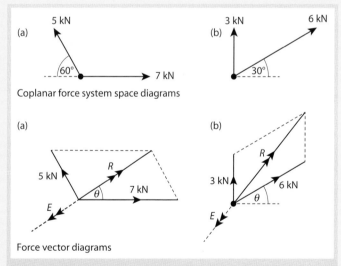

Figure 11.30 Coplanar force system space diagrams and force vector diagrams

Remember, the resultant of a system of forces is their combined pulling effect on a body. The equilibrant is the additional force that must be applied, equal and opposite to the resultant, to keep the body in a state of static equilibrium.

CONTINUED ▶▶

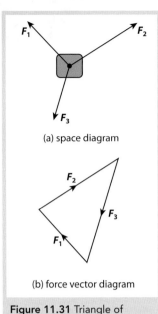

Figure 11.31 Triangle of forces

Triangle of forces

When three coplanar forces act on a body and hold it in a state of static equilibrium as shown in Figure 11.31(a) the lines of action of the forces must all pass through a common point; that is, they must be concurrent.

The force vectors form a closed triangle when drawn nose to tail as in in Figure 11.31(b). This is called **vector addition**.

Provided that you know the magnitude and direction of two of the forces, F_1 and F_2, you can construct the triangle and measure the magnitude and direction of the third force, F_3. Similarly, if you know the magnitude and direction of only one of the forces, F_1, together with the directions of the other two, you can still construct the triangle and measure the magnitude of F_2 and F_3.

The fact that a body can only be in static equilibrium under the action of three coplanar forces if the forces act through a single point (when the forces are concurrent) is worth remembering, as it may come in useful when you progress to more advanced work.

Worked example 11.9

If the body shown in Figure 11.32 is in a state of static equilibrium, find the angle θ that the 8 kN force must make with the horizontal.

From triangle of forces vector diagram, angle $\theta = 40.5°$

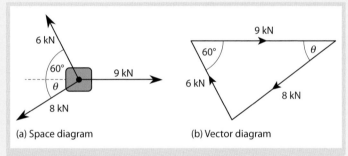

(a) Space diagram   (b) Vector diagram

Figure 11.32 Space diagram and vector diagram

Polygon of forces

Consider now a body acted on by three or more concurrent coplanar forces in such a way that it is not in equilibrium.

When the force vectors are added together, the vector diagram is not a closed triangle. There is a gap between the tail of F_1 and the nose of F_3. The line joining these, which is shown dotted in Figure 11.33(b), gives the magnitude and direction of the resultant, R, of the three forces; if the body is not secured, it will be pulled in this direction.

The additional force, F_4, which must be added to the system to maintain static equilibrium, is equal and opposite to the resultant as shown in Figure 11.33(a). This is of course the equilibrant of the system.

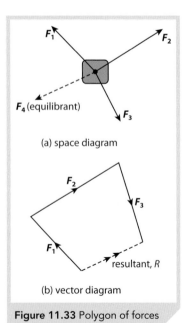

(a) space diagram

(b) vector diagram

Figure 11.33 Polygon of forces

You can use this method of solution to find the resultant and equilibrant of any number of concurrent coplanar forces. It is just that your polygon of forces will have more sides. It is good practice to work clockwise around the body when adding the force vectors together, as in Figure 11.33(b). Remember to always add them nose to tail so that the force vectors chase each other around the polygon as indicated by the arrow-heads.

Worked example 11.10

Determine the magnitude and direction of the resultant and equilibrant of the coplanar force system shown in Figure 11.34.

From vector diagram, $R = 9.75$ kN and makes an angle $\theta = 34.0$ to the horizontal as shown. The equilibrant, E, is equal and opposite to the resultant, R.

(a) Space diagram   (b) Vector diagram

Figure 11.34 Space diagram and vector diagram

Principle of moments

One of the conditions for static equilibrium is that the sum of moments of the forces acting on a body must be zero so that there is no rotation clockwise or anticlockwise. This is sometimes called the **principle of moments** and for static equilibrium it can be written that:

Clockwise moments = Anticlockwise moments

The principle can be used to find the support reactions of a simply supported beam as shown in Worked example 11.10. The load that acts on a member of any kind is said to be an **active force**. If the load and its supports are in static equilibrium we say that the supports exert an equal and opposite **reactive force**, which is why we use the term **support reaction**.

Key terms

Principle of moments – a condition for static equilibrium that states that clockwise and anticlockwise turning moments must be equal.

Active force – an external force acting on a body.

Reactive force – the equal and opposite force exerted by the body.

Support reaction – the reactive force exerted by the supports of a body.

Worked example 11.11

Determine the load carried by each support of the simply supported beam shown in Figure 11.35.

Figure 11.35 A simply supported beam

Begin by equating moments about the right-hand support to find the reaction R_1

Clockwise moments = Anticlockwise moments

$R_1 \times (2.65 + 1.75) = 8 \times 1.75$

$R_1 \times 4.4 = 8 \times 1.75$

$R_1 = \dfrac{8 \times 1.75}{4.4}$

$R_1 = 3.18$ kN

Now equate moments about the left-hand support to find the reaction R_2

Clockwise moments = Anticlockwise moments

$8 \times 2.65 = R_2 \times 4.4$

$\dfrac{8 \times 2.65}{4.4} = R_2$

$R_2 = 4.82$ kN

Finally, check that the two reactions that you have calculated add up to the downward load of 8 kN.

$R_1 + R_2 = 3.18 + 4.82 = 8$ kN, so the answers are correct.

Linear motion

Getting started

The maximum speed that you are allowed to travel on British motorways is currently 70 miles per hour (mph). If you were to break the law and travel at 75 mph, how much time would you save on a 70 mile journey? Would it be worth the risk of a fine?

Introduction

In this topic we will be looking bodies that are moving along a straight path with uniform motion. By uniform motion we mean that a body is travelling at a steady velocity or is speeding up or slowing down at a steady rate. Movement is always opposed by friction and we shall also be looking at the work done and power expended in overcoming frictional resistance.

Distance, time, speed and acceleration

The distance travelled by a moving body is usually denoted by the letter s, and measured in metres or kilometres. The time taken is denoted by the letter t, and is generally measured in seconds or hours. Speed is the rate at which distance is covered. Velocity is not quite the same. It is the rate at which distance is covered in a particular direction. Both are denoted by the letter v, which is generally measured in metres per second (ms^{-1}) or kilometres per hour (kmh^{-1}).

Graph of displacement v time

When a body is travelling at a constant velocity along a straight path, a graph of distance travelled against time is as shown in Figure 11.36.

The graph is a straight line whose gradient gives the value of the steady uniform velocity. If the body travels through a distance s, in time t, the uniform velocity v, is given by:

$$v = \frac{s}{t} \ (\text{ms}^{-1}) \quad (20)$$

When the body is travelling with initial velocity u, and accelerates to final velocity v at a steady rate, that is, increases its velocity by the same amount each second, a graph of velocity against time is as shown in Figure 11.37.

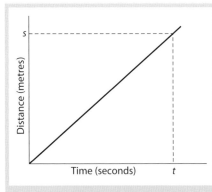

Figure 11.36 Distance v. time graph

Acceleration

Acceleration is the change of velocity per second. It is denoted by the letter a, and is generally measured in metres per second per second (ms^{-2}). When a body is speeding up its acceleration is said to be positive. When it is slowing down or retarding, its acceleration is negative and should always be given a negative sign in calculations.

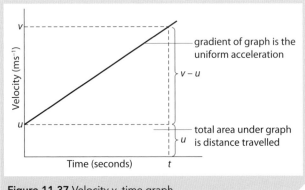

Figure 11.37 Velocity v. time graph

You can obtain three pieces of information from the graph shown in Figure 11.37. The first is that the body did not start from rest but had an initial velocity u.

The second is that the acceleration a (ms^{-2}), is uniform because the graph is a straight line. Furthermore, the gradient of the graph gives you the value of the acceleration.

$$\text{Acceleration} = \frac{\text{Change of velocity}}{\text{Time taken}}$$

$$a = \frac{v - u}{t} \quad (21)$$

Transposing this gives:

$$at = v - u$$

$$\text{or } v = u + at \quad (22)$$

These are useful formulae for finding the acceleration when you know the change in velocity or for finding the final velocity when you know the value of the uniform acceleration.

The third piece of information that you can obtain from the velocity v. time graph is the distance, s, travelled during the period of acceleration. This is given by the area under the graph which is made up of a rectangle and a triangle.

$$\text{Distance travelled} = \text{Total area under graph}$$

$$s = ut + \frac{1}{2}(v - u)t$$

From equation 22 above, $v - u = at$, and substituting for this gives:

$$s = ut + \frac{1}{2}at.t$$

$$s = ut + \frac{1}{2}at^2 \quad (23)$$

The distance travelled can also be found by multiplying together the average velocity and the time taken.

$$\text{Distance travelled} = \text{Average velocity} \times \text{Time taken}$$

$$s = \frac{1}{2}(v + u)t \quad (24)$$

These are both useful formulae for calculating distance travelled when you know the value of the other terms.

In all of the above formulae you need to know the time taken for the increase in velocity and distance travelled. Two more useful formulae can be found by combining equations 21 and 24 in such a way that the time, t, is eliminated.

Making t the subject of equation 21 gives:

$$t = \frac{v - u}{a}$$

Substituting for t in equation 24 gives:

$$s = \frac{1}{2}(v + u)\frac{(v - u)}{a} = \frac{(v + u)(v - u)}{2a}$$

It can be shown that multiplying the bracketed terms together gives:

$$s = \frac{v^2 - u^2}{2a} \quad (25)$$

CONTINUED ▶▶

Transposing gives:

$$a = \frac{v^2 - u^2}{2s} \quad (26)$$

and:

$$v^2 - u^2 = 2as$$
$$v^2 = u^2 + 2as \quad (27)$$

These are useful alternative formulae for finding distance travelled, acceleration and final velocity.

A summary of the formulae for motion with uniform acceleration is given in Table 11.2.

> ### Remember
>
> When solving problems on uniform acceleration and retardation, always look carefully at the data you are given. Select which you think is the best formula for finding distance travelled, velocity or acceleration. Afterwards, check your answer by using an alternative formula.

Table 11.2 Uniform acceleration formulae

To find distance travelled	$s = \frac{1}{2}(v + u)t$
	$s = ut + \frac{1}{2}at^2$
	$s = \frac{v^2 - u^2}{2a}$
To find acceleration	$a = \frac{v - u}{t}$
	$a = \frac{v^2 - u^2}{2s}$
To find final velocity	$v = u + at$
	$v^2 = u^2 + 2as$

Worked example 11.12

A forging of mass 75 kg is accelerated uniformly from rest along a horizontal surface to a final speed of 2.75 ms⁻¹ in a time of 3.5 seconds. The coefficient of kinetic friction between the casting and surface is 0.35. Calculate a) the frictional resistance, b) the uniform acceleration, c) the distance travelled, d) the work done in overcoming friction, e) the average value of the power dissipated in overcoming friction.

a) Finding weight of casting

$$W = mg = 75 \times 9.81$$
$$W = 736 \text{ N}$$

Finding frictional resistance

$$F = \mu R_N$$

On a flat surface, $R_N = W$

$$F = \mu W = 0.35 \times 736$$
$$F = 258 \text{ N}$$

b) Finding uniform acceleration

$$a = \frac{v - u}{t} = \frac{2.75 - 0}{3.5}$$
$$a = 0.786 \text{ ms}^{-2}$$

c) Finding distance travelled

$$s = \frac{1}{2}(v + u)t = \frac{1}{2}(2.75 + 0) \times 3.5$$
$$s = 4.81 \text{ m}$$

Provided that you have calculated the uniform acceleration correctly you could also use the formula

$$s = ut + \frac{1}{2}at^2 = (0 \times 3.5) + \frac{1}{2}(0.786 \times 3.5^2)$$
$$s = 4.81 \text{ m}$$

continued

You could also have used the formula

$$s = \frac{v^2 - u^2}{2a} = \frac{2.75^2 - 0}{2 \times 0.786}$$

$$s = 4.81 \text{ m}$$

d) Finding work done in overcoming friction

Work done = Fs = 258 × 4.81

Work done = 1,241 J or 1.24 kJ

e) Finding average power dissipated in overcoming friction

$$\text{Avg. power} = \frac{\text{Work done}}{\text{Time taken}} = \frac{1241}{3.5}$$

Avg. power = 355 W

Worked example 11.13

A braking force of 175 N causes a fork-lift truck to be retarded uniformly from an initial velocity of 10 ms⁻¹ to a final velocity of 3 ms⁻¹ while travelling through a horizontal distance of 12 m. Calculate a) the uniform retardation, b) the time taken, c) the work done, d) the maximum power dissipation.

a) Finding value of uniform retardation

$$a = \frac{v^2 - u^2}{2s} = \frac{3^2 - 10^2}{2 \times 12}$$

$$a = -3.79 \text{ ms}^{-2}$$

The negative sign denotes retardation and must be retained in part b).

b) Finding time taken

$$a = \frac{v - u}{t}$$

$$t = \frac{v - u}{a} = \frac{3 - 10}{-3.79}$$

$$t = 1.85 \text{ s}$$

c) Finding work done

Work done = Fs = 175 × 12

Work done = 2,100 J or 2.1 kJ

d) Finding maximum power dissipated

Max power dissipated = Force × Max velocity = 175 × 10

Max power dissipated = 1,750 W or 1.75 kW

Just checking

1 What can you find from the area under the curve of a velocity–time graph?

2 How do you define acceleration and how can you find it from a velocity–time graph?

Fluids and gases

Introduction

In this topic we will be looking at pressure measurement in gases and liquids, and in particular how the pressure increases with depth below the surface of a liquid.

A fluid may be described as a substance that takes on the shape of its container. A fluid can be either a liquid or a gas. The pressure in a fluid is the normal force per square metre that it exerts on the walls of its container or on a body that is immersed in the fluid. The SI unit of pressure is the **Pascal** (Pa), which is defined as a force of 1 Newton acting at right angles on an area of 1 square metre. The Pascal is a very small unit and pressures are more often measured in *kPa* or *MPa*.

Atmospheric pressure (p_a)

We are surrounded by the earth's atmosphere which exerts a very high pressure on us. At the earth's surface its average value is:

p_a = 101,325 Pa or 101.325 kPa

Luckily the pressure inside our bodies is the same as that outside, otherwise we would be crushed by the surrounding air.

An experiment that is often carried out to demonstrate the pressure of the atmosphere is to boil a small quantity of water in a metal container. A screw-top 5 litre metal container as used for motor oil is ideal. When all of the air has been driven out by steam, the container is sealed. Cold water is then allowed to run over its surface, causing the steam to condense. The pressure inside the container is then much smaller than the outside atmospheric pressure, which is seen to crush it very quickly.

An alternative unit for measuring pressure is the bar where:

1 bar = 100,000 Pa or 100 kPa

This is almost equal to atmospheric pressure and is found to be a convenient unit for measuring the pressure in a wide range of industrial processes. Atmospheric pressure is measured using a barometer, of which there are two common types. The Fortin-type mercury barometer is often used in science laboratories, while the aneroid type is more widely used by meteorologists in weather forecasting. The word 'aneroid' indicates that the instrument does not contain a liquid. The barometer that you may have on the wall at home is a basic type of aneroid barometer.

Gauge pressure (p_g)

A pressure gauge that you see on a steam boiler or a compressed air receiver measures the difference between the pressure on the inside and atmospheric pressure on the outside. This difference is called **gauge pressure** (p_g). There are a number of different types of pressure gauge, ranging from the simple U-tube manometer to Bourdon- and diaphragm-type gauges. However, unless you are told otherwise, you can assume that they all record gauge pressure.

Absolute pressure (p)

Gauge pressure is usually all that you need to know for controlling industrial processes but in some applications the total pressure of the fluid inside a container is needed. An accurate reading of atmospheric pressure is then required, which must be added on to the gauge pressure reading. That is:

Absolute pressure = Gauge pressure + Atmospheric pressure

$p = p_g + p_a$ (28)

In later work you will investigate the expansion and compression of gases where **absolute pressure** has to be used in calculations.

Density

The density of a substance is its mass per cubic metre and is represented by the Greek letter ρ, 'rho'. In the case of water, 1 litre has a mass of 1 kg and, because there are 1,000 litres in a cubic metre, its density is 1,000 kgm^{-3}.

Acceleration due to gravity

The acceleration due to gravity of a body in free fall near the earth's surface is 9.81 ms^{-1}. Its value is often denoted by the letter g. It is numerically the same as the earth's gravitational field strength at its surface. This is why we multiply the mass of a body or substance by g to find its weight.

Key terms

Absolute pressure – the sum of gauge pressure and atmospheric pressure.

Pressure at depth in a fluid

As you know, the pressure of the water increases as you dive to the bottom of a swimming pool. The pressure depends on depth, the density of the fluid and, as you will see, it also depends which planet you are on.

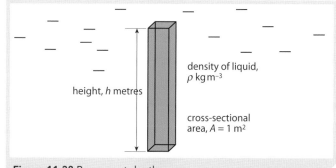

height, h metres

density of liquid, ρ kgm^{-3}

cross-sectional area, $A = 1$ m²

Figure 11.38 Pressure at depth

Consider a column of liquid in a tank or swimming bath of height h metres and cross sectional area 1 m² as shown in Figure 11.38. Let the density of the liquid be ρ kgm^{-3}. The pressure at the base of the column is caused by the weight of liquid pressing down on it. The liquid around the column has no effect on the pressure at its base.

The mass m, of the column is its volume multiplied by its density.

$m = hA\rho$

But the cross-sectional area is 1 m², giving:

$m = h\rho$

The weight of the column is its mass multiplied by g.

Weight = mg

Weight = $h\rho g$

This is the force acting on an area of 1 m², which by definition is the pressure at the base. However, this does not take into account the atmospheric pressure pushing down on the surface of the liquid, and so it is a measure of the gauge pressure, pg, at the base of the column.

$p_g = h\rho g$ (29)

CONTINUED ▶▶

The gauge pressure at depth is generally all that is needed when calculating the thrust exerted by a liquid on the side of a tank, a lock gate or the wall of a dam. As you can see from equation 29, it depends on three things:

- the depth h metres below the free surface of the liquid
- the density ρ kgm^{-3} of the liquid
- the force / acceleration due to gravity $g = 9.81$ms^{-2} (this depends which planet you are on).

The force of gravity is less on Mars because it is a smaller planet, and quite a lot less on the moon. If liquids are ever stored in these locations the pressure at depth will be correspondingly less.

Worked example 11.14

A hatch cover on the deck of a submarine is 850 mm in diameter. Determine the pressure and force acting on it at a depth of 125 m. The density of the sea water is 1,025 kgm^3.

Finding pressure on hatch cover

$p_g = h\rho g = 125 \times 1,025 \times 9.81$

$p_g = 1.26 \times 10^6$ Pa or 1.26 MPa

Finding area of hatch cover

$$A = \frac{\pi d^2}{4} = \frac{\pi \times 0.85^2}{4}$$

$A = 0.567$ m²

Finding force acting on hatch cover

$\mathbf{F} = p_g A = 1.26 \times 10^6 \times 0.567$

$\mathbf{F} = 714 \times 10^3$ N or 714 kN

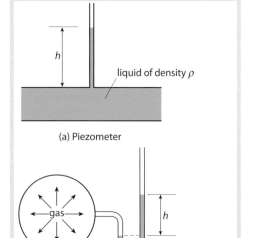

(a) Piezometer

(b) U-tube manometer

Figure 11.39 Pressure measuring devices

Pressure measurement

Piezometers and manometers are simple pressure measuring devices that make use of equation 30.

The piezometer shown in Figure 11.39(a) is a glass tube tapped into a pipe containing a liquid whose pressure is greater than the outside atmospheric pressure. This causes a column of liquid to rise to a height h metres in the tube. The pressure at the base of the column given by equation 29 is the gauge pressure of the liquid in the pipe.

$$p_g = h\rho g$$

The U-tube manometer shown in Figure 11.39(b) can be used to measure the gauge pressure in a pipe or vessel containing a gas. When the gas pressure is equal to the outside atmospheric pressure, the liquid in the manometer rests at the same level in each limb of the U-tube. When the gas pressure is greater than atmospheric the manometer liquid is pushed around the bend so that the difference in the levels is the height h metres. Here again, equation 29 can be used to calculate the gauge pressure of the gas.

The earliest form of mercury barometer used to measure atmospheric pressure is shown in Figure 11.40. Its use is discouraged today because of the dangerous vapour given off by an open bath of mercury. It consists of a glass tube, closed at one end and filled with mercury. With a thumb placed over the open end, it is then up-ended and placed beneath the surface of the mercury bath. When the thumb is removed the mercury falls down the tube, creating a vacuum above it. It settles at a height hm, of around 760 mm above the surface of the bath where it is balanced by the outside pressure of the atmosphere.

Atmospheric pressure is often given in millimetres of mercury which can be converted to Pascals using equation 29.

$$p_a = h_m \rho_m g \quad (30)$$

The Fortin mercury barometer, as used in science laboratories, operates on the same principle but with the mercury reservoir fully enclosed.

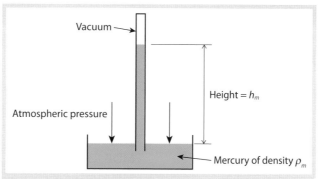

Figure 11.40 Mercury barometer

Worked example 11.15

The gas inside a vessel is measured using a U-tube manometer containing water. If the difference in levels between the two limbs is 345 mm, determine a) the gauge pressure in the vessel, b) the absolute pressure in the vessel. The density of water is 1,000 kgm^{-3} and that of mercury is 13,600 kgm^{-3}. Atmospheric pressure recorded on a Fortin barometer is 760 mm of mercury.

a) Finding gauge pressure in vessel

$$p_g = h_w \rho_w g$$
$$p_g = 0.345 \times 1,000 \times 9.81$$
$$p_g = 3.38 \times 10^3 \text{ Pa or 3.38 kPa}$$

b) Finding atmospheric pressure

$$p_a = h_m \rho_m g$$
$$p_a = 0.76 \times 13,600 \times 9.81$$
$$p_a = 101.4 \times 10^3 \text{ Pa or 101.4 kPa}$$

Finding absolute pressure in vessel

$$p = p_g + p_a$$
$$p = 3.38 + 101.4$$
$$p = 104.78 \text{ kPa}$$

Assessment activity 11.2

2B.P5 | 2B.P6 | 2B.P7 | 2B.M3 | 2B.D2 | 2B.P8 | 2B.M4

The training manager has asked you to produce a series of learning documents that will be of help to new mechanical and plant maintenance apprentices. You will need to begin by defining the parameters of static and dynamic mechanical systems. These must include mass, earth's gravity, weight, force, pressure, density, relative density, moment of a force, displacement, velocity, acceleration/retardation, limiting coefficient of kinetic friction and frictional resistance to motion. You will then need to describe the conditions required for the static equilibrium of a body and demonstrate graphically how to find the resultant and equilibrant of a system of concurrent coplanar forces.

Your next task will be to explain and demonstrate the plotting of a velocity–time graph and how to find from it the uniform acceleration and retardation of a body. You will also need to demonstrate the calculation of work done in overcoming friction and the power dissipated for a body moving at constant velocity along a horizontal surface.

For your last task you will need to define gauge and absolute pressure and demonstrate the calculation of pressure at depth in a liquid. Finally, with the help of a suitable diagram, you will need to describe how a U-tube manometer is used to measure gas pressure.

Tips

- Make sure that you have defined the full range of parameters.
- Illustrate your description of the conditions for static equilibrium with a diagram.

- State the scale chosen on your vector diagram and clearly label the coplanar forces, their resultant and equilibrant.

Appendix

Appendix 1: Abbreviations

2D – two-dimensional
3D – three dimensional
AC – alternating current
A/C – across corners
A/F – across flats
Alum – aluminium
ASSY – assembly
BDMS – bright drawn mild steel
BH – Brinell hardness number
BS – British Standard
BSI – British Standards Institution
CAD – computer aided design
CBORE – counterbore
CHAM – chamfer
CI – cast iron
CIM – computer integrated manufacturing
CL – centre line
CNC – computer numerical control
CRMS – cold rolled mild steel
CRS – centres
CSK – countersunk
Dural – duralumin
DTI – dial test indicator
EMF – electromotive force
FSH – full service history
GRP – glass reinforced plastic
HDMI – high definition multimedia interface
HEX HD – hexagon head

I/D – inside diameter
ISO – International Organization for Standardization
LED – light emitting diode
LDR – light dependent resistor
MDF – medium density fibreboard
MB – megabyte
Φ – diameter (preceding a dimension)
O/D – outside diameter
PAT – portable appliance testing
PCB – printed circuit board
Phos Bronze – phosphor-bronze
PPE – personal protective equipment
PVC – polyvinylchloride
PTFE – polytetrafluoroethylene
PE – potential energy
PCD – pitch circle diameter
R – radius (preceding a dimension, capital only)
SG iron – spheroidal graphite cast iron
SS – stainless steel
SMT – surface mount technology
SWG – standard wire gauge
THK – thick
TIG – tungsten inert gas welding
TYP – typical or typically
USB – universal serial bus
VA – volt amperes
VPN – Vickers pyramid harness number

Appendix 2: SI unit prefixes and symbols

Multiple	Prefix	Symbol
10^{12}	tera	T
10^{9}	giga	G
10^{6}	mega	M
10^{3}	kilo	k
10^{2}	hecto	h
10^{1}	deka	da
10^{-1}	deci	d

Multiple	Prefix	Symbol
10^{-2}	centi	c
10^{-3}	milli	m
10^{-6}	micro	μ
10^{-9}	nano	n
10^{-12}	pico	p
10^{-15}	femto	f
10^{-18}	atto	a

Appendix 3: Standard symbols for electronic components

Connected wires

Unconnected wires

Cell

Battery or cells

Earth

Fuse

Transformer

DC supply

AC supply

Lamp

Resistor

Variable resistor

Variable capacitor

Capacitor with pre-set adjustment

Voltmeter

Ammeter

Switch

Capacitor

Capacitor (polarised)

LED

Diode

Amplifier

Bell

Buzzer

Transistor

Appendix 4: Information on selected engineering materials

Table A1 Tempering temperatures

Component	Tempering temperature (°C)	Oxide colour film
Lathe tools	230	Pale straw
Drills	240	Dark straw
Screw-cutting taps and dies	250	Brown
Punches and rivet snaps	260	Brown/purple
Press tools and axes	270	Purple
Cold chisels and screwdriver blades	280	Dark purple
Springs	300	Blue

Table A2 Ferrous metals

Material	Carbon content and other elements	Properties	Applications
Mild steel	0.1–0.3% carbon	Strong, fairly malleable and ductile.	Wire, rivets, nuts and bolts, pressings, girders – general workshop material.
Medium carbon steel	0.3–0.8% carbon	Strong, tough and can be hardened by heat treatment.	Hammer heads, cold chisels, gears, couplings – impact-resistant components.
High carbon steel	0.8–1.4% carbon	Strong, tough and can be made very hard by heat treatment.	Knives, springs, screw-cutting taps and dies – sharp-edge tools.
Grey cast iron	3.2–3.5% carbon	Weak in tension but strong and tough in compression, very fluid when molten.	Lathe beds, brake drums, engine cylinder blocks and cylinder heads, valve bodies.
Stainless steel	Up to 1.0% carbon Up to 27% chromium Up to 0.8% manganese	Resistant to corrosion, strong, tough.	Food processing and kitchen equipment, surgical equipment, decorative items.

Table A3 Non-ferrous metals

Material	Composition	Properties	Applications
Copper	Almost pure	Very ductile and malleable, good conductor of heat and electricity, resistant to corrosion.	Electrical wire and cable, water pipes, soldering iron bits, alloying to make brasses and bronzes.
Zinc	Almost pure	Soft, rather brittle, good fluidity when molten, resistant to corrosion.	Protective coating, alloying to make brasses.
Tin	Almost pure	Very soft and malleable, highly resistant to corrosion.	Protective coating, alloying to make solders.
Lead	Almost pure	Extremely soft, heavy and malleable, highly resistant to corrosion.	Roofs, lining of tanks, alloying to make solders.
Aluminium	Almost pure	Soft, light and malleable, resistant to corrosion.	Wide range of domestic products and containers, wide range of alloys.
Brasses	Up to 70% copper Up to 40% zinc Up to 1% tin	Very ductile with high copper content. Very strong, tough and fluid when molten with high zinc content.	Tubes, pressings, forgings and castings for a wide range of engineering and marine components.
Tin – bronzes	Up to 96% copper Up to 22% tin Up to 2% zinc Up to 0.5% phosphorus	Very malleable and ductile with high copper content. Very strong, tough and fluid when molten with high tin content.	Springs, electrical contacts, bearings, gears, valve and pump components.
Aluminium alloys	Up to 97% aluminium Up to 5% silicon Up to 3% copper Up to 0.8% magnesium Up to 0.8% manganese	Ductile, malleable with good strength and good fluidity when molten.	Electrical power lines, ladders, aircraft and motor vehicle components, light sand and die castings.

Table A4 Common thermoplastic materials

Common name	Properties	Applications and uses
Low-density polythene	Flexible and tough with good solvent resistance, degrades if exposed to sunlight or ultraviolet radiation.	Flexible squeeze containers, packaging, pipes and tubes, cable and wire insulation.
High-density polythene	Similar to low-density polythene but harder, stiffer and stronger.	Food containers and crates, pipes, moulded components, tubs, kitchenware and utensils, items of medical equipment.
Polypropylene (or polypropene)	High tensile strength and high melting point, can be produced as a fibre.	Ropes and slings, electronic components, kitchen utensils, items of medical equipment.
PVC	Good solvent resistance, can be made tough and hard or soft and flexible.	Building materials such as window frames, piping and guttering when made in the hard condition. Electrical insulation, clothing and upholstery when made in the soft condition.
Polystyrene	Tough and rigid but can be brittle and liable to attack by chemical solvents, can be produced as a light cellular foam.	Packaging foam and disposable drinking cups. Used for refrigerator mouldings and other appliances in its solid form.
Perspex	Transparent strong and tough, can be softened and moulded, liable to attack by chemical solvents.	Protective guards on workshop machinery, lenses, corrugated roofing sheets, aircraft windows, light fittings.
PTFE	High solvent resistance with a low-friction surface, tough, flexible and heat-resistant.	Non-stick coatings for kitchen utensils, bearings, seals and gaskets.
Nylon	Very strong, tough and flexible, good solvent resistance but does absorb water and deteriorates with exposure to outdoor conditions.	Gears, cams, bearings brushes, textiles.
Terylene	Strong and flexible with good solvent resistance.	Reinforcement in rubber belts and tyres, textiles, electrical insulation.

Table A5 Common thermosetting plastics

Common name	Properties	Applications and uses
Bakelite	Hard, resistant to heat and solvents, good electrical insulator and machinable, colours limited to brown and black.	Electrical components, vehicle distributor caps, saucepan handles, glues, laminates.
Melamine	As above but harder and with better resistance to heat. Very smooth surface finish.	Electrical equipment, tableware, control knobs, handles, laminates.
Epoxy resins	Strong, tough, good chemical and thermal stability, good electrical insulator, good adhesive.	Container linings, panels, flooring material, laminates, adhesives.
Polyester resins	Strong, tough, good wear resistance, and resistance to heat and water.	Boat hulls, motor panels, aircraft parts, fishing rods, skis, laminates.

Answers to Assessment Practice questions

Unit 1, Assessment practice 1.1

1. Give **three** hazards associated with using workshop machinery. [3]

Answers could include:

- Loose clothing entanglement
- Swarf entering the eyes
- Burns or cuts from hot material being removed

2. A small engineering company produces bespoke printed circuit boards for a range of products. Name the five main stages in PCB manufacture. [5]

Answer:

1 Design the layout
2 Produce the artwork
3 PCB etching
4 Drilling the board
5 Populating the board

3. Match the two processes to the correct description. [2]

Answer:

| Forging | Heating a metal, then applying a force to change its shape or size permanently |
| Casting | Pouring/injecting liquid metal into a mould, which then cools in the shape of the desired product |

Unit 1, Assessment practice 1.2

1. Which type of production has the following characteristics: high unit cost, low initial investment, skilled labour? Select one of the options. [1]

Answer: C One-off production

2. Give one advantage of using mass production to produce Blu-Ray DVD players. [1]

Answers could include:

- Lower cost per unit
- Faster production rates
- Automation usually means reduced labour costs
- Non-stop production is possible

Unit 1, Assessment practice 1.3

1. Give **three** hazardous tasks that robots can perform. [3]

Answers could include:

- Task 1: Handling nuclear waste
- Task 2: Handling extremely hot or cold materials
- Task 3: Carrying out paint spraying activities

2. Give **one** advantage of using PLCs in a parcel-sorting office. [1]

Answers could include:

- PLCs not very good at handling large amounts of data
- PLCs not very good at handling complex data
- PLCs are not very good for displaying data
- PLCs require programming – can be costly in terms of time

3. Match the **two** types of technology to the correct description. [3]

Answer:

| CAM | The use of CAD information to execute a series of machinery operations. |
| CAD | A type of software that is used to create drawings of products. |

Unit 1, Assessment practice 1.4

1. Give two advantages of using optical fibres in the communications sector. [2]

Any two of the following answers:

- Transmits data at a higher speed
- Reduced transmission errors
- Much greater amount of information can be carried
- Much cheaper than other materials
- Easier to maintain and install due to thinner nature of product

2. Give three benefits of using hydrogen fuel cells. [3]

Answers:

Benefit 1: No impact on carbon footprint

Benefit 2: Very efficient method of producing energy

Benefit 3: Simple construction so low production cost

Unit 1, Assessment practice 1.5

1. Explain **two** characteristics of Kaizen that ensure continuous improvement within an engineering company. [4]

Any two of the following answers:

- Ideas come from the workforce (1) therefore similar process adopted making it easier to implement (1)
- Small changes are implemented (1) making it more likely to succeed (1)
- Workers are responsible for the changes (1) increasing workforce motivation (1)

3. Give three advantages of Just-In-Time manufacturing. [3]

Answers:

Advantage 1: Products are made to order

Advantage 2: Less storage space required for materials and/or finished components

Advantage 3: Reduces production times through automation and layout changes

Unit 1, Assessment practice 1.6

1. A company is considering using tidal power to generate electricity. What would be the most appropriate location? [1]

Answer: B Near the mouth of an estuary

Unit 1, Assessment Zone

1. Describe the process of turning a product. [2]

Answer: The process involves the use of a lathe to produce a cylindrical shape. The work is held in a chuck and rotated whilst a cutting tool produces the required shape and size.

2. Using workshop materials such as a centre lathe can be dangerous. Give **three** safety procedures that you must follow when using a centre lathe. [3]

Any three of the following answers:

- You must wear safety goggles/glasses.
- Make sure work is secure in the chuck.
- Ensure that guard is in position.
- Loose clothing should be secure.
- Tie long hair back.
- Do not distract others while they are using the machine.
- Ensure chuck key is removed from chuck before starting the machine.
- Do not touch rotating parts whilst machine is on.
- Do not remove swarf with your hands.

3. TNC Engineering produces injection moulded components for the automotive industry. When parts are rejected after production they recycle the plastic material. Describe **two** advantages of recycling these plastic materials. [4]

Answers could include:

- Reduces the need to extract raw materials (1) therefore has minimal impact on the earths finite resources (1)
- Takes a non-biodegradable material out of landfill (1) preventing harm to wildlife (1)
- Manufacturer can re-use the material to make additional parts (1) reducing costs of purchasing new material (1)

4. Energy sources can be classed as either renewable or non-renewable. Complete the following table by identifying whether the energy sources oil, wave power and solar are renewable or non-renewable [3].

Answers:

Energy source	Renewable Energy	Non-renewable energy
Oil		✓
Wave power	✓	
Solar	✓	

5. State the main difference between MIG welding and Oxy-Acetylene welding. [1]

Answer: MIG Welding uses electricity to generate heat for welding whereas Oxy-Acetylene uses a mixture of gases.

Unit 9, Assessment practice 9.1

1. Figure 9.6 shows a working drawing of a part used in a racing bicycle. Which of the three sectional lines, shown on the plan view, has been used to create the sectional elevation? [1]

Answer: (a) X-X

2. Figure 9.7 shows an aerospace component manufactured by Freeair limited. Produce a three-view representation of the part using first angle projection. [3]

Individual answers.

Unit 9, Assessment practice 9.2

1. Look back at Figure 9.8. The diamond shape symbol is a: [1]

Answer: Yes/No decision

2. Look back at Figure 9.8. The oblong symbol is a: [1]

Answer: Start/stop decision

3. Explain one advantage of a flow diagram. [2]

Answer: A flowchart is easy to understand because it is a simple graphical technique that shows the information flow in a system, indicating how data flows from start to finish.

Unit 9, Assessment practice 9.3

1. A component has the dimension 15mm +0.2.

(a) What is the maximum size of the component? [1]

Answer: 15 + 0.2 = 15.2 mm

(b) What is the minimum size of the component? [1]

Answer: 15 – 0.8 = 14.8 mm

2. An engineering drawing uses the symbol shown in Figure 9.12. Which of the following does the symbol represent? [1]

Answer: (b) concentricity

3. Explain why it is often difficult to see where spot welds have been used on assembled components. [2]

Answer: Spot welds are used where two surfaces are joined. The weld occurs in between the joined surfaces so, like two pieces of paper that have been glued together, you cannot see inside the join.

Unit 9, Assessment practice 9.4

1. What kind of safety sign features a white picture on a blue background? [1]

Answer: (a) Mandatory

2. Which of the following is a safe condition sign? [1]

Answer: (b) Emergency stop

3. What shape and colour are warning signs? [2]

Answer: Warning signs are always triangular with black text on a white background.

Unit 9, Assessment practice 9.5

1. What does SOP stand for? [1]

Answer: (a) Standard Operating Procedure

2. Which of the following is used when a maintenance activity is required on a production line? [1]

Answer: (b) Job card

3. Explain how quality control documentation is used in a production environment. [2]

Answer: Quality control documentation specifies the size, colour, weight, appearance etc. of a finished product and it is used to check that the product meets its intended specification.

Unit 9, Assessment practice 9.6

1. When preparing to machine a part the feed and speed to use would be indicated on a… [1]

Answer: (a) production plan

2. A colour carded graphical sequence of operations is known as…? [1]

Answer: (b) a Gantt chant

3. Explain the importance of the critical path in project planning. [2]

Answer: The critical path indicates the longest sequence of events in a project indicating the key events that should not be delayed.

Unit 9, Assessment Zone

1. Which welding feature is indicated by the symbol below? [1]

Answer: Single U butt weld

2. Describe two features of a safe condition sign. [2]

Answers could include:

- Green background
- White image
- White text
- Rectangular or square shape

3. Engineering companies will use a production plan when they start a project. Explain the reasons why a production plan is needed. [4]

Answers could include:

- Will show start/end dates
- Identify tools/machines/equipment needed
- Identify materials and components
- State feeds/speeds for machines
- Show the order to produce/assemble parts
- Identify quality control checks

4. A number of drawing types are used to explain electronic circuits. Explain the features of circuit diagrams. [4]

Answers could include:

- Circuit diagram – shows all components
- Shows how components join together
- Components are shown in a grid layout
- Components drawn to scale

5. Sketch the line types that are used to indicate: hidden detail, centre lines and outlines. [3]

Answer:

Hidden detail: ----------------------

Centre lines: —·—·—·—·—·—·—·—

Outlines: ——————————————

Answers to Assessment Activities (Unit 10 only)

Unit 10, Assessment activity 10.1

1a. A diesel engine cylinder contains 0.125 m³ of air at the start of its compression stroke. If this is compressed into a volume of 7.35×10^{-3} m³ at the end of the stroke, calculate its compression ratio correct to three significant figures.

Answer: 17.0 or 17.01

1b. An engineering component costs £2.25 and a buyer requires a batch of 110. What will be the cost if a discount of 15% is allowed for this quantity? Give your answer to 2 decimal places.

Answer: £210.38

2. A gantry crane moved a casting from rest along a workshop with uniform acceleration. If its velocity after 12 s is 2.75 ms^{-1}, what is its acceleration? Give your answer to three significant figures.

Answer: 0.146 ms^{-2}

3. A vehicle travelling at a steady speed starts to accelerate. Its velocity is recorded at one-second intervals and the readings are shown in the following table. Plot a graph of velocity v against time t. From the graph, determine the velocity of the of the vehicle as it started to accelerate, the acceleration of the vehicle and the law that connected the two variables, v and t.

Answer: 1.4 ms^{-1}, 1.19 ms^{-2}, $v = 1.19t + 1.4$

4. For different lengths of the cantilever shown in Figure 10.11, the load at the point of failure is shown in the following table. Plot a graph of length, L against load carrying capacity W, and determine the law that connects the two.

Answer: $LW = 0.6$ or $W = 0.6/L$

Unit 10, Assessment activity 10.2

1. Calculate the area of the panel shown in Figure 10.34.

Answer: 1.06 m^2

2. Calculate the volume of vessel shown in Figure 10.35.

Answer: 2.96 m^3

3. Calculate the length of each member in the roof truss shown in Figure 10.36.

Answer: AB = 2.66 m, BD = 3.26 m, BC = 5.0m, AD = 3.01 m, DC = 2.23 m

Glossary

555 timer IC – an integrated circuit chip, often used in timer circuits.

A

Abrasion – wearing away by frictional contact with another material.

Absolute coordinates – measured from the start point/origin, like plotting a graph in x–y.

Absolute pressure – the sum of gauge pressure and atmospheric pressure.

Absolute value – the numerical value of a number, regardless of its sign.

Acid rain – rainfall that contains trace elements of acid.

Active force – an external force acting on a body.

Acute angle – an angle less than 90°.

Adjacent – the side that lies next to one of the other angles and, together with the opposite side, forms the right-angled corner.

Aesthetic – aesthetic changes to a product make it more attractive but do not have any functional purpose.

Alloy – a mixture of metals. (It may also be a mixture of a metal and a non-metal as long as the final product has metallic properties.)

Aluminium – one of the most widely used and lightest non-ferrous metals.

Annealing – heat treatment of a metal to remove work hardness.

Anode – the terminal connected to the positive power supply.

Arithmetic – the science of calculation using numbers.

Armature – the rotating part of an electric motor.

Assembly drawing – a drawing showing components assembled together.

Astable circuit – a type of circuit that can be used to make lights flash.

B

Base – a number that is to be raised to a power.

Batch production – where a pre-determined number of products is produced.

Bilateral tolerance – a tolerance that deviates in both directions, e.g. 15 mm ± 0.3 mm.

Blind hole – a hole that does not go all the way through the workpiece.

Blow moulding – a process where molten plastic or resin is injected into a mould and air is then blown into the mould, forcing the material into a uniform thickness in the shape of the mould.

Bluetooth – open wireless technology for exchanging data over short distances.

BODMAS – **B**rackets, **O**rder, **D**ivision, **M**ultiplication, **A**ddition, **S**ubtraction.

Boring bar – a type of turning tool used on a lathe to carry out boring operations along the axis of a workpiece, for example, increasing the size of a drilled hole.

Boring tools – tools used to create a large hole by increasing the size of a drilled hole.

Brass – an alloy of copper and zinc.

Brittleness – a material's inability to withstand sudden impact and shock loading. Brittle materials are easily shattered.

C

CAD (computer-aided design) system – computer software that can be used to produce engineering drawings during the design process.

CAD template – a standard layout that CAD operators use to produce drawings. It includes a border, title block and standard logo for the company or organisation. It also features standard settings such as units, types of line and colours.

Calibration – the process of comparing the performance of an instrument against a known standard. For accurate measurements to be taken the tools must be regularly calibrated. This activity is undertaken by specialist organisations although instruments such as verniers and micrometers can be tested with the use of slip gauges.

CAM (computer-aided manufacture) – involves the use of software to control machine tools and other manufacturing systems such as robots.

Carbon fibre reinforced plastic – a composite material consisting of epoxy or polyester resins reinforced with carbon fibres.

Case hardening – the heating of mild steel components in the presence of a carbon bearing material to increase the surface carbon content.

Cast iron – contains 3.0–3.5% carbon, which makes it very fluid and able to be cast into complicated shapes.

Castings – components that have been formed by pouring molten metal into a mould.

Cathode – the terminal connected to the negative or ground power supply.

Centre drill – a small drill used to make tiny location spots or 'centres' in a workpiece in preparation for turning operations on a lathe.

Ceramics – non-metallic, inorganic materials produced mainly from naturally occurring earths and clays (e.g. bricks, tiles and pottery).

Change note – when a change to a technical document or drawing is made a change note is often issued; this is an official note that is circulated to all key departments where it is signed to confirm that staff are aware of the changes and previous copies of the drawing/document have been discarded.

Chuck – used to secure the workpiece in a lathe.

Circuit diagram – a drawing that shows how an arrangement of components can be combined to form a circuit.

CNC (computer numerical control) machining – a system that allows the movements of a machine to be programmed rather than requiring a skilled operator.

Coating – a layer of material deposited on a surface to enhance its properties.

Commutator – that part of the armature through which the electric current is supplied.

Component – a single part that is sometimes used by itself but is usually assembled with other parts. Fasteners such as nuts and bolts are components, as are complex engineered products such as gears, integrated circuits or filter elements.

Composite material – a material that is made from two or more constituents for added strength and toughness.

Compressive forces – press on a material, tending to squash it.

Computer numerically controlled (CNC) machining – the manufacture of products using machines controlled by computers.

Conductors – materials that have low resistance to the flow of electrons.

Constant of proportionality – the gradient of a proportional relationship graph.

Contactor – a heavy-duty relay.

Coordinates – a set of values that show an exact position in space.

Copper – a non-ferrous metal with a characteristic red colour.

Corrosion – a chemical reaction, usually in the presence of moisture or oxygen in the atmosphere, that causes a metal to become degraded.

Counterboring – producing a cylindrical, round-bottomed hole which enlarges an existing hole allowing a fastener to sit below the surface of the workpiece.

Countersinking – producing an angled start to a hole used for a screw or bolt head.

Cubed – a number multiplied by itself twice.

Cutting speed – the speed the workpiece moves relative to the tool.

Cycle time – the time taken to produce each moulded component.

D

Darlington Pair – a combination of two transistors where the second one benefits from the gain of the first one.

Dead centre – a type of lathe centre without a bearing; it must be lubricated regularly to prevent friction.

Decimal – part of a whole expressed as the sum of tenths, hundredths, thousands and so on.

Dedicated machines – machines used specifically for a particular process and nothing else.

Density – the number of kilograms contained in a cubic metre of a material.

Dependent variable – a variable whose changing values we can control.

Diamagnetic – a diamagnetic material cannot be made into a magnet but will align at right angles to the lines of force if placed in a magnetic field.

Down-cut – a method of material removal where the cutter rotates in the same direction as the table is feeding the work.

Drawing – pulling a ductile material through a circular die to form rods and tubes.

Drill bit – the tool that is used to produce the drilled holes (sometimes called a twist drill).

Drilling – a process that removes material by moving a rotating cutter into contact with a workpiece; drilling produces holes in the workpiece.

Ductility – a material's ability to be pulled or drawn out in length to make thin rods and wire.

E

Elasticity – a material's ability to increase or decrease in size in proportion to the load that is applied. When unloaded, an elastic material returns to its original shape.

Electrical conductivity – the ability of a material to conduct an electric current.

Electrical power – the energy consumed per second by an electric circuit. It is measured in Watts (W). Heat, light and work are forms of energy into which electrical energy is often transferred.

Electrical resistivity – the extent to which a material resists the passage of electrical current.

Electrochromic materials – materials whose transparency can be changed by the application of electrical potential difference.

Electromotive force (emf) – the voltage across the terminals of a battery before anything is connected to it.

End mill – the most common tool used in milling, with cutting teeth at one end and along the sides.

Engineering – a profession that involves applying scientific and mathematical principles to design, develop and manufacture products and systems.

Environmental degradation – the decay of timber and plastic materials because of the presence of moisture and/or sunlight.

Epoxy resins – thermosetting polymers formed by mixing together a liquid resin and a hardener.

Equilibrant – the force equal and opposite the resultant that is required to hold a body in static equilibrium.

Ergonomic – designed to be safe, comfortable and easy to use.

Exponential decay – decrease at an ever-faster rate.

Exponential growth – increase at an ever faster rate, as seen in the world's population.

Extracted – removed and taken away.

Extraction – the removal of natural resources such as gas, coal and oil from beneath the earth's surface.

Extrusion – pushing a malleable material through a shaped die to make tubes and other kinds of cross-section.

F

Fabrication drawing – a drawing showing how a structure is built up.

Face mill – a cutter with multiple cutting tips – often called inserts – designed to move across the face of the workpiece.

Faceplate – a circular metal plate with slots machined into it, used instead of a chuck if an awkward workpiece has to be secured in a lathe.

Facing tool – a tool used to remove material from the end of a workpiece to produce a flat surface.

Feed gates – the point where either the plastic or metal is fed into the die.

Feed rate – the distance the tool travels during one revolution of the workpiece.

Feedback – a small proportion of the output is fed back into the system to make sure it works correctly. Negative feedback tends to keep a signal under control, whereas positive feedback increases the output signal constantly.

Ferromagnetic – containing large amounts of iron, nickel and cobalt; able to be made into a magnet.

Ferrous metal – a material that is composed of or contains a large quantity of iron.

Fibreboard – a composite material made from fine compressed wood fibres of differing size.

Field effect transistor – a type of transistor that works as an amplifier and has digital properties, meaning it is either turned on or off.

Fixed steady – a type of clamp, used to support a long workpiece, clamped to the bed of the lathe.

Flow chart – a block diagram that shows a sequence of events.

Flux density – the flux passing through an area of 1 m² at right angles to the field.

Forgings – components that are formed to shape by hammering or pressing.

Form – the shape/style of a product.

Formica – also known as urea-methanal resin. A transparent, tough and hard-wearing thermosetting polymer.

Forming tool – a type of turning tool which produces a very specific shape or profile such as a radius or stepped feature.

Fossil fuels – types of fuel formed from plant or animal remains, for example, coal, oil and natural gas.

Fraction – part of a whole expressed in the form of a ratio.

Function – the purpose of a product.

G

Gain – the increase in the signal power produced by the transistor.

Gauge pressure – a measure of pressure in excess of atmospheric pressure as shown on a pressure gauge.

Geometrical tolerances – used to determine the shape of a feature to given tolerances (e.g. roundness, flatness, parallelism).

Glass reinforced plastic (GRP) – a composite material consisting of epoxy or polyester resins reinforced by glass fibres in the form of matting.

Gradient – the slope of a graph.

Graph – a means of displaying the changes in value of the two variables.

Grid – used with the snap tool, the grid is a series of dots that are evenly spaced and allow you to edit objects and plot lines, a bit like using graph paper.

Grinding – a process that removes material by abrasion. A grinding wheel, rotating at high speed, is brought into contact with the workpiece. Because the grinding wheel is very hard it causes the softer workpiece to wear or abrade.

H

Hardness – a material's resistance to wear, abrasion or indentation.

Hazard – something that could cause injury or harm.

Heat sink – a piece of equipment used to absorb heat when soldering a circuit in order to protect sensitive components.

High carbon steel – contains 0.8–1.4% carbon.

Hypotenuse – the longest side of a right-angled triangle that is opposite the right angle.

I

Incineration – disposal of waste materials by burning under controlled conditions.

Indentation – piercing the surface of a material.

Independent variable – a second variable that changes as a result of change in the dependant variable.

Index – the power a number is to be raised to.

Indexing head – a device bolted to the machine table that allows the workpiece to be indexed or rotated to selected angles.

Ingots – blocks of metal from primary processing.

Injection moulding – producing products by injecting plastic into a mould.

Input – the sensing part of the circuit.

Installation drawing – a drawing that shows you how to install a piece of equipment.

Insulators – materials which have a high resistance to the flow of electrons.

Inversely proportional – related variables where, as one increases, the other decreases in the same proportions.

Isometric projection – a 3D representation of a 2D object.

J

Job card – a document that details what has to be done in terms of maintenance, production, manufacture and so on.

K

Kevlar® – an extremely strong polymer fibre, which can also be used as reinforcement for epoxy resin.

Kinetic energy – energy created as a result of movement of a body/mass, whether it is vertical or horizontal.

Knurling tool – a type of turning tool which produces a diamond pattern, known as a knurl, on the outside of the workpiece.

L

Landfill – a huge area of land where general household waste is disposed of; disposal of waste materials by compaction and burying.

Latching – when a component remains turned on, even after the trigger has been removed, it is said to have latched.

Lathe – a machine used for turning operations, which grips and rotates the workpiece while a cutting tool is applied to the surface to remove material.

Lathe centre – an accurately machined cone-shaped tool that is clamped in a lathe's chuck to position a workpiece precisely and securely.

Lead – a heavy, grey, non-ferrous metal that is very malleable and highly resistant to corrosion.

Life cycle – the different stages a product goes through from design through to disposal.

Lightweighting – designing or redesigning products to use a minimal amount of material.

Likelihood – the chances of an injury or harm occurring.

Linear relationship – the relationship between two variables whose graph is a straight line but does not pass through the origin.

Linear tolerances – used to determine the accuracy of a dimension to given tolerances (e.g. length, width, diameter).

Live centre – a type of lathe centre with a bearing incorporated, allowing it to rotate, so that it does not require lubrication.

Lubricants – used to reduce the friction between surfaces.

M

Magnetic field – a force field produced around a magnet.

Magnetic flux – the imaginary lines of force in a magnetic field.

Maintenance – the process followed to keep a product working properly.

Malleability – the ability of a material to be spread or deformed in many different directions, until it breaks.

Mandatory – an action that must be taken.

Manufacture – the process followed to make a product.

Mass production – where thousands of products are produced at once.

Materials and substances hazardous to health – materials requiring special storage, specific handling equipment and disposal procedures to protect the workforce and the environment.

MDF (medium density fibreboard) – a type of fibreboard manufactured by a dry process at a lower temperature than hardboard.

Medium carbon steel – contains 0.3–0.8% carbon; stronger and tougher than mild steel.

Melamine – also known as methanal-melamine resin. A thermosetting polymer which is similar to formica but harder and more resistant to heat.

Melting point – the temperature at which a change of state from solid to liquid occurs.

Mensuration – the branch of mathematics dealing with measurement.

Metric system – a system of measurement made up of multiples and submultiples of 10.

Mild steel – contains 0.1–0.3% carbon. Also known as 'low carbon' steel.

Milling – a process that removes material by moving a workpiece into contact with a rotating cutter.

Monostable circuit – a type of circuit that can be used as a timer.

Motherboard – the part of the computer that holds the processor and memory. All of the other parts, such as graphics cards, disc drives and input devices, are connected to this, usually by cables inside the computer.

N

Natural growth and decay – a form of exponential growth and decay.

NiCad – short for Nickel Cadmium, commonly used in rechargeable batteries.

Non-ferrous metals – metals that do not contain iron or in which iron is only present in relatively small amounts.

Normalising – heat treatment of a metal to remove internal stresses and refine the structure.

Nylon – a type of thermoplastic, also known as polyamide.

O

Oblique projection – a method of taking a 2D view of an object and adding lines to give a 3D impression of the object.

One-off production – where a single product is produced.

Operational amplifier (Op-Amp) – an integrated circuit that can be used as both a comparator and invertor.

Opposite – the side that is opposite one of its other angles.

Orthographic projection – a specific arrangement of 2D views.

Output – the part of the circuit which either moves, makes a noise or gives off light.

P

Paramagnetic – a paramagnetic material cannot be made into a magnet but will align along the lines of force if placed in a magnetic field.

Parting off – producing deep grooves, which will cut off the workpiece at a specific length.

Pascal – the unit of force defined as a force of 1 Newton acting evenly over an area of 1 square metre.

PCB etching – removing unwanted conductive material from the surface of a circuit board through a chemical process.

Percentage – a fraction that is expressed as the number of parts in 100.

Perfect square – a number whose square root is a whole number.

Performance – a product's ability to do the job it is intended to do.

Peripheral Interface Controllers (PICs) – programmable integrated circuits used in many household products.

Physical layout diagram – a drawing showing how items should be positioned relative to each other but not connected.

Piezoelectric materials – materials that produce an electric charge when subjected to pressure or stress.

Planned maintenance programme – operations and repairs that are carried out at regular intervals.

Plastic deformation – when a force is applied to a material, it changes its shape or size permanently, even after the force has been removed.

Plasticity – a material's ability to deform when a load is applied. A plastic material stays in its deformed shape when the load is removed.

Plotter – a mechanical drawing machine that reproduces what you have drawn on-screen onto paper or drawing film. Nowadays, any large inkjet or laser printer is often called a plotter.

Plywood – a composite material made of thin layers of wood bonded together with their grain directions running alternately at right angles.

Polar coordinates – measured in terms of length and angle, like using a protractor.

Polarised – components which will only work when they are connected into a circuit in a certain direction. They have different methods of identifying which is the anode and which is the cathode. A LED for example has a long leg for the anode and a flat side on the plastic case for the cathode. Placing a polarised component the wrong way can often be the reason a circuit does not work immediately.

Polycarbonate – a thermoplastic which has similar properties to Perspex but is stronger, scratch-resistant and highly transparent.

Polyester resins – thermosetting polymers with similar properties to epoxy resins, good heat resistance and a hard-wearing surface.

Polyethylene (PET) – a tough and flexible thermoplastic material, also known as polythene or PET.

Polymers – long intertwined chains of molecules, rather like spaghetti. They consist mostly of hydrogen and carbon atoms with the atoms of other elements such as chlorine attached to give them their different properties. Plastics and rubbers are classed as polymer materials or just polymers for short.

Polystyrene – the common name for polyphenylethene, a type of thermoplastic.

Polythene – a tough and flexible thermoplastic material, also known as polyethylene or PET.

Potential difference – the voltage between any two points in an electric circuit.

Potential divider circuit – by using resistors of different values, the voltage from a supply can be divided into fixed fractions to power different parts of a circuit.

Potential energy – energy that results from a body or a mass's position or configuration.

Power – the number of times that a number has been multiplied by itself.

Precedence – the order in which you should carry out arithmetical calculations.

Primary processing – extraction of raw material from metallic ores, crude oil and timber.

Principle of moments – a condition for static equilibrium that states that clockwise and anticlockwise turning moments must be equal.

Process – the part of a system which converts the signal from the input into some form of output.

Product design specification – a detailed list of a product's requirements that takes into account function, performance, cost, aesthetics and production.

Profile cutters – cutters designed to produce a specific shape or profile such as gears or corner radii.

Projection – the system used in drawing to arrange different 2D views of a 3D object. Specific symbols are used.

Properties – the qualities or power of a substance.

Proportional relationship – the relationship between two variables whose graph is a straight line passing through the origin.

PVC – polyvinyl chloride or polychloroethene, a type of thermoplastic.

Pythagoras' theorem – the square on the hypotenuse of a right-angled triangle is equal to the sum of the squares on the other two sides.

Q

Quality control documentation – documents that record information about whether products or services meet their specification or not or how many are within specification.

Quantum tunnelling composites (QTC) – materials whose electrical conductivity increases with the application of pressure or stress.

Quench hardening – heating medium and high-carbon steel components to a specified temperature and quenching in oil or water.

R

Raw material – the material as it is without anything being done to it.

Reactive force – the equal and opposite force exerted by the body.

Reactivity – the degree to which a material will readily combine in a chemical reaction.

Reamers – tools used to produce a very smooth surface finish after drilling, to ensure a very accurately sized hole.

Reaming – a technique used to produce an exceptionally smooth surface finish in previously drilled holes.

Recessing tool – a type of turning tool often used after boring operations to produce internal features such as a recessed groove.

Rectangular hyperbola – shape of the graph when inversely proportional variables are plotted.

Recycle – reuse waste materials during the manufacture of new products.

Reject – refuse to accept something because it is inadequate or inappropriate.

Relative coordinates – measured from the current point, like using a ruler.

Relay – a magnetically operated switch.

Repair/modification drawing – a drawing used to show where repairs or modifications are required to an existing component/assembly.

Resistance – opposition in a conductor to the flow of electric current.

Resultant – the single force that can replace a coplanar system and have the same effect.

Risk – the likelihood that there will be some harm done and the severity of the harm from a hazard.

Risk assessment – identification of hazards, associated risks and their control.

Rotary table – a device bolted on top of the machine table that allows horizontal rotary movement of the table to provide accurate angular movement.

S

Saddle – part of a lathe which allows a travelling steady to be moved along as machining takes place.

Safe condition – a sign that indicates a safety action.

Sawmills – mills where timber is sawn into planks.

Scale – the distance on a graph that represents an increase or decrease of 1 unit of a variable.

Schematic diagram – a simple way of presenting complex information.

Scientific notation – same as standard form.

Scleroscope – an instrument used for assessing surface hardness using the height of rebound of a hardened steel ball.

Secondary processing – changing the raw material into a more usable form.

Semiconductor – a material that, in certain conditions, allows electricity to pass through it.

Sensor – a component that reacts to a change in the environment.

Severity – how serious the harm or injury would be.

Shape memory alloys – alloys containing combinations of copper, zinc, nickel, aluminium and titanium, which return to a pre-formed shape when heated.

Shape memory polymers – polymer materials that return to a pre-formed shape when heated.

Shear strength – the maximum shearing load that each unit of the sheared area of a material can carry before it fails.

Single point threading – used when a thread form needs to be cut into the workpiece.

Sketch – a quick form of engineering drawing drawn in proportion with dimensions added.

Slitting saws – discs with saw teeth around the perimeter designed for cutting deep thin slits into the workpiece.

Slot drill – a type of end mill designed to plunge into the workpiece like a drill and then move across to create a groove.

Slotting cutters – cutters with multiple tips designed to move through a workpiece to create a channel or slot.

Smart material – a material that can have one or more of its properties changed in a controlled manner by an external stimulus.

Smelting – extracting a metal from its ore.

Snap – a feature that allows you to move the mouse in even spaces or steps, a bit like 'dot to dot'.

Solvent – a chemical, usually in liquid form, that attacks plastics and rubbers.

Space diagram – a labelled diagram that shows a system of coplanar forces acting on a body.

Spotfacing – producing a very shallow version of a counterbore – often used to ensure a small flat area for a seal or washer.

Square law – a relationship where one variable increases in proportion to the square of the other.

Squared – a number multiplied by itself.

Stainless steel – contains chromium and nickel in addition to iron and carbon, which makes it very tough and resistant to corrosion.

Standard form – a very large or very small number converted to one with a single digit between 1 and 10 before the decimal point (the mantissa) and multiplied by a power of 10 (the exponent) to give it the same value.

Starting point – the point from which absolute coordinates are measured, also called the origin or (0,0). This is usually in the bottom left-hand corner of the screen.

Steel – a mixture of iron and carbon.

Sub-assembly drawing – a drawing that shows several components, which form part of a larger assembly, assembled together.

Superalloy – a high performance alloy which is extremely strong, resistant to corrosion and resistant to high temperature creep.

Support reaction – the reactive force exerted by the supports of a body.

Surface finish – how smooth the surface is. If you run the tip of your fingernail over a surface you will get an indication of how smooth it is. Imagine a saw blade – the distance between the high point and low point is the measure used for surface finish. Surface finish is measured in mm where 1mm = 0.000001 m.

Sustainable product – a product that has a minimal impact on the environment throughout each stage of its life cycle.

Switch – a component that mechanically controls current in a circuit.

T

Tapping – a technique used after drilling a hole, in order to produce an internal thread.

Taps – tools used to cut threads after a hole has been drilled.

Tempering – reducing the hardness and brittleness in quench-hardened components by reheating to a specified temperature followed by natural cooling or quenching.

Tensile forces – pull on a material tending to lengthen it.

Tensile strength – the ability of a material to withstand tensile (stretching) forces without fracturing.

Test report – a document that outlines the results of a test and the test conditions/parameters.

Thermal conductivity – the ability of a material to conduct heat energy.

Thermal expansion – increase in the dimensions of a material owing to temperature rise.

Thermoplastic – a polymer material that can be softened by heating.

Thermosetting polymers – polymer materials which cannot be softened by heating.

Threads – a spiral form used to locate a threaded part, e.g. a bolt.

Thyristor – similar to a transistor, a thyristor will stay switched on once it has been triggered until the power source is removed.

Time constant – the time taken for a capacitor to fully charge or discharge. Equal to five times the time period (t = 5CR).

Titanium – a lightweight, non-ferrous metal which is highly resistant to corrosion.

Tolerance – how far above, or below, the required size the finished size is allowed to be to be considered accurate or to specification. Accuracy is expressed in terms of a tolerance. For example a $\Phi 12 \pm 1$ mm dimension means a feature should have a diameter of 12 mm with a tolerance so it is compliant if it falls between 11 mm and 13 mm.

Tool changes – some machining processes require several different tools. Whenever a new tool is needed, you must stop the machine, remove the guards, remove the original tool, insert and secure the new tool, and replace the guards.

Tools – the part of an engineering machine used to remove material from a workpiece. Different tools are fitted to a machine to carry out different operations.

Torque – a measure of the turning effect of the force.

Toughness – a material's ability to resist sudden impact and shock loading.

Toxic – hazardous to health.

Transistor – an electronic component which has three connections: a base, a collector and a gate. It can be used as an amplifier or as an electronic switch.

Transposition – manipulation of a mathematical or engineering formula to make the quantity you require the subject of the formula.

Travelling steady – a type of clamp, used to support a long workpiece, which can be moved along as machining takes place.

Trigonometry – study of the relationship between the sides and angles of triangles.

Tungsten carbide – a non-ferrous metal which is made from equal parts of tungsten and carbon.

Turning – a process that removes material by rotating or turning a workpiece using a lathe. The cutting tool is moved, usually parallel to the surface, removing material while it contacts the rotating workpiece.

Turning tool – a tool used to remove material from the workpiece.

Twist drills – tools used to produce holes in the workpiece.

U

Unilateral tolerance – a tolerance that only deviates in one direction, e.g. 10 mm + 0.05 mm or 17 mm - 0.01 mm.

Unit cost – the costs associated with manufacturing each individual product.

Up-cut – a method of material removal where the cutter rotates in the opposite direction as the table is feeding the work.

User requirements – qualities which will make a product attractive to potential users.

V

Variable – a quantity with changing values.

Variable resistor – a type of resistor which can be adjusted to allow varying amounts of current to flow in a circuit.

Vector addition – force vectors added together to find the resultant force.

Vector diagram – a diagram in which forces are drawn to scale and acting in a given direction.

Volatile organic compound (VOC)

Volatile organic compound (VOC) – any chemical compound with a boiling point of 250°C or less that can endanger a person's health or cause damage to the environment.

W

Warning signs – signs that reminds people of dangers in the area.

Waste management – collecting, transporting, processing and disposing of waste material.

Welding drawing – a drawing showing how parts are to be welded together.

Wiring/circuit drawing – a drawing showing you how to put together an electrical/pneumatic/hydraulic circuit.

Workpiece – the piece of material that is being machined in order to produce a finished component.

Z

Zinc – a soft but rather brittle non-ferrous metal.

Index